Volume IV

Comic Medievalism

ISSN 2043–8230

Series Editors
Karl Fugelso
Chris Jones

Medievalism aims to provide a forum for monographs and collections devoted to the burgeoning and highly dynamic multi-disciplinary field of medievalism studies: that is, work investigating the influence and appearance of 'the medieval' in the society and culture of later ages. Titles within the series will investigate the post-medieval construction and manifestations of the Middle Ages – attitudes towards, and uses and meanings of, 'the medieval' – in all fields of culture, from politics and international relations, literature, history, architecture, and ceremonial ritual to film and the visual arts. It welcomes a wide range of topics, from historiographical subjects to revivalism, with the emphasis always firmly on what the idea of 'the medieval' has variously meant and continues to mean; it is founded on the belief that scholars interested in the Middle Ages can and should communicate their research both beyond and within the academic community of medievalists, and on the continuing relevance and presence of 'the medieval' in the contemporary world.

New proposals are welcomed. They may be sent directly to the editors or the publishers at the addresses given below.

Professor Karl Fugelso
Art Department
Towson University
3103 Center for the Arts
8000 York Road
Towson, MD 21252–0001
USA

Dr Chris Jones
School of English
University of St Andrews
St Andrews
Fife KY16 9AL
UK

Boydell & Brewer Ltd
PO Box 9
Woodbridge
Suffolk IP12 3DF
UK

Previous volumes in this series are printed at the back of this book

Comic Medievalism
Laughing at the Middle Ages

Louise D'Arcens

D. S. BREWER

First published 2014
D. S. Brewer, Cambridge
Paperback edition 2017

ISBN 978 1 84384 380 1 hardback
ISBN 978 1 84384 478 5 paperback

D. S. Brewer is an imprint of Boydell & Brewer Ltd
PO Box 9, Woodbridge, Suffolk IP12 3DF, UK
and of Boydell & Brewer Inc.
668 Mt Hope Avenue, Rochester, NY 14620–2731, USA
website: www.boydellandbrewer.com

A CIP catalogue record for this book is available
from the British Library

The publisher has no responsibility for the continued existence or accuracy
of URLs for external or third-party internet websites referred to in this book,
and does not guarantee that any content on such websites is, or will remain,
accurate or appropriate

This publication is printed on acid-free paper

For Robert, Eva and Mimi
with love and thanks

Contents

Illustrations

The author and publishers are grateful to all the institutions and individuals listed
for permission to reproduce the materials in which they hold copyright. Every
effort has been made to trace the copyright holders; apologies are offered for any
omission, and the publishers will be pleased to add any necessary acknowledgement in subsequent editions.

Acknowledgements

I am fortunate to have been able to complete this book as part of an Australian Research Council (ARC) Future Fellowship, which I received for the project FT120100931 'Comic Medievalism and the Modern World'. The ARC Centre of Excellence for the History of Emotions has also supported me with Associate Investigator funding, which has enabled me to run a seminar directly relevant to the subject of this book. Some of the preliminary research for this study was undertaken while I was the recipient of a collaborative ARC Discovery Grant. I would like to acknowledge the support of the ARC in enabling me to complete a number of large projects over the last several years. I wish also to thank the University Research Committee at the University of Wollongong for awarding me a 'near-miss' grant that assisted my research and the preparation of this manuscript.

I have numerous colleagues and friends in the field of medievalism studies whose stimulating conversation, and generous and astute suggestions, have improved my thinking, research and writing. There are many, many people who could be named, but I will limit myself to thanking Andrew Lynch, Stephanie Trigg, John Ganim, Chris Jones, David Matthews, Stephen Knight, Eileen Joy, Clare Monagle, Lawrence Warner, Kim Wilkins, Clare Bradford and Narelle Campbell. In the area of film studies, I would like to thank Adrian Martin and Gino Moliterno for their guidance and helpful conversations, and for helping me track down the wonderful *Brancaleone* films.

My colleagues at the University of Wollongong, especially my colleagues in the English Literatures Program, are a true pleasure to work with. I would like to thank all of my Program colleagues for being consistently collegial, un-egoistic and fun to be around. Leigh Dale in particular has been a source of constant encouragement, as well as being the voice of sanity at some key moments. Thanks also to Noel Broadhead for assistance in seeking image permissions.

At Boydell & Brewer, I would like to thank Caroline Palmer for her guidance, patience and understanding throughout the (occasionally delayed) course of this book's development. As with so many academic books, this one was written in a period of intense work and family commitment, and Caroline has been accommodating and encouraging. My thanks also to Chris Jones and Karl Fugelso for their guidance during the proposal stage of this book, and to the anonymous reader who provided helpful feedback on the draft manuscript.

Some of the chapters in this book draw on material published elsewhere. I would like to thank the editors of the following publications for their kind permission to use material from the following: 'Dario Fo's *Mistero Buffo* and the Left-Modernist Reclamation of Medieval Popular Culture', in Gail Ashton and Daniel T. Kline (eds), *Medieval Afterlives in Popular Culture* (New York: Palgrave Macmillan, 2012), pp. 57–70, and 'Laughing in the Face of the Past: Satire and Nostalgia in Medieval Heritage Tourism', *Postmedieval* 2:2 (2011), 155–70.

My thanks go to my research assistant David Urry for his work in retrieving materials for the book, and for putting my idiosyncratic citation system into order. David lost his beloved mother during the course of this book's writing, so his persistence is very much appreciated. Thanks also to Chris Tiffin for compiling the index.

I am very fortunate to have many supportive friends, as well as some family members whose kindness to me seems limitless. My mother Paulina and my father Brian have stepped in at some crucial times when the dual pressures of parenting and academic work became too much, and I will always be grateful to them. My adorable daughters Eva and Mimi accepted (almost) uncomplainingly the sight of their mother at her computer screen for months on end, including over their summer holidays, and cheered me with their little-girl humour. Finally, I could not ask for a more supportive partner than my husband Robert Sinnerbrink, whose role in the production of this book has ranged from reading drafts and suggesting references through to cooking dinner and taking the kids out so I could write. He is patient, understanding, kind and clever, and is the reason I have been able to complete this book.

I

THE SET UP

Introduction: Laughing at, with and in the Middle Ages

> Comedy is tragedy plus time.
> Woody Allen, *Crimes and Misdemeanors*[1]

MEDIEVALISM – THE CITATION, interpretation or recreation of the Middle Ages – has had a major presence in the cultural memory of the modern West. Whether the medieval period is evoked as a superseded age of ignorance and cruelty, a venerable origin of national cultures or a lost age of beauty and social unity, it provides a reservoir of images and ideas that have been crucial to defining what it is to be 'modern'. For today's audiences viewing medievalism via the body of heroic and fantastic texts emerging out of the nineteenth-century tradition, it would seem that it is a deeply serious business. If any humour is attributed to these magisterial texts and their descendants, it is an unintended humour arising out of their ponderous stylistics, earnest cultural aspirations and historical gaffes. Erudite readers have long revelled in deriding the anachronisms in Walter Scott's *Ivanhoe*, while the pomposity of nineteenth-century historical verse, such as Adam Lindsay Gordon's Teutonic verse drama *Ashtaroth*, has drawn mirth from even its earliest audiences.[2] This tenor of high serious-ness also characterises some of the most inadvertently hilarious instances of medievalist material culture, such as the Eglinton Tournament of 1839, which was conceived as a refined spectacle of revived chivalry, but ended up as a

---

[1] *Crimes and Misdemeanors*, dir. Woody Allen (Jack Rollins & Charles H. Joffe Productions, 1989).
[2] Frank Maldon Robb, ed., *Poems of Adam Lindsay Gordon* (London: Oxford University Press, 1912).

muddy debacle and an object of sustained public mockery.[3] Over a century later, the straight-faced quasi-archaic dialogue of fantasy fiction continues to elicit sniggers from those who are not among the genre's fans. But to limit the comedy of medievalism to the unintended side-effect of either its historicist or its fantastic ambitions risks overlooking the many other avowedly comic forms that have figured in the long history of medievalism. To that end, this book will cast its net wide in order to demonstrate that humour has been, for centuries, an essential and ingeniously wielded tool of medievalism.

In conversation with scholars of the Middle Ages and of medievalism, my experience has been that they frequently demonstrate an authoritative knowledge of the rich tradition of comic medievalism, often reeling off inventories of personal favourites that are much more comprehensive than that which can be treated in this first book on the subject. Many freely confess not only to enjoying these texts, but to using them in their teaching, where the amusement they afford proves a highly effective pedagogic entry point for meditating on such key medievalist questions as cultural memory, reception, adaptation, authenticity, presentism and anachronism. This pervasive practical recognition of comedy's value as a mode of medievalist representation has not, however, been matched by widespread scholarly reflection on the particular contribution comedy has made to medievalism as a cultural field.

This dearth has persisted even in spite of a steady interest in humour within medieval culture, from such earlier and broader historical–theoretical accounts as Johan Huizinga's *Homo Ludens: A Study of the Play Element in Culture* or Mikhail Bakhtin's influential (if contested) *Rabelais and his World*, through to contributions by medievalists within larger 'humour in history' collections, innumerable separate studies of humour in the work of Chaucer and Boccaccio, in vernacular genres such as the fabliaux, *cantigas d'escarnho e de mal dizer*, and Anglo-Saxon riddles, as well as in the Latin tradition. These have been supplemented by themed edited volumes such as Thomas J. Farrell's *Bakhtin and Medieval Voices*, Herman Braet, Guido Latré and Werner Verbeke's *Risus Mediaevalis: Laughter in Medieval Literature and Art*, and Albrecht Classen's *Laughter in the Middle Ages and Early Modern Times*, and by anthologies such as Derek Brewer's *Medieval Comic Tales*.[4] By contrast, so far only a single journal article by Clare A. Simmons has taken

---

3   Albert D. Pionke, 'A Ritual Failure: The Eglinton Tournament, the Victorian Medieval Revival, and Victorian Ritual Culture', *Studies in Medievalism* 16 (2008), 25–45.

4   See, for instance, Thomas J. Farrell, *Bakhtin and Medieval Voices* (Gainesville, FL: University Press of Florida, 1995); Herman Braet, Guido Latré and Werner Verbeke, eds, *Risus Mediaevalis: Laughter in Medieval Literature and Art* (Leuven: Leuven University Press, 2003); Jacques Le Goff, 'Laughter in the Middle Ages', in *A Cultural History of Humour: From Antiquity to the Present Day*, ed. Jan Bremmer and Herman Roodenburg (Cambridge, MA: Polity Press, 1997); Albrecht Classen, ed., *Laughter in the Middle Ages and Early Modern Times: Epistemology of a Fundamental Human Behavior, its Meaning, and Consequences* (Berlin: de Gruyter, 2010); and Derek Brewer, ed., *Medieval Comic Tales*

up the explicit reflexive question of what role humour plays in post-medieval understandings of the medieval past.[5] It is true that humour is notoriously difficult to anatomise, and carries with it the risk that its mysterious alchemy will curdle under the glare of analysis; so while there has been no shortage of medievalist scholarship that discusses popular comic texts, particularly in the area of cinema (see, for example, accounts of *Monty Python and the Holy Grail* by Nickolas Haydock, Laurie A. Finke and Martin B. Shichtman, and John Aberth,[6] or Scott A. Nollen's discussion of the film *Robin Hood: Men in Tights*),[7] this has not led to the development of a critical language with which to understand their comic dynamics, their unique ethical demands, their social functions or the 'affective-historical' responses they generate. With this book I aim to move humorous medievalism out of the margins of scholarly discussion and make it the subject of focused study that takes up these larger questions, exploring some of its myriad forms and social functions.

Comic representations of the medieval past have abounded in Western culture. From the earliest parodies of medieval chivalry such as Chaucer's *Tale of Sir Thopas*, with its misfiring hero and its floundering narrative, through to the scatological 'gross-out' humour of contemporary children's history books, the pedagogic parody of televisual 'jocumentary', or the post-modern ironic stance of comic heritage tourism, as long as there has been medievalism, people have been encouraged to laugh *at*, *with* and *in* the Middle Ages. This comic Middle Ages, as I will go on to demonstrate, is not simply a series of responses to a temporal period, but rather is better charac-terised as the ongoing comic (re)formulation of ideas about the Middle Ages based on a cluster of practices, rituals, beliefs, people and events that have come to be constituted as quintessentially 'medieval'. By examining a range of comic forms including early modern chivalric satire, eighteenth-century verse, Victorian burlesque, Marxist farce, medievalist cinema, contemporary comic-historical books and television programmes and heritage tourism, the book aims to identify what has been perceived as uniquely funny about 'the Middle Ages' in different times and places, and how this has influenced modern ideas both about the Middle Ages and about modernity. This gene-alogy of medievalist comedy will trace the development and permutations of

(Cambridge: D. S. Brewer, 1996). See also Holly Crocker, ed., *Comic Provocations: Exposing the Corpus of Old French Fabliaux* (New York: Palgrave Macmillan, 2006).

5   Clare A. Simmons, 'Small-Scale Humor in the British Medieval Revival', in *The Year's Work in Medievalism: 2004*, ed. Gwendolyn Morgan (Eugene, OR: Wipf and Stock, 2006).

6   Nickolas Haydock, *Movie Medievalisms: The Imaginary Middle Ages* (Jefferson, NC: McFarland, 2008), pp. 10–12; Laurie A. Finke and Martin B. Shichtman, *Cinematic Illuminations: The Middle Ages on Film* (Baltimore, MD: Johns Hopkins University Press, 2010), pp. 48–52, 74–7; John Aberth, *A Knight at the Movies: Medieval History on Film* (New York: Routledge, 2003).

7   Scott A. Nollen, *Robin Hood: A Cinematic History of the English Outlaw and his Scottish Counterparts* (Jefferson, NC: McFarland, 1999, reprinted 2008), pp. 185–7.

its various styles and registers (satire, parody, irony, camp, kitsch, wit, jokes, farce, scatological humour), reading these through some of the major theories of humour. It does not attempt to offer new definitions for these forms, all of which have been treated exhaustively within humour scholarship, but rather seeks to discuss what happens, to them and to the Middle Ages, when they are mobilised to give comic expression to modern ideas of 'the medieval'. In so doing it aims to offer fresh insight into comic medievalism as a vehicle for commentary on the present as well as the past, exploring the many ways it has enabled modern societies to express their anxieties about such issues as social change and historical progress, political and religious structures and cultural tolerance.

A better understanding of comic medievalism can disclose several under-examined dimensions of medievalism as a phenomenon. First, it can shed valuable light on the affective range of our relationship to the medieval past. Mirth, amusement and laughter have tended to be neglected responses in the existing scholarship on affect in medievalism, which has so far concentrated on emotional states founded on yearning and loss, such as nostalgia, and historical melancholy. It is true that Linda Hutcheon and others have argued that nostalgia need not be entirely antithetical to a comic, or at least an ironic recognition of the mediated nature of our contact with the past, and scholars of nostalgia have pointed out nostalgia's high tolerance of the inauthentic in its apparent quest for an originary past;[8] but this recognition has deepened rather than diminished the continued examination of the ache (*algos*) and pathos at the core of nostalgic longing, such that Helen Dell has recently pointed to it as part of the agonised poignancy of medievalist nostalgia.[9] Alongside these analyses of medievalist pain, a small number of scholars have called for a greater recognition of the pleasurable nature of both scholarly and popular creative engagements with the Middle Ages. Aranye (then Louise O.) Fradenburg was prescient when, in 1997, she claimed:

> medievalism has promoted such an ethos of pietas with respect to the past ... that passion often seems very distant to its purposes. As a corollary, because of their association with an enjoyment opposed to pietas, 'popular' manifestations of medievalism also often seem very distant to the purposes of academic medievalism. But the differences between academic and popular medievalism are of course made, and sometimes are made to occlude similarities.[10]

---

8   Linda Hutcheon, *A Theory of Parody* (London: Methuen, 1984).
9   Helen Dell, 'Nostalgia and Medievalism: Conversations, Contradictions, Impasses', *Postmedieval* 2 (2011), 115–26.
10   Aranye Fradenburg, '"So That We May Speak of Them": Enjoying the Middle Ages', *New Literary History* 28 (1997), 205–30 (p. 209).

Fradenburg argued for the 'irresistible ... value now of reclaiming the issue of enjoyment for social and culturalist and historicist projects' in order to combat the powerful utilitarian imperatives of the institution that have led medievalists to 'elide the issue of our enjoyment', reinstating a continuum of *jouissance* that embraces scholarly and non-scholarly medievalism alike.[11] A decade later, Stephanie Trigg and Tom Prendergast turned again to this theme, this time querying the disciplinary ethic that 'abjects' medievalist research by casting suspicion not only on the manifestly unscholarly pleasure medievalist authors and filmmakers take in 'creating' the Middle Ages, but also on the pleasure such texts afford scholars of medievalism: '[i]t is as if we have found ourselves in a garden and been embarrassed by the evident lack of labour required to enjoy it ... [there] is no need to invest in a laborious procedure of policing a spurious border or creating enclosures in order to justify the pleasure that we take in things medieval'.[12] While these arguments are valuable due to their emphasis on the possibility of pleasurable affective engagement with 'the medieval', construed broadly as encompassing the period and its long cultural afterlife, the pleasure they allude to is a more diffuse *jouissance*, less eruptive and pointed than the amusement solicited by the comic medievalist texts treated in this book. Focusing on mirth and laughter, then, this book will expand our understanding of medievalism's affective reach by exploring how texts that generate these emotional responses foster, or, conversely, block, attachments to the medieval past.

This book also aims to make a distinctive intervention into the study of humour, which has so far largely ignored the phenomenon of historicist humour. The ethics and politics of laughing at an 'other' have preoccupied the field of humour studies for some time, particularly those attempting to identify the line between humour and offence and assessing the aptness of the so-called 'superiority' and 'relief' theories, in which humour either has the effect of establishing the laughing group's superiority over the laughed-at group via ridicule, or conversely, performs the more benign function of diffusing social tension by channelling and hence warding off fear of the laughed-at group.[13] But because this scholarship addresses itself to analysing the role of humour in establishing relationships (and especially hierarchies)

---

[11] Ibid., p. 205.

[12] Tom Prendergast and Stephanie Trigg, 'What is Happening to the Middle Ages?' *New Medieval Literatures* 9 (2008), 225–6.

[13] Christy Davies, *The Mirth of Nations* (Piscataway, NJ: Transaction Publishers, 2002), and *Jokes and their Relation to Society* (Berlin: Mouton de Gruyter, 1998); Sharon Lockyer and Michael Pickering, eds, *Beyond a Joke: The Limits of Humour* (Houndmills, Basingstoke: Palgrave Macmillan, 2005); Paul Lewis, 'The Muhammad Cartoons and Humour Research: A Collection of Essays', *Humor* 21.1 (2008), 1–46; Andy Medhurst, *A National Joke: Popular Comedy and English Cultural Identities* (New York: Routledge, 2007); John Morreall, *Comic Relief: A Comprehensive Philosophy of Humor* (Chichester, UK: Wiley-Blackwell, 2009).

between contemporaneous or cohabiting groups, the theorising of historicist humour – laughing at the past as 'other' to the modern – is virtually absent from the literature. Not even the widely held belief among humour scholars that humour is a vehicle for the perpetuation or undermining of axiomatic social values has led to the analysis of the social values implicit within comic representations of the past, despite the significance of these representations to reinforcing or challenging a whole range of ideological truisms. One book has recently appeared on this topic, Hannu Salmi's helpful edited volume *Historical Comedy on Screen* (2011), but this has emerged from film studies, even though it engages with theoretical questions from humour scholarship. Some medievalist cinema does feature in Marcia Landy's contribution to the volume – almost inevitably, *Monty Python and the Holy Grail*, but also Mario Monicelli's two *Brancaleone* films, which will be discussed in Chapter 5 of this book – yet these are not analysed *qua* the specific question of comic perceptions of the Middle Ages, but under the volume's broader rubric of exploring how 'the register of comedic narration provides alternative ways of perceiving the past and of shaping … spectators' relationship with history'.[14] *Laughing at the Middle Ages* will both broaden the textual ambit and narrow the historical focus of Hannu's volume by exploring the theoretical questions of what it means to laugh specifically at the medieval past, and whether the historical 'object' of this humour generates a unique form of comic practice with its own set of ethical considerations and its own characteristics.

Its historicism means that comic medievalism is inevitably bound up with theories of temporality, which determine not just how we view the past, but how we view its relationship to the present. Looking at these texts thus opens up a new avenue into the study of literary and historical periodisation. Periodisation as a mode of historical organisation has been placed under increased critical pressure for some years now within medieval studies, along with the stake-holding involved in dividing the 'modern' from the 'pre-modern', which has led to the latter being artificially divested of any qualities deemed (often equally artificially) 'modern'.[15] This challenge has been working in tandem with the work of those such as Carolyn Dinshaw and Carla Freccero who have queried the ideological stakes of linear and progressivist conceptions of time, arguing instead for the strategic value of conceptualising historical continuity, co-temporality and the 'queer' asynchronous persistence of the pre-modern past within modernity.[16] Periodisation is pertinent to a

[14]   Hannu Salmi, *Historical Comedy on Screen* (Bristol, UK: Intellect, 2011), p. 29.

[15]   Margreta De Grazia, 'The Modern Divide: From Either Side', *Journal of Medieval and Early Modern Studies* 37 (2007), 453–67; Kathleen Davis, *Periodization and Sovereignty: How Ideas of Feudalism and Secularization Govern the Politics of Time* (Philadelphia: University of Pennsylvania Press, 2008).

[16]   Carolyn Dinshaw, *Getting Medieval: Sexualities and Communities, Pre- and Postmodern* (Durham, NC: Duke University Press, 1999), Carla Freccero, *Queer/Early/*

consideration of comic medievalism because, as I will go on to discuss, it is common for comic representations of the Middle Ages to rest on post-medieval assumptions about how humour, comedy and laughter operated in the medieval past; assumptions that inform the style as well as the content of these texts. By investigating whether post-medieval texts are attempting to continue, revive or, conversely, displace perceived 'medieval comic traditions', this book will determine the extent to which they rely on or challenge the notion of a division between the medieval and the modern.

Ironically, the importance of humour to modern perceptions of the Middle Ages is best exemplified in a resolutely non-comic text, Umberto Eco's *The Name of the Rose*.[17] Eco's monastic detective novel meditates on many themes, but the one that is of most pertinence here is its portrayal of the relationship between laughter and institutional power in the later Middle Ages. Through the novel's murder mystery plot, in which a succession of monks die after handling a poisoned manuscript containing the forbidden 'lost' second book on comedy from Aristotle's *Poetics*, Eco portrays a society riven by zealous opposition over the nature of laughter and the purpose and value of humour. Through its portrayal of this conflict, Eco's novel offers us three parallel representations of 'the Middle Ages', each embodied by a different character, which together encapsulate the most widely disseminated post-medieval perceptions of humour in the medieval period.

First is a censorious authoritarian culture epitomised by the ancient librarian-monk Jorge of Burgos, who poisons the sole surviving copy of Aristotle's book because he believes that 'laughter is weakness, corruption, the foolishness of our flesh' which makes us doubt the power of good and evil. Jorge repeatedly cites patristic *auctoritates* against mirth, as well as the Benedictine Rule's prohibition both of laughter and of words that provoke laughter, and he fears Book II of *The Poetics* because its appeal to learned men would mean that in their hands laughter and humour would become intellectual arts that would cancel fear of authority and of the divine.

Second is a Middle Ages in which the comic impulse endures as a toler-ated substratum of 'official culture'. This society is embodied by the Fran-ciscan intellectual William of Baskerville. Though prevented from reading the poisoned text, William is able to figure out that Aristotle 'sees the tendency to laughter as a force for good, which can have an instructive value', exposing truths hidden in plain sight.[18] William embodies for Eco a long ecclesias-

Modern (Durham, NC: Duke University Press, 2006), and Carolyn Dinshaw, *How Soon is Now? Medieval Texts, Amateur Readers, and the Queerness of Time* (Durham, NC, and London: Duke University Press, 2012).

    [17] Umberto Eco, *The Name of the Rose*, trans. William Weaver (London: Vintage, 1998).

    [18] Ibid., p. 472. For accounts of laughter in the novel, see Rocco Capozzi, 'Palimpsests and Laughter: The Dialogical Pleasure of Unlimited Intertextuality in *The Name of the*

tical subculture that tolerated or even promoted parody and satire, a culture exemplified by the abiding popularity of the early Christian biblical parody *The Feast of Cyprian*. In addition, William's participation in jocular monastic tradition is due to his membership of the order founded by the 'holy fool' St Francis. He describes Francis's use of buffoonish spectacle as a reformist tactic, situating clowning and the solicitation of laughter as central to the order's agenda of holy simplicity and social justice.

Thirdly, we encounter a Middle Ages in which the comic and laughter exist as a keystone of a larger folk resistance which is nevertheless in constant danger of being managed or suppressed by the institutional authorities of church and state. This Middle Ages is embodied in the character of Salvatore, the erstwhile homeless peasant who became a Dolcinite heretic and is now being harboured within the monastery walls. As becomes apparent in the text's harrowing inquisition scenes, this comic link between the people and the sects emerging in the wake of Francis attracts the deep antagonism of church authorities, for whom laughter is on a heretical continuum ending in anarchy.

Eco's medievalist novel is a powerful exemplification of how humour offers a conceptual frame within which the medieval past can be narrated, and its power–knowledge nexus portrayed to modern audiences. And while not itself comic (although William delivers some slyly ironic ripostes), its three formulations of humour in the Middle Ages in many respects condense the mass of post-medieval responses to the topic, which can be divided into three main categories:

1) Representations featuring a Middle Ages that is risible, either for its ludicrously self-serious authoritarianism, its benighted superstitiousness or its unself-conscious vulgarity, which allows us to laugh *at* it. Such representations engage in a kind of modern-centric Schadenfreude, taking pleasure in the misfortune of those born into unenlightened pre-modernity. One of the most celebrated examples of this is the American humourist Mark Twain's *A Connecticut Yankee in King Arthur's Court* (1889), a satire on post-Walter Scott romantic medievalism, in which Camelot is ridiculed by the novel's time-travelling Yankee narrator Hank Morgan on all three counts, as being pompous, credulous and coarse. The courtiers are briefly seen to enjoy jokes, it should be said, but these are 'worm-eaten' and infantile, so that their sense of humour is itself an object of Hank's derision, placed on a continuum with their mindless acceptance of oppressive hereditary rule and their childish faith in the bogus 'magic' of Merlin.

Rose', *Italica* 66 (1989), 412–28, and Diego Fasolini, 'The Intrusion of Laughter into the Abbey of Umberto Eco's *The Name of the Rose*: The Christian Paradox of Joy Mingling with Sorrow', *Romance Notes* 46 (2006), 119–29.

2) Representations of a Middle Ages which, via a playful collapsing of temporal distinctions between the Middle Ages and later epochs, fosters in members of post-medieval cultures a comic identification with the period, tracing transhistoric lines of cultural continuity that enable a kind of modern laughing *in* the Middle Ages. A much-loved instance of this is British comedian Bill Bailey's stand-up routine 'Pubbe Gagge', as seen on the recording of his 2001 *Bewilderness* tour.[19] This ingenious forty-four line comic tale of a drunken lads' night out, narrated mostly in decasyllabic rhyming couplets with heavy comic emphasis on the final 'e', 'in the style of Geoffrey Chaucer' ('Three fellowes wenten into a pubbe̲ | And gleefullye their handes did rubbe̲ | In expectatione of revelrie̲ | For 'twas the houre that is called happye̲') presents the pub gag as a local genre spanning six centuries, linking Chaucer to Bailey via the *Dick Emery Show* of the 1970s. By mentioning the 'lewdness and debaucherie' of Emery's very politically incorrect sketches, Bailey cheekily suggests that they contribute, like his and Chaucer's tales, to a continuous comic tradition portraying a long-thriving ritual of British life.

3) Representations of the Middle Ages whose resilient folk comedy offers a model for modern forms of comic resistance, enabling us to laugh *with* the Middle Ages. A poignant example of this can be found in Soviet director Andrei Tarkovsky's film *Andrei Rublev* (1966). In the episode entitled 'Buffoon, 1400', when a *skomorokh* (itinerant jester) is rounded up violently by soldiers after entertaining some peasants with a ribald song about the local feudal boyar (lord), it appears the satire-intolerant institutional forces of the age have triumphed; but he resurfaces over two decades later, in the film's final episode, where it is revealed that after years of imprisonment, and with half his tongue cut out, his anti-authoritarian spirit remains undimmed. Having declined the domesticating commission to be the Prince's jester, he continues his boisterous clowning for the people, his final words in the film, 'you ain't seen nothing yet', a defiant vow which, for all Tarkovsky's cagey denials of the scene's allegorical import, resonated loudly within his restrictive Soviet context.

These three responses each seem to be invested in different notions of historical periodisation and temporality, wherein medieval and post-medieval periods are either joined or divided along the fault-line of humour. In many cases these differing historical paradigms go hand-in-hand with forms of social commentary, which in turn issue different moral, ethical or political imperatives to their audiences. Comic texts such as Twain's that laugh

---

[19] Bill Bailey, *Bewilderness*, dir. John Kaye Cooper (Talent Television, 2000).

at the Middle Ages seem to affirm a progressivist model of history which emphasises the breach between periods, and arguably validates and advocates for modernity for its implicitly more evolved culture. Texts such as Bailey's that laugh *in* the Middle Ages subscribe to a model of historical continuity that queries both progressivism and periodisation. In so doing, it calls for a kind of transhistorical sympathy with medieval people based on a comic recognition of the universal humanity they share with modern people. This shared humanity is powerfully corporeal, but also inheres in a notion of humanity's perpetual negotiation with the dynamics of power. Texts such as Tarkovsky's that laugh *with* the Middle Ages operate according to recursive historical logic that promotes the notion that social progress might be achieved through recovery of medieval practices. The ethico-political task in such cases is to recover the lost practices of subversive humour bequeathed to modernity by medieval forebears in order to challenge the hegemonic forces within modern society.

The reason historical modelling, social commentary and ethico-political agenda are so commonly linked in comic medievalism is because so much of it operates under the star of satire. Its comic modalities range widely, but its intent is commonly to call attention, via the medieval, to the many unexamined contradictions underpinning the values of modernity, and to provide Western culture with a historical mirror in which it can reflect on and even reform itself. It can be argued that medievalism and satire are, in fact, uniquely compatible bedfellows: working from the premise that post-medieval representations of the Middle Ages are intrinsically tied to, and reflective of, the anxieties and desires of the contexts in which they are produced, it is not surprising that this is a phenomenon that is implicitly as forward-looking in its aspirations as it is backward-looking in its inspirations. When medievalism utilises humour, moreover, to address these post-medieval concerns, a potent, often very amusing and highly variable form of historical satire emerges. Its apt yet uneasy fusion of reformist intent, comic modality and historical content makes it a complex and often contradictory phenomenon that relies simultaneously on cruelty and sympathy toward the Middle Ages, and on both ridiculing and valorising the medieval vis-à-vis modernity in a prankish game of rejection and reclamation. Salmi asks of historical comedy, '[t]he important question … is at whom is the ridicule directed: the contemporary reader, or the people of the past?'[20] In the case of comic medievalism, with its satiric double-vision, the answer is very often 'both'.

One hugely popular illustration of this is the 'Medieval Helpdesk' skit from a 2000 episode of the Norwegian television show *Øystein og jeg*.[21] In this skit

---

[20] Salmi, *Historical Comedy*, p. 22.

[21] 'Medieval Helpdesk', *Øystein og jeg* (Norsk Rikskringkasting, 2000). Skit with English subtitles (NRK, 2001). URL: http://www.youtube.com/watch?v=pQHX-SjgQvQ.

a medieval 'tech guy', with typical cheery perfunctoriness, coaches a bamboo-zled monk, Brother Ansgar, through the shift from parchment rolls to bound books. A favourite with medievalists, this densely clever skit has also struck a particular nerve with the public: it has become a virally popular YouTube clip that has been translated into several languages and inspired numerous continuations and remakes, and internet sites have regularly ranked it among the funniest ten clips about technology, frequently in the number one posi-tion. Interpreted superficially, this skit would appear to be ridiculing the rudimentary nature of medieval 'information technologies' as well as the era's perceived hostility to innovation, where an object like the humble book could be incomprehensible and threatening. But its ingenious transposition of the dynamics of the familiar IT 'helpdesk' exchange on to an earlier watershed in the history of literacy elevates it to the realm of double-visioned satire, addressing itself via the Middle Ages to the sense of disorienting inevita-bility that surrounds today's culture of accelerated change in information technologies. While its humour appeals partly to modern viewers' sense of having progressed beyond the Middle Ages, cheekily likening those who fail to keep up to the progress-averse Ansgar (see, even the static Middle Ages had tech upgrades!), its use of familiarising situational comedy invites the sympathetic laughter of identification with the hapless monk's struggle to absorb the shock of the new.

The children's animated film *How to Train Your Dragon* (2010) provides another example. While its historical humour revolves around depicting the jovial violence of the larger-than-life hiberno-Viking Gobber the Belch and his fledgling dragon-slayers, its satiric portrayal rests on the familiar secular-modernist trope of the irrational medieval society that responds to a perceived threat (the raiding dragons) with reactive fear and retribution.[22] The film does not have a Hank Morgan-style modern time-traveller; but its protagonist Hiccup, with his American ironical-teen idiom and preference for the soft power of training dragons over their destruction or imprisonment, appears to represent a kind of proleptic modern alternative to the benighted ways of his heroic clan. But just as it seems the modern is exposing and displacing the medieval, the film's narrative moves into an allegorical register which reveals that its satire is in fact directed at contemporary America, and that the paranoid violence of the medieval clan has its modern parallel in the US war on terror and failure to grasp the foundations of Islamic insurgency. In a departure from the Cressida Cowell novel on which it is based, the film develops a narrative in which Hiccup discovers that the dragons terrorising the skies above the village are not in fact vindictive destroyers but rather enslaved minions tasked with perpetually feeding a monstrous Über-dragon

[22] *How to Train Your Dragon*, dir. Dean DeBlois and Chris Sanders (Dreamworks Animation, 2010).

whose headquarters are an inaccessible and as-yet undiscovered dragon nest like Osama Bin Laden's (then still unexposed) hideout. Whether viewers accept or reject the consolations offered by this allegory, which exonerates the United States by suggesting that Islamic terrorists are simply the victims of fundamentalist Islamism, the key point here is that the text's satire of the Middle Ages also functions as a commentary on the present. If the past and the present appear to be exposed as equally flawed, however, in such comic-satiric texts the model of historical progress is still upheld, and the modern is still ultimately valorised over the medieval, because implicit within them is the assumption that we moderns should know better. Whatever is risible in medieval culture – whether its undemocratic institutions, its pre-scientific irrationality or its violent habits – is no laughing matter when encountered in the modern period because it marks a failure to evolve socially and morally.

These selected instances point to the fundamental instability of comic medievalism. This instability does not entirely dismantle the tripartite taxonomy discussed above, but it does call into question the neatness of its divisions, as many texts use multiple comic forms to laugh at, with and/or in the Middle Ages at the same time. There is rarely an uncomplicated 'othering' of the Middle Ages: even in *A Connecticut Yankee*, the arrogantly modern Hank observes parallels between the labour inequities of the sixth century and the nineteenth, leading William Dean Howells in 1890 to say of the novel '[it] makes us glad of our republic and our epoch; but it does not flatter us into a fond content with them'.[23] As Steve Guthrie has recently argued, it is important for scholars of medievalism not to fall back too readily on received notions of the medieval as always othered in popular culture.[24]

Symptomatic of this comic breach of periodisation is the very liberal use of anachronism, a much-noted but still under-theorised phenomenon in the context of medievalism studies, which is only just beginning to be rigorously examined.[25] Anachronism is arguably the clearest evidence of what John Morreal has called 'incongruity humour', summarised by Simon Critchley as humour 'produced by the experience of a felt incongruity between what we know or expect to be the case, and what actually takes place in the joke'.[26] In some cases this involves the introduction of incongruous modern elements into medieval scenes, either to highlight modernity's progression beyond the

[23] W. D. Howells, *My Mark Twain: Reminiscences and Criticisms*, edited with an introduction by Marilyn Austin Baldwin (Baton Rouge: Louisiana State University Press, 1967), p. 124.

[24] Steve Guthrie, 'Time Travel, Pulp Fictions, and Changing Attitudes toward the Middle Ages: Why You Can't Get Renaissance on Somebody's Ass', in *Medieval Afterlives in Popular Culture*, ed. Gail Ashton and Daniel T. Kline (New York: Palgrave Macmillan, 2012), pp. 99–111.

[25] For a good recent analysis, see Tison Pugh and Angela Jane Weisl, *Medievalisms: Making the Past in the Present* (London: Routledge, 2013).

[26] Simon Critchley, *On Humour* (New York: Routledge, 2002), p. 3.

medieval (the medieval sketches from the BBC series *Horrible Histories*, to be discussed in Chapter 6), or to make a point about how little humanity has changed ('Pubbe Gagge'), or to endow the Middle Ages with a particular set of 'modern' qualities ('Medieval Helpdesk'); in other, rarer cases, the medieval intrudes into a later period to assert its influence over modernity (Jean-Marie Poiré's madcap film, *Les Visiteurs* (1993), to be discussed in Chapter 5). Using Thomas M. Greene's influential fivefold taxonomy, the most readily identifiable category of anachronism within comic medievalism appears to be his fourth, 'creative anachronism', a deliberate (rather than naïve) usage which 'bring[s] a concrete present into relation with a specific past and play[s] with the distance between them'.[27] The ludic nature of this anachronism, as recognised here by Greene, makes it especially apposite for comic usage. But while Greene argues that creative anachronism 'involves a deliberate dramatization of historical passage', such a description does not apply straightforwardly to much comic medievalism, which, even as it dramatises history's 'diachronic passage', pleats it into synchrony, simultaneity and a paradoxical, circular temporality.[28] Returning to 'Pubbe Gagge', for instance, Bailey does not present himself simply as an heir of Chaucerian bawdy, but rather as telling a 'very old pub joke' that is simultaneously both his and Chaucer's inheritance and creation, a point reinforced by the gag's cross-historical idiom ('after wine and meade and sack | man muste have a massive snack') and by Bailey's mock-Middle English delivery. It explicitly evokes, furthermore, a paradoxical temporality: having described the tale as 'like a sketch by Dick Emery', Bailey-Chaucer goes on to say 'Except that Dick Emery is not yet born | So such a comparisonne may not be drawn', an utterance that confounds audiences with its baffling multi-temporality (and gets the biggest laugh in the process). To cite Zachary S. Schiffman's recent addition to Greene's typology, Bailey's gag, along with so many other comic medievalist texts, exhibits an 'awareness of anachronism as "error"', but embraces the comic potential of this error to bring about a 'synchronic encounter' of the medieval past and the present that teases us out of (historical) thought and into laughter.[29]

A few words should be offered about the use of some key terms in this book, including the general, but not exclusive, preference for the term 'comic' medievalism over the more general designation of 'humorous' medievalism. It is widely acknowledged among theorists in humour studies that attempts

---

[27] Thomas M., Greene, 'History and Anachronism', in *Literature and History: Theoretical Problems and Russian Case Studies*, ed. Gary Saul Morson (Stanford: Stanford University Press, 1986), pp. 205–20 (p. 210); also, Pugh and Weisl, *Medievalisms*, pp. 83–100.

[28] Greene, 'History and Anachronism', p. 210.

[29] Zachary Sayre Schiffman, *The Birth of the Past* (Baltimore, MD: Johns Hopkins University Press, 2011).

to use terms such as 'humour', 'comedy' and their cognates as though they allude to essential and discrete phenomena is not just over-ambitious, but in fact counterproductive. In his major study *Linguistic Theories of Humour*, Salvatore Attardo observes that 'traditional lexical categories may lead to the erroneous belief that there are clean-cut distinctions [between humour and the comic] in reality', and calls instead for a more heuristic approach to terminology that answers to the needs of the specific field. He points, moreover, to the special value of taking this approach when dealing with cultural and historical texts, which are less interested in diagnosing humour as a universal human behaviour or affective category.[30] Following this, I have adopted definitions of the terms 'humour' and 'comedy' which respond more closely to the dual critical-historical nature of this study. First, as a critical study of textual strategies and their reception, its more prominent usage of 'comic medievalism' is modelled in part on that used by Brett Mills in *Television Sitcom*, which distinguishes between the comic as an often highly crafted set of techniques designed to generate mirth, and humour as the more general, incidental and often 'unscripted' experience of amusement in everyday life, which exceeds the comic.[31] Nevertheless, because comedy contains the humorous – that is, the comic content of texts necessarily involves some technical or aesthetic arrangement of humour as 'raw material' – the words 'humour' and 'humorous' are still used to describe content that generates mirth. The other strategic reason for the more insistent use of 'comic' and 'comedy' is that they reflect the study's commitment to arguing for historical continuity and recursion as fundamental premises of medievalism. The term 'humour' is regularly described as 'modern' in humour studies in a way that not only reifies a break between the medieval and the modern, but also uncritically perpetuates a belief that modern mirth is more sophisticated and civilised than earlier forms. Comedy and the comic, conversely, are forms that are acknowledged as crossing the pre-modern/modern divide, adapting themselves to historical change, but still challenging the progressivist claims about the supercession of the medieval by the modern. For this reason, the medievalism that laughs in, with and at the Middle Ages is comic medievalism.

The principal aim of this book is to develop a critical discourse for understanding how and why the medieval period has yielded such an enduring and rich seam of mirth for later ages, and through this to see what medievalism's intersection with humour can illuminate about the affective, creative, historicist dimensions of medievalism in general. To that end, this is not a comprehensive study of the history of laughing at the Middle Ages, tracing

---

[30]   Salvatore Attardo, *Linguistic Theories of Humour* (Berlin and New York: Mouton de Gruyter, 1994), pp. 1–5, esp. p. 3.
[31]   Brett Mills, *Television Sitcom* (London: BFI, 2005), p. 18.

a trajectory of emergence and stages of development up to the present. This is partly because such a task, even treated synoptically, would be far too vast for a single book, given the long, international history of medievalism; but it is also because medievalism as a cultural phenomenon resists a smooth developmental narration. The Middle Ages have been recruited (to use Bruce Holsinger's suggestive term[32]) to speak to later ages unpredictably, contingently and opportunistically, so joining the dots of medievalism's genealogy would be less like plotting a smooth arc than mapping a constellation, with its crossing lines and angles doubled back on themselves to form irregular shapes. The texts selected for analysis, then, are conceived not as points on a historical trajectory but as representative samples to test out the conceptual framework tendered in this introduction, as well as because they represent distinctive varieties of medievalist humour and distinctive 'visions' of the Middle Ages as (deliberately or inadvertently) funny, or they capture significant moments in the development of comic medievalism. The structure is loosely genealogical, insofar as the earlier texts mostly precede the later ones; but they are also grouped into sections according to what they do with the Middle Ages.

Borrowing its title from the terminology of joke-telling, Part I, 'The Set Up', introduces the book's critical frame for interpreting the myriad of comic representations of the Middle Ages. Encompassing the current introductory chapter and Chapter 1, this part of the book identifies and calibrates the different comic and historical dynamics within medievalist texts, sets up the case for comic texts' unique querying of the distinction between the medieval and the modern and explores, by way of an analysis of Cervantes's *Don Quixote*, the relationship between the key comic medievalist forms of parody, satire and farce. It also locates a self-reflexive 'meta-medievalist' impulse inherent within comic medievalist texts, and argues for its significance not only in shaping their comic contours but also in disclosing their comic meditations on what it means to represent the medieval past.

Following on from this introduction, Chapter 1 'The Cervantean Paradigm: Comedy, Madness, and Meta-Medievalism in *Don Quixote*' argues that an examination of *Don Quixote* is vital to establishing the terms of any genealogy of comic medievalism, not primarily because of the novel's chronological precedence as the most famous among the early comic medievalist texts, but, more compellingly, because by anatomising Cervantes's capacious and sometimes dissonant fusion of parodic and farcical elements under the auspices of satire, it is possible to develop an aesthetic blueprint for modern comic medievalism that will be tested and contested by later iterations of comic medievalism. The chapter also suggests that as a meta-medievalist

---

[32] Bruce Holsinger, *The Premodern Condition: Medievalism and the Making of Theory* (Chicago, IL: The University of Chicago Press, 2005), p. 5.

text Cervantes's novel additionally offers an early template for medievalism studies' examination of medieval afterlives, both enacting and commenting on the processes by which medieval texts come to be disseminated and resignified in post-medieval settings, showing that even from its earliest days, medievalism – both its interpretive modes and its social effects – has been subject to as much commentary and evaluation as the Middle Ages themselves. It also investigates the extent to which Cervantes's ambivalence toward the Middle Ages, which leads him both to engage in and critique medievalism, can also be regarded as a constitutive feature of medievalist comic forms that maps out the key ways in which the Middle Ages can be laughed at, in and with.

Part II, 'Oldies but Goodies: Comic Recovery', explores 'methodological comic medievalism'. Rather than examining comic representations of the Middle Ages, its two chapters focus on ways in which the medieval period has come to be associated in the post-medieval world with particular forms of comedy and humour. These chapters examine two very different ways in which medieval comic precedents have been reanimated as a way to understand comic forms and practices that are strongly aligned with notions of modernity and progress.

Chapter 2, 'Scraping the Rust from the Joking Bard: Chaucer in the Age of Wit', focuses on the Enlightenment reclamation of Chaucer. It examines the diverse and ambivalent ways in which readers and writers in the long eighteenth century (starting in the late seventeenth century) invested heavily in an idea of Chaucer as a 'joking bard', and explores how this preoccupation with Chaucerian jocularity intersected with attempts either to retrieve a lost comic tradition or, conversely, to identify a continuous presence of wit in English culture and beyond. Examining Enlightenment theories of wit, the chapter focuses on a number of comic engagements with Chaucer by such well-known writers as Edmund Spenser, Alexander Pope and John Gay, contextualising these within the broader culture of Chaucer commentary, as well as modernisation, imitation, and Chaucer continuation. It also examines how this comic engagement emerged in tandem with vital developments in the editing of the poet's works, and thus argues that the less-examined recovery of the Joking Bard needs to be examined in the context of the period's widespread and varying evaluation of his role in the development of the English language. It explores in particular the tension between this period's medievalism and the anti-medievalist presentism that underpinned the widely held eighteenth-century conviction that Chaucer's 'rusted' wit could only be rescued by divesting it of its 'unpolish'd' versification and its ribald excesses – that is, of its medievalness.

Chapter 3, 'Medievalist Farce as Anti-Totalitarian Weapon: Dario Fo as Modern *Giullare*', looks at how the Nobel Prize-winning playwright Dario Fo's self-perception as a comedian-activist has long drawn on tropes drawn from his extensive research into medieval comic entertainment. Focusing on Fo's *Mistero Buffo: The Comic Mysteries* and *Francis the Holy Jester*, the chapter examines how Fo's own radical buffoonery was developed directly out of his conception of a Middle Ages in which anarchic folk humour had the power to expose the abuses and hypocrisies of those in power. Dwelling closely on his attempt to reanimate the peripatetic figures of the medieval *giullare* and St Francis of Assisi, the chapter argues for Fo's medievalism as a key weapon in his satiric armoury against social injustice, capitalism and the turbulence of Italian politics. It also considers the role of Fo's physical comedy, and his adaptation of farce, as an instrument of his satiric agenda. Fo's work is placed in the context of a longer left-modernist tradition that was strongly committed to an exploration, and revival, of medieval 'folk' humour. The chapter also addresses the dissent between Fo and his direct contemporary Pier Paolo Pasolini over the revolutionary possibilities of representing the medieval past, and examines how Umberto Eco's *The Name of the Rose* responds to the legacy bequeathed by Fo and the medievalism of the modernist left.

Part III, 'Hit and Myth: Performing and Parodying Medievalism', surveys the proliferation of comic representations of the Middle Ages on stage and screen, looking at how they epitomise the cannibalising, and self-cannibalising, tendency not only of popular performance but also of medievalism as a cultural phenomenon. Both chapters in this section show the convergence of parody with satire, and again highlight the ambivalence popular comic culture nurses towards the medieval past.

Chapter 4, 'Pre-Modern Camp and Faerie Legshows: Travestying the Middle Ages on the Nineteenth-Century Stage', offers a critical overview that ranges across the rich culture of comic medievalism on the Victorian stage, comprising burlesque, pantomime, harlequinade, opera bouffe and fairy spectacle, focusing on these plays' promiscuous looting of medieval history, legend and folklore for the purposes of topical humour. By considering these performance texts historically and in relation to changing formulations of camp aesthetics, it argues that these forms, for all their avowed triviality and ephemerality, are worth revisiting for what they expose about the complicated nature of representing the medieval in popular comedic performance. This complication is located primarily in the tension between their ambitious antiquarian representational form, and their relatively facile content, which often evinced a blithe unconcern with the fact that their subjects were indeed medieval. The chapter explores how the imperatives of ephemeral parodic satire inevitably compromise the medievalism on which these performances depend. In considering these issues, this chapter will explore the question of whether these plays' camp medievalism is symptomatic, or even paradigmatic, of performative comic adaptations of the Middle Ages.

Chapter 5, 'Up the Middle Ages: Performing Tradition in Comic Medievalist Cinema', continues the critical overview approach taken in Chapter 4, surveying the expansive corpus of comic medievalist cinema, from well-

known films such as *Monty Python and the Holy Grail* through to a number
which, while less famous, feature fascinating comic visions of the past. Because
medievalist cinema is characterised by a prolific breadth of genres and comic
techniques, no single idiom is nominated to characterise it. Nevertheless, its
links to parodic theatre are maintained, in that rather than seeing cinematic
medievalism as an independent comic tradition, the chapter examines how
numerous films overtly ground their comic techniques in perceived long
performance traditions reaching back to the Middle Ages. It also considers
the valence of these films' witty meta-parodic nods to those earlier and
contemporary 'straight' medievalist films that have been so instrumental in
forming popular views of the Middle Ages. Exploring key examples, it also
gauges comic medievalist cinema's satiric potential as well as its limitations,
dwelling on its engagement with sexual politics and the ideologies of class
and social progress in the modern West. Finally, through a discussion of the
subgenre of the medieval time-travel film, the chapter considers cinema's
capacity to undertake comically philosophical meditations on time and the
role of the medieval past in forming, or indeed reforming, the present.

Part IV, 'That's Edutainment: Comedy and History', shifts from fictional
representations of the Middle Ages to focus on the complex stylistic and
ethical negotiation between comedy and history in contemporary formats
that offer what can be described as forms of comic pedagogy or 'edutainment'. It examines these formats' strategic responses to the competing pressures of historical accuracy and/or nostalgic recovery.

Chapter 6, '"The Past is a Different and Fairly Disgusting Country": The
Middle Ages in Recent British Jocumentary', examines the representation of
the medieval past, and in particular the 'British Middle Ages', in three television series: Tony Robinson's *Worst Jobs in History* and Terry Jones's *Medieval
Lives* and *Horrible Histories*, based on the hugely successful book series by
British author Terry Deary. It traces the ways in which these series represent
the medieval past as edutainment, paying particular attention to the question of how they are able to partake of the authority of documentary at the
same time as adopting an ironic disposition toward the genre and engaging
the 'lower' pleasures of laughter and amusement. It considers this question
through an examination of their intersecting range of comic techniques
and of their allusions to the history of comedy as well as to social histories.
Through examining these questions, it will explore the ways in which these
series invite a different treatment from other more avowedly fictive forms of
comic medievalism. It ends by assessing these three jocumentaries' attempts
to address their divided pedagogical and comic ambitions by embracing an
unstable logic in which historical alterity is both acknowledged and disavowed.

Chapter 7, 'Smelling the Past: Medieval Heritage Tourism and the Phenomenology of Ironic Nostalgia', explores, through selected British examples,
how medievalist heritage tourism, as a phenomenological or experiential

counterpart to jocumentary, balances historicism, nostalgia and irony in its attempts to reconcile its aim to deliver an experience of 'living history' with its postmodern scepticism about the possibility of experiencing nostalgic possession and medieval presence. Examining a number of comic medievalist tourist attractions, this chapter explores the way they attempt to resolve this dilemma by operating in a paradoxical 'comic-nostalgic' register that combines the distancing strategies of ironic edutainment with an intimate phenomenological evocation of the past. Engaging closely with the question of how nostalgic historicism and irony can coexist, this chapter focuses in particular on the ways this industry makes conspicuous use of 'medieval' odour to achieve this touristic register, arguing that the transitivity of odours works to reinforce the boundaries between the pungent Middle Ages and modernity yet simultaneously offers a comically repellent experience of disgusting pre-modernity. Despite this abjecting of the past, however, this chapter suggests that the satiric intent of heritage tourism is frequently aimed at the anxieties and hypocrisies of contemporary society rather than at the Middle Ages.

The Afterword, 'Laughing into the Future', offers a brief reflective culmination to the study by revisiting the distinctions between comedy that laughs *at* the Middle Ages, *with* the Middle Ages and *in* the Middle Ages, and by considering whether there is anything these diverse forms share. It offers a reflection on which theories of humour offer the most productive paths into understanding the post-medieval comic reception of the Middle Ages, and on the relative success and limitations of the various comic modes discussed throughout the book. It will, finally, point to future directions that the study of comic medievalism might take, posing critical questions that have emerged through the course of the book that merit future analysis.

1

The Cervantean Paradigm: Comedy, Madness and Meta-Medievalism in *Don Quixote*

T HE MAN CRASHES TO THE DIRT FLOOR and lies motionless, unhorsed by the blow of a lance to his chest. His alarmed opponent leaps from his horse and runs to the man's aid. 'Well done, good sir', says the vanquished knight, 'you are the victor; but we will meet again.' As the weary men rise, gauntlets clasped above their heads in camaraderie, the crowd roars at the lengthy and violent spectacle it has just witnessed. The date is 1996; the place is the Buena Park outlet of the theatre-restaurant chain Medieval Times; and the men are Chip Douglas and Steven Kovacs, the two protagonists of the dark comedy *The Cable Guy*, directed by Ben Stiller. In this, the film's famous 'Medieval Times' scene, the unstable Chip (the eponymous cable guy), obsessed with gaining Steven's friendship but also consumed by lonely malice, has secretly arranged for the two of them to engage in public mock combat 'to the death', according to the 'King' of Medieval Times, 'to resolve a grievance'. What ensues is an onslaught in which reality dissolves into violent chivalric fantasy, with Chip wielding a sword, a flail, a battle axe and a lance with such clear intent to harm that the Medieval Times performers are as frightened of him as Steven is. Later, though, after he has been unhorsed, he congratulates Steven on his 'warrior's instinct', and the two have (temporarily) formed the bond Chip has been desperately chasing but which the wary Steven has so far evaded.[1]

This scene is arresting for its brutally comic take on medievalism as a form of delusion. It is true that Chip's medievalism is not the only expression of his escalating psychosis, but neither is it incidental. At first his devotion to Medieval Times (he attends twice a week and describes it without irony as 'the best restaurant in town') seems benign, a kind of shorthand for

---

[1]   *The Cable Guy*, dir. Ben Stiller (Columbia Pictures, 1996).

his goofiness and social ineptitude. Finke and Shichtman have argued that it can be seen as part of Chip's understandable desire for respite from the alienation of a technologised society in which organic human relations have been replaced by remote cable connections: in short, through medievalism he seeks a nostalgic 'cure for the trauma of modernity'.[2] As he becomes more and more violent in his staged battle with Steven, however, it is clear that his love of chivalric combat is also a symptom of a deeper wound, emerging out of a yearning for homosocial relations in which love and aggression are intertwined and codified: a yearning which, the audience learns, has its origins in his unfulfilled wish as a lonely boy for a brother to play and fight with, like the kids he sees on television.

There is much about Chip that reflects, as Finke and Shichtman suggest, a subjectivity formed unhappily in the crucible of modern media and commodity culture. But his character also fits a template of delusional chivalry that reaches back across centuries to a seminal comic forebear: Miguel de Cervantes's fanatical self-appointed knight errant Don Quixote in the 1605–15 masterpiece *The Ingenious Gentleman Don Quixote of La Mancha* (henceforth *Don Quixote*). The echoes are undeniable. First, just as Don Quixote's 'brains [have] dried up', and he has lost much of his estate, as a result of his insatiable reading of chivalric romances, so too Chip's compulsive diet of television, with its idealised portraits of couple-formation and family life, has 'rotted his brain', costing him his job and leaving him unable to form relationships.[3] The dialogue of both characters is a tissue of allusions to the texts they have imbibed: in Don Quixote's case his speech combines generalised chivalric pastiche with specific citations of romances including his favourite, *Amadís of Gaul*, while Chip strings together memorised lines from films and TV programmes to form a confabulated approximation of everyday banter. At Medieval Times, he mouths verbatim the cod-chivalric shtick of the 'King', and later in the arena he switches between medievalesque archaisms and references to the iconic 'Amok Time' episode of *Star Trek*, in which Kirk duels with Spock. Further, both he and Don Quixote have adopted pseudonyms that connect them to their fantasy worlds, although they differ insofar as Don Quixote merely styles his name in the fashion of his heroes, while the cable guy's pseudonym 'Chip Douglas' is lifted directly from a character in the wholesome 1960s family sitcom *My Three Sons*. Finally, as comic protagonists, Chip and his iconic forebear share an amusing but alarming tendency to veer between the poles of affable derangement and extreme violence, the latter emerging in response to perceived violations of their delusional ideal

---

[2]   Laurie A. Finke and Martin B. Shichtman, *Cinematic Illuminations: The Middle Ages on Film* (Baltimore, MD: Johns Hopkins University Press, 2010), p. 16.

[3]   Miguel de Cervantes, *Don Quixote*, trans. Edith Grossman, intro. Harold Bloom (London: Vintage Books, 2005), p. 21.

worlds. So while Chip might be a medievalist only on a part-time basis, he is quixotic all the time.

In addition, then, to being profoundly important to the development of the novel, the whole future course of which, some have argued, is anticipated within its pages, *Don Quixote* casts a long shadow over the later development of comic medievalism. This is not to suggest that all subsequent comic medievalist texts pay tribute to this novel, or even that they are directly influenced by it, but rather that the capaciousness of its medievalism and its nuanced use of several comic registers forecast the many ways in which future ages have come to take comic approaches to the Middle Ages. Allusions to *Don Quixote* in scholarly accounts of comic medievalist texts are so frequent as to be almost a convention, suggesting that no genealogical account of this phenomenon would be complete without assessing what this novel has bequeathed to modernity's view of the Middle Ages. This framing chapter, then, does not aim to offer an exhaustive analysis of Cervantes's massive novel, but instead to focus on the complex paradigm of comic medievalism formulated in it, exploring its relationship to the critical framework outlined in this book's introduction and analysing how this early text maps out the ways in which the Middle Ages can be laughed at, in and with.

I should begin by saying that although the novel's combination of subject matter and comic registers would appear to make it an agenda-setting text for comic medievalism, on closer inspection the case is more complicated. For a start, unlike many of the texts to be discussed in later chapters of this book, Cervantes's tale is less concerned with presenting a comical representation of the medieval period itself than with exploring the comic outcomes arising from an unchecked fanaticism for medieval culture. It appears to be actually laughing at medievalism, and thus is more readily describable as comic *meta*-medievalism. The novel's stated premise, repeated no fewer than three times in the Prologue alone, is to offer an 'invective against books of chivalry', one which 'intends ... to undermine the authority and wide acceptance that [these books] have in the world and among the public' with 'the goal of demolishing [their] ill-founded apparatus ... despised by many but praised by so many more'.[4] The target, therefore, is not simply the books themselves but their popularity and influence in contemporary society. This objective is reiterated at the conclusion of Book II, when the fictional author of the original 'history' of Don Quixote, the Arab historian Cide Hamete Benengeli, is quoted as saying 'my only desire has been to have people reject and despise the false and nonsensical histories of the books of chivalry'.[5] This meta-textual dimension partly explains why scholars of medievalism are also drawn to the novel; it shows that even from its earliest days, medievalism

---

4   Ibid., p. 8.
5   Ibid., p. 940.

– both its interpretive modes and its social effects – have been subject to commentary and evaluation. Far from simply offering a comic representation of the Middle Ages, Cervantes's book goes further by both enacting and commenting on the idiosyncratic processes through which medieval texts come to be disseminated and resignified in post-medieval settings, offering an early template for medievalism studies' examination of medieval afterlives. In portraying Don Quixote's improvised adventures of knight errantry, it traces equally the misadventures of medievalist reception.

The crucial error resulting from Don Quixote's obsessive reading of these books, and one which reflects one of the novel's central dialectics, is his inability to distinguish history from romance, or fact from fiction: 'he became so convinced in his imagination of the truth of all the countless grandiloquent and false inventions he read that for him no history in the world was truer'.[6] For all his singularity as a character, in thus confusing fact and fiction he embodies a common anxiety that had been expressed for some decades by Spanish chroniclers, who were determined that their works should be distinguished from chivalric tales, with all their mendacious extravagances.[7] Even more alarming is the material effect of Don Quixote's misreading. His belief in the factuality of heroic romance leads him to reject the everyday, substituting it with a delusional world in which he repeatedly accosts unsuspecting strangers and assigns them involuntary roles in his dissociative chivalric fugue. In the novel's much-loved early chapters this leads to numerous comic episodes in which bemused prostitutes are addressed with florid encomia, innocent travellers are attacked and forced to pay tribute to the peerless beauty of Don Quixote's imagined mistress Ducinea del Toboso and, most famously, the local farmer Sancho Panza is persuaded by grandiose promises into serving as Don Quixote's squire. Throughout the novel everything that happens to him is re-narrated by him as a chivalric encounter, from the famous battle with the windmills in Book I:8 through to the fumble he shares with the Asturian servant girl Maritornes in Book I:16, whose rough clothes and uncomely features he duly re-imagines as rich and beauteous. His delusions extend even to the olfactory realm, so that Maritornes's breath, instead of smelling like 'yesterday's stale salad, seemed to him a soft, aromatic scent, wafting from her mouth'.[8] So impregnable is the edifice of Don Quixote's fantasy that his one momentary glimpse of reality is swiftly repelled and made to conform to his romance worldview. This takes place in the episode in Book II:10 when Sancho tries to convince him that three plain peasant girls are actually his beloved Dulcinea and her

<hr>

6   Ibid., p. 21.
7   See B. W. Ife, *Reading and Fiction in Golden-Age Spain: A Platonist Critique and Some Picaresque Replies* (Cambridge, UK: Cambridge University Press, 1985), pp. 12–18.
8   Cervantes, *Don Quixote*, p. 113.

damsels. This scene is remarkable because in a moment of unprecedented clarity, Don Quixote is thunder-struck by the fact that he 'could see nothing except a peasant girl, and one not especially attractive, since she was round-faced and snub-nosed';[9] but Sancho immediately, and successfully, convinces him that he is under a wicked enchantment that distorts his vision, after which he falls to his knees and venerates the exasperated young woman. In *Mimesis* Erich Auerbach suggests that this episode hovers between the comic and the tragic, exposing just how vulnerable Don Quixote's bookish delusions have made him; nevertheless the fact that literary fantasy ultimately survives its perilous brush with reality leads Auerbach to declare the scene, and indeed the novel, comic.[10]

In positing *Don Quixote* as a blueprint of meta-medievalist commentary, I do not wish to nominate it as some kind of stand-alone originary text, because it is certainly not isolated as an early example of comic medievalism. That the increasingly hackneyed chivalric conventions of medieval literature had for some time been ripe for parody is evident in Geoffrey Chaucer's hilariously abortive tail-rhyme, 'The Tale of Sir Thopas', the first of the Chaucer pilgrim's two tales in *The Canterbury Tales*. This tale's anticipation by over two centuries of Cervantes's themes was, as I point out in Chapter 2, noted by eighteenth-century devotees to Chaucer's 'wit', and has continued to draw commentary up to the present. 'Sir Thopas' differs from Cervantes's book in that rather than containing overt commentary on the ridiculousness of chivalric literature and its redundancy in the present, or featuring a deluded reader of romance as its main character, Chaucer's tale engages in performative critique: the genre's exhaustion is lampooned via the content and structure of the tale itself, and the bad reader of romance is the narrator himself. The muddle of cliché (a knight, a giant, an elf-queen, a forest), prosaic deflation epitomised in the dull Flemish setting of Poperyng, and apparently inadvertent ribaldry with strong suggestions of onanism ('pryking'), all present romance as a genre made stale by overuse. The narrative structure, meanwhile, enacts the exhaustion of chivalric romance: the tale of conflict between Thopas and his antagonist, the giant Sir Oliphaunt, labours along irresolutely and culminates undramatically in Thopas retreating from the rocks being slung by Oliphaunt in a comic reversal of David and Goliath's confrontation. The Chaucer pilgrim's heavily padded narration similarly sputters out into nothingness, with each Fytte, as Malcolm Andrew pointed out some time ago, literally halving in length as he flounders in a derivative puddle, struggling to sustain his narrative and thereby to maintain his listeners' attention:

---

9   Ibid., p. 518.
10   Erich Auerbach, *Mimesis: The Representation of Reality in Western Literature*, trans. William Trask (Princeton: Princeton University Press, 1953), p. 347. For Auerbach's full argument, see the chapter 'The Enchanted Dulcinea', pp. 334–58.

the 'Listeth, lordes, in good entent' with which he first hails his audience degenerates by the third Fytte into the agitated plea 'Now holde youre mouth, par charitee', until he is cut off unceremoniously by the Host, who condemns him for his 'drasty' rhymes.[11]

Another text that is almost directly contemporary with Cervantes's, and which engages in a remarkably similar burlesque of the early modern consumption of medieval chivalric romance, is Francis Beaumont's City Comedy *The Knight of the Burning Pestle*, first performed in 1607 by the children's company of London's second Blackfriars Theatre. Although the play's first publisher, Walter Burre, declared that it predated the publication of Thomas Shelton's 1612 English translation of *Don Quixote* by 'about a yeare', Sheldon P. Zitner argues that Shelton's unpublished manuscript had been in circulation since 1607, and so Beaumont may have had some knowledge of Cervantes's content when writing his script.[12] This play, in which Rafe the Grocer's apprentice determines to become a 'grocer errant' after reading such 'worthy books' of chivalry as *Palmerin of England* and *Amadís of Gaul*, dubbing himself The Right Courteous Knight of the Burning Pestle, would appear to owe a debt to Cervantes's narrative premise. Similarly, Cervantes's unromantic planes of La Mancha and Chaucer's forest outside of Poperyng are echoed in the 'perilous Waltham Down' where Rafe's adventures take place. Although the play's complexity extends to a meta-commentary on middle-class tastes, weighing the relative merits of 'realist' citizen drama against the glamour of chivalric scenarios, its prosaic burlesque of chivalric motifs make it, at its heart, a Quixotic drama.

A further complication that merits consideration even when describing *Don Quixote* as 'meta-medievalist' is that the chivalric tales mentioned

---

[11] Geoffrey Chaucer, 'The Tale of Sir Thopas', *The Riverside Chaucer*, ed. Larry D. Benson, 3rd edn (Boston, MA: Houghton Mifflin Co., 1987), pp. 213–16, nn. 917–23. As medievalist scholars have for some time pointed out, 'Sir Thopas' is not the only, or the first, text to tease out the absurd potential in chivalric romance. Indeed, the medieval romance tradition itself includes a rich and varied use of comic modes. Along with the widespread commentary on the comic impulse in famous tales such as *Sir Gawain and the Green Knight*, see, for instance, Dennis Howard Green's earlier study of *Irony in the Medieval Romance* (Cambridge: Cambridge University Press, 1978). More recently, Erik Kooper has produced an edition of *Sentimental and Humorous Romances: Floris and Blancheflour, Sir Degrevant, The Squire of Low Degree, The Tournament of Tottenham and the Feast of Tottenham* (Kalamazoo, MI: Medieval Institute Publications, 2005). As Geraldine Heng's account of anthropophagic humour in *Richard Coer de Lyon* reminds us, humour in the medieval romance is not necessarily subversive, but can constitute a 'skilful expansion of romance resources … that enlarg[es] the narrative constituency of romance and the effectivity of the ideological medium'. See her *Empire of Magic: Medieval Romance and the Politics of Cultural Fantasy* (New York: Columbia University Press, 2003), p. 67.

[12] Sheldon P. Zitner, ed., 'Introduction', to Francis Beaumont, *The Knight of the Burning Pestle* (Manchester: Manchester University Press, 1984, revised 2004), pp. 10–11.

throughout the text, despite their recognisable use of conventions developed in medieval literature, are not described by Cervantes or any of his characters as 'medieval' per se. E. C. Riley's assertion that 'the golden age of chivalry [Don Quixote] wanted to resurrect had little to do with the real Middle Ages; it was an age that never was, the imaginary story book age of "Once upon a time"' is certainly borne out in the characters' vague allusions to 'knights of yore' (the term used by the innkeeper who knights Don Quixote), who are themselves nostalgic evocations of a legendary heroic past. [13] Yet, as B. W. Ife argues, the novel's portrayal of its protagonist's consumption of knightly tales 'has anachronism as its central theme'; [14] so in order for this anachronistic conceit to be comic, chivalry must be perceived not as timeless but, rather, as out of date. As such, the novel relies on evoking a clear epochal rupture between a perceived 'age of chivalry' and Don Quixote's present. Don Quixote, amid all his delusion of seeing himself as a knight errant, still recognises himself as a historical subject in a way that enables him to embrace proudly the status of anachronism. This is apparent in his explicit claim, in Book I Chapter 47, to be reviving chivalry as a discontinued pre-modern practice; he sees himself not as a 'knight of yore' living in a heroic past, but as 'a new knight in the world, the first to resuscitate the now forgotten practice of errant chivalry'.[15] He later frames this anachronistic personal mission within a grand historical narrative of decline, offering a lengthy denunciation of the present which, despite mentioning no specific dates or eras, nevertheless nostalgically contrasts the post-chivalric present with a vanished world which unmistakably has its origins in medieval romance:

> our decadent age does not deserve to enjoy the good that was enjoyed in the days when knights errant took it as their responsibility to bear on their own shoulders the defense of kingdoms, the protection of damsels, the safeguarding of orphans and wards, the punishment of the proud, and the rewarding of the humble. Most knights today would rather rustle in damasks, brocades, and the other rich fabrics of their clothes than creak in chain mail; no longer do knights sleep in the fields, subject to the rigors of heaven, wearing all their armor from head to foot; no longer does anyone, with his feet still in the stirrups and leaning forward on his lance, catch forty winks, as they say, in the way knights errant used to do ... sloth triumphs over diligence, idle-

---

[13] E. C. Riley, 'Literature and Life in Don Quixote', in *Cervantes' Don Quixote: A Casebook*, ed. Roberto González Echevarría (Oxford: Oxford University Press, 2005), p. 126; Cervantes, *Don Quixote*, p. 25.

[14] B. W. Ife, 'The Historical and Social Context', in *The Cambridge Companion to Cervantes*, ed. Anthony J. Cascardi (Cambridge: Cambridge University Press, 2002), pp. 11–31 (p. 11).

[15] Cervantes, *Don Quixote*, pp. 405–6.

ness over work, arrogance over valor, and theory over the practice of arms, which lived and shone only in the Golden Age and in the time of the knights errant.[16]

Don Quixote's grandiose perception of his revival of knighthood's lost glory contrasts amusingly with the no-nonsense modernity of the narration of his adventures, which highlights his anachronistic status for comic effect, revelling in the risible spectacle his chivalric antics present to his contemporaries. The historical incongruity of his performance and appearance is registered in their reactions to him, which range from alarm to anger and, in many cases, hilarity, as his interlocutors struggle to contain their laughter: of his early encounter with the prostitutes at the inn, for instance, it is said 'when they heard themselves called maidens ... they could not control their laughter'.[17] Despite its stark tonal difference, however, the plain-speaking narration colludes with Don Quixote's self-description by aligning him with an image of knighthood that is strongly coded as medieval, depicting him as spouting chivalric clichés while dressed in armour which 'had belonged to his great-grandfathers [and] spent many long years stored and forgotten in a corner'.[18] Notwithstanding the absence of terminology identifying the Middle Ages, then, the medieval period is conceptually strongly evident both for Don Quixote and for the narrator, and its appeal to Don Quixote is strongly accounted for.

The novel's meta-medievalism need not be regarded as operating entirely separately from the comic medievalism woven throughout it, in which the Middle Ages are, for the most part, heartily laughed at. From the very beginning of the novel, the twinned nature of the novel's satire is apparent. There is no doubt that Don Quixote's fixation on heroic romance is presented as absurd, but this is in large part because the object of his mania, medieval literature, is itself (to cite again the novel's framing sections) 'ill-founded' and 'false and nonsensical'; in short, risible. One of the chief comic techniques used to expose the absurdity of romance, and one which certainly sets the paradigm for future comic medievalism, is verbal parody. In the opening section narrating Don Quixote's descent into madness, it is not just the volume of reading he does that robs him of sanity, but the mind-numbing density of the phrasing which he has struggled unsuccessfully to parse, parodied wickedly in the *trobar ric*-like sentence '[t]he reason for the unreason to which my reason turns so weakens my reason that with reason I complain of your beauty'.[19] Such ornate speech is Don Quixote's preferred enunciative mode throughout the novel, while Sancho Panza, meanwhile, becomes more

[16] Ibid., p. 465.
[17] Ibid., p. 26.
[18] Ibid., p. 22.
[19] Ibid., p. 20.

and more adept at 'managing' his master by addressing him from within the discursive framework of chivalry, so as the novel develops his speech increasingly draws on its concepts and phrases, becoming more comically elaborate as the narrative continues.

Examining these speeches helps disclose the complexity of parody as a comic medievalist register, for its aim to ridicule medieval culture is achieved through the use, and thereby the continuation or even revival, of medieval forms. In other words, in order to laugh *at* the Middle Ages, it must laugh *in* the Middle Ages. This is borne out in Cervantes's verbal parodies, the success of which, according to Anthony J. Close, lies first of all in their 'marginal' rather than 'crude' exaggeration of chivalric and courtly rhetoric, which Cervantes amplifies rather than caricatures. This finely tuned parody, Close argues, transfers the weight of the absurdity in many scenes on to 'the grotesque mismatch between style and addressee',[20] with his principal example being the scene where Don Quixote addresses the peeved 'peasant Dulcinea' as 'highest virtue that can be desired, summit of human courtesy, sole remedy for this afflicted heart that adoreth thee!'[21] To Close's sound observation that Cervantes's readers would have regarded such mismatched exchanges as comic 'failure[s] of decorum', I would add that these encounters are also amusing because there is a historical mismatch between the speeches and their addressees. It is not simply that many of the characters are too déclassé to be spoken to in this way, but also that they are too modern.

Chivalric parody is also engaged in performatively at the level of narrative, in the many scenes where Don Quixote's knight errantry brings him into conflict with people (and objects) who cross his path. The occasions when he consults his memory about how his literary counterparts would have behaved, or indeed when he acts without reflection but in accordance with the literary canons of knight errantry, lead to situations that are disastrous but nevertheless humorously familiar to readers acquainted with the ultra-violence favoured in many medieval heroic texts. Similarly to the novel's verbal parodies, the comic essence of these episodes lies in the incongruity between Don Quixote's knightly deeds and his context. This is taken to a particularly ludicrous extreme in Book II:26 when he unleashes his noble fury on a group of puppets. Watching Master Pedro's puppet show, the plot of which is 'taken literally from the French chronicles and Spanish ballads' about Charlemagne's son-in-law Don Gaiferos, he becomes so involved in the plot that, emulating the heroes of its source texts, he violently hacks the

---

[20] Anthony J. Close, 'The Legacy of Don Quijote and the Picaresque Novel', in *The Cambridge Companion to the Spanish Novel: From 1600 to the Present*, ed. Harriet Turner and Adelaida López de Martínez (Cambridge: Cambridge University Press, 2003), pp. 15–30 (p. 27).
[21] Cervantes, *Don Quixote*, p. 518.

enemy 'Moorish' puppets to pieces.[22] By trading so heavily in this kind of incongruity between chivalric deed and modern context, Cervantes exposes to ridicule the inherently absurd conventions of medieval literature, which are shown to be entirely inappropriate to the modern world. It is worth reiterating, however, that in order to do this, Cervantes himself performs in the modern what he ridicules in the medieval. In so doing, he also makes the modern look ridiculous, relying on the mock-heroic technique that Alexander Pope would later call *bathos*, where the high (the idiom of chivalric honour) is brought into contact with the low (early modern Spain), so that the incongruity not only deflates the high, but also emphasises the indignity of the low,[23] whether this be puppets, peasants or prostitutes. This performative collapse of the dichotomy between laughing subject and comic object is central to what James Wood describes as the 'comedy of forgiveness', a compassionate ridicule that does not preclude self-mockery.[24] It is this very ambiguity that infuses Cervantes's parody, and medievalist parody in general, with both its pleasure and its ambiguity, its rich quality of laughing both at and in the Middle Ages.

This ambiguity is aptly described by Robert Phiddian, who describes the economy of parody as comprising '[s]upplementary logics of criticism, reformulation, and homage'. Speaking specifically of *Don Quixote*, he argues that it 'illustrates this supplementary relationship to its host genre, in that it attacks and ironizes romance, yet also becomes implicated in its logic and energy'. Phiddian's description of 'the very peculiar and intense intimacy that builds up between a parody and its host genre [which] oscillates and steadfastly refuses to be stabilized into any straightforward pattern of criticism or logical argument' perfectly captures the mischievous parasitism that feeds not just Cervantes's engagement with medieval romance, but many other engagements with discourses of the 'medieval' that will appear throughout this book.[25]

Further enriching the novel's many parodic scenes is their use of premodern farcical and buffonic modes, forms that will re-emerge regularly throughout the history of comic medievalism. *Don Quixote* abounds with scenes of physical comedy in which the characters, Don Quixote and Sancho in particular, endure thrashings, trampling, mishaps, punishments and pranks, and find themselves in situations of misrecognition, hardship, abjection and humiliation. The question of farce and buffoonery in *Don Quixote* has been

[22]   Ibid., pp. 628–36.

[23]   Alexander Pope, 'Peri Bathous, or the Art of Sinking in Poetry', in *Alexander Pope: The Major Works*, ed. Pat Rogers (Oxford: Oxford University Press, 2006), pp. 195–238.

[24]   James Wood, *The Irresponsible Self: On Laughter and the Novel* (New York: Picador, 2005), p. 19.

[25]   Robert Phiddian, 'Are Parody and Deconstruction Secretly the Same Thing?' *New Literary History* 28:4 (1997), 673–96 (p. 682).

a contentious one in scholarship on Cervantes in two ways. First, acknowledging their inclusion jars with some commentators' strong commitment to
the belief that the novel sits safely on the modern side of an epochal divide
in which humour, which is perceived as modern and consists of sophisticated
forms such as parody, irony, wit and satire, has superseded comedy, which is
pre-modern, 'pre-novelistic' or 'popular', and is deemed to consist principally
of un-ironic farcical humour with little to no ideological, social or existential reflection. Michael Scham is among those who argue that Cervantes's
humour is modern because of its 'suggestive scepticism', which is expressed
in its epistemological questioning of the distinction between the rational and
the insane.[26] This largely corresponds with the views of James Wood and
Milan Kundera, both of whom are well-known advocates of a Cervantean
radical doubt that they take to be specifically modern and therefore remote
from the relatively simplistic and 'stable' forms of pre-modern humour.[27]
Commentators falling into this category not only tend to accept untested the
progressivist assumptions underlying this account, but in many cases (with
the exception of Scham) prefer only to touch on Cervantes's comic impulses
insofar as they can be interpreted under the rubric of him as a philosopher
of a distinctly modern cast.

For the second group, whose work is more attuned to the question of
cultural continuities and the trans-temporality of comic forms, the contentious issue is not so much whether Cervantes uses earlier farcical or buffonic
elements as what he does with them. Earlier commentators such as Auerbach
were less concerned about the implications of describing the novel's juxta-
position of seriousness and indignity as 'the acme of farce'.[28] More recently,
however, this has become more fraught, with scholarly divisions emerging over
the question of Cervantes's relationship to the 'coarser' traditions of popular
culture. James Iffland, one of a number of scholars who have read Cervantes
through the lens of Bakhtin's landmark *Rabelais and his World*, argues that
many of the novel's comic elements (such as those mentioned above) are
grounded firmly in the 'popular–festive matrix' of medieval folk culture, and
that many of its episodes partake of the folk 'carnivalesque' logic of grotesquery and social inversion.[29] A. J. Close, on the other hand, in addition to
de-medievalising the farcical elements in Cervantes by situating them within

---

[26] Michael Scham, 'Don Quijote and the Art of Laughing at Oneself', *Cervantes* 29
(2009), 31–55. See also Adrienne L. Martín, 'Humor and Violence in Cervantes', in *The
Cambridge Companion to Cervantes*, ed. Anthony J. Cascardi (Cambridge, UK: Cambridge
University Press, 2002), pp. 60–185 (pp. 161–2).

[27] Wood, *The Irresponsible Self*, p. 10; Milan Kundera, *The Curtain*, trans. Linda Asher
(New York: Harper Collins, 2005), p. 109.

[28] Auerbach, *Mimesis*, p. 342.

[29] James Iffland, 'Laughter Tamed', *Bulletin of the Cervantes Society of America* 23:2
(2003), 395–435 (pp. 415–18).

a longer 'Aristophanic' tradition, claims that in *Don Quixote* the vulgarity of traditional comic forms has been mitigated by the author's subscription to the contemporary urbane values of 'discretion and taste' which, along with restorative laughter, form the core of his comic poetics.[30] Notwithstanding this, he does argue that Cervantes's text takes inspiration from such earlier and 'lower' forms as early theatrical comedy and the picaresque novels of the late sixteenth century, with their low-life characters whose peripatetic and haphazard lives are like the downmarket, realist mirror-images of the idealistic knight errant.[31] In all, Close concludes that the omnivorous style of *Don Quixote* enables it to absorb elevated forms and blend these 'grotesquely' with 'innumerable motifs derived from comic tradition' which includes picaresque, ballads and farce, but in a way that conforms to the decorous tastes of urbane culture.[32] Despite his recognition of this multi-temporal blend, Close's view about farce reflects a lingering crypto-progressivist desire to raise Cervantes above his pre-modern influences, and, according to critics such as Iffland, invests too heavily in seeing the author as compliant with the Golden Age literary academies' domestication of the comic under the strictures of decorum.[33] A less hierarchical formulation of the relationship between medieval source and modern adaptation can not only acknowledge that the novel's farcical and decorous modes simultaneously complement and threaten to exceed one another, but can also recognise the extent to which this predicts comic medievalism's continued tendency to hold the medieval and the modern in a paradoxical state of cooperative tension.

The ambivalence that informs Cervantes's use of medievalist parody and farce is even evident in the scene containing the book's most explicit condemnation of chivalric literature. In Book I:47 the Canon of Toledo encounters Don Quixote imprisoned in an oxcart. When the Canon learns from the village priest that it is Don Quixote's knightly mania that has ultimately landed him there, he launches into a broadside against the romance genre, telling the priest that in addition to romances' disjointed episodic narratives,

> the style is fatiguing, the action incredible, the love lascivious, the courtesies clumsy, the battles long, the language foolish, the journeys nonsensical, and, finally, since they are totally lacking in intelligent artifice, they deserve to be banished, like unproductive people, from Christian nations.[34]

---

[30] Anthony J. Close, *Cervantes and the Comic Mind of His Age* (Oxford: Oxford University Press, 2009), pp. 17, 79.

[31] Ibid., p. 308.

[32] Ibid., p. 337.

[33] Iffland, 'Laughter Tamed', pp. 424–33.

[34] Cervantes, *Don Quixote*, p. 412.

This speech at first presents an arresting contrast to the lighter and essentially performative mode of critique that dominates most of the novel. It is, however, mitigated almost immediately afterwards, with the Canon changing his tune and delivering a lengthy speech in which he not only praises chivalric literature as a vehicle for ingenuity, learning, insight and beauty, which can 'teach and delight at the same time',[35] but admits he has himself drafted the first hundred pages of a romance. Through this kind of playful recuperative logic, in which medieval forms are not so much transcended as preserved, continued, revived and praised even as they appear to be mocked, Cervantes avoids a wholesale demolition of the genre. The novel also stops short of any call for censorship: just as the Canon's pronouncement that chivalric tales 'deserve to be banished ... from Christian nations' does not stand unchallenged, so too during the inquisition of Don Quixote's extensive library in Book I:6, the village priest, who has a thorough acquaintance with the genre, saves a number of romances based on their literary and exemplary merit. The fact that the remaining volumes are consigned to the flames because 'he wearied of seeing more books, and so without reflection, he wanted all the rest to be burned' implies that many more good books met with an unfair fate. The matter-of-factness of the statement quietly emphasises the hasty, indiscriminate destructiveness of this act.[36] It is difficult, as Georgina Dopico Black has argued, to imagine that Cervantes's first (and subsequent) audiences could read this scene without thinking of the Inquisitorial Indices of Prohibited Books that were compiled in the mid-sixteenth century and expanded throughout the seventeenth, or of the scrutinising of libraries and the book burnings that were official instruments of censorship. Furthermore, since, in Black's words, 'the anatomical body, the textual body, and the national body are ... stubbornly intertwined in early modern Spain', it was not a long stretch to recall the *autos-da-fé* in which the bodies of the dubiously guilty were burned.[37] The Canon's call for the 'banishment' of chivalric books from Christian nations is similarly charged with the memory of the expulsion of Spain's Jews in 1492 as well as evoking the increased cultural repression of the country's Morisco population that would culminate in their expulsion in 1609. *Don Quixote's* capacity to incorporate rather than expel what it critiques makes it not only a capacious and humane book, but, crucially, a template for a comic medievalist tradition to come.

What all this suggests, then, is that Cervantes is actually rewriting the knight-errant romance; he is engaging in a medievalism in which he renovates the genre. The preferred model of a romance that incorporates realism

---

[35] Ibid., p. 414.

[36] Ibid., p. 52.

[37] Georgina Dopico Black, 'Canons Afire: Libraries, Books, and Bodies in Don Quixote's Spain', in *Cervantes' Don Quixote: A Casebook*, ed. Roberto González Echevarría (Oxford and New York: Oxford University Press, 2005), pp. 95–123 (p. 109).

is described by the priest during the inquisition of Don Quixote's library, when he describes the late fifteenth-century *History of the Famous Knight Tirant lo Blanc* as 'of its style ... the best book in the world' because 'in it knights eat, and sleep, and die in their beds, and make a will before they die, and do everything else that all the other books of this sort leave out'.[38] This description is particularly striking given that at the end of Book II Cervantes's narrative closes on just this note, with Don Quixote (who has now reclaimed his real name Alonso Quixano) dying in his bed having not only dictated his will but renounced, indeed denounced, his delusional knight errantry. This reflexive joking about the value of renovated romance is arguably corroborated by the Canon's praise of books of chivalry. His claims that the 'good thing' about books of chivalry is 'the opportunity for display that they offer a good mind' and that 'the free writing style of these books allows the author to show his skills as an epic, lyric, tragic, and comic writer',[39] are surely winking allusions to Cervantes's own virtuosic achievement in this very book. More forthrightly, in Chapter I:28 the narrator asserts that his 'agreeable and artful' story about Don Quixote's deliberate 'resolve to resuscitate ... the lost and dying order of knight errantry', is especially apt 'for our own time, which is so in need of joyful entertainment'.[40] This combination of meta-medievalism and medievalism reveals the temporal porosity between medieval and modern; their mutual dependence. As with so many of the texts to be dealt with in this book, the medieval and modern collapse into one another in a way that ultimately comments on the modern, in this case modern literary production and consumption.

As is also the case with many of the medievalist texts to be discussed in this book, the relationship between *Don Quixote*'s satire of literary reception and its more broadly directed social satire is not straightforward. One readily available explanation for this can be located in the novel's own elusiveness. To cite a comparative example, in his 1883 memoir *Life on the Mississippi* Mark Twain explicitly attributes the continuation of Southern slavery and the American civil war to the renovated love of chivalry in the American South. Arguing that this feudal mentality, which was vital to 'the making of Southern character', had its origin in reading habits, he referred to it as 'Sir Walter disease', claiming that it grew out of his contemporaries' avid and widespread consumption of the novels of Sir Walter Scott. According to Twain, 'it was [Scott] that created rank and caste [in the South], and also reverence for rank and caste, and pride and pleasure in them', an attitude which, he believed, had deleterious social and political results.[41] By contrast,

---

38 Cervantes, *Don Quixote*, p. 50.
39 Ibid., pp. 413–14.
40 Ibid., p. 227.
41 Mark Twain, *Life on the Mississippi* (Boston: James R. Osgood and Company, 1883), p. 469.

Cervantes's objections to the genre appear, to use Close's words, to be 'more aesthetic than moral';[42] dispensing with the moral criticisms conventionally levelled against chivalric books, the Prologue condemns their mendacity, triviality and implausibility, but does not offer any explicit socially oriented reason why they should lose their influence in seventeenth-century Spain. This reticence could partly explain the development of a dominant strain of interpretation that has focused more heavily on the novel's sophisticated metafictionality and its satire of reading practices than on its engagement with its social and historical context.

The ambiguity of the novel's frame is reinforced by the subtlety of the narrative voice. The satiric style used by Cervantes walks a fine line, exposing its central character without resorting to a derisory or mocking voice. This is achieved through the development of a style in which the laudatory third-person voice of romance narrative is split into opposing registers, the florid medieval-heroic register of Don Quixote and the plain-speaking modern-quotidian register of the narrator, which are then juxtaposed without being fully synthesised. In the gap between these registers nestles irony, where the narrator invites the reader to engage in the deflationary practice of meas-uring the distance between the ideal (Don Quixote's view of himself and the world) and the real (what he and the world are really like). Just as Cervantes uses this to meta-medievalist ends, in later chapters it will be seen that this technique is also regularly used in more recent comic medievalist texts, which make liberal use of irony. One memorable instance of this kindly irony can be found in Book I:35, in which the plain-speaking narrator's ludicrous description of Don Quixote, his thin and grubby frame barely covered by an abbreviated nightshirt as he slashes wineskins in his sleep, is juxtaposed against the hero's solemn declaration, on waking, that he has just slain a giant. The satiric suppleness of scenes such as this, in which laughter and pity are equally invoked, is further enhanced, as discussed earlier, by the virtuosic relish with which Cervantes parodies chivalric language. Scham, arguing that '[t]he conventionality ... may be a set-up for another prosaic deflation, but ... Cervantes delights in the very material he travesties',[43] aligns this inclusive method with that used by Erasmus, with whose 'forgiving' satire Cervantes was familiar.[44]

The use of straight-faced narrative to generate oblique satire leads Ife to suggest that one reason 'readers and critics of Cervantes have found it diffi-cult to detect what he really thinks about his material' is because instead of offering direct commentary, he uses the novel's ironic register and the events within his narrative as 'circumstantial evidence ... to act as testimony to a

42 Close, 'The Legacy of Don Quijote', p. 22.
43 Scham, 'Don Quijote and the Art of Laughing at Oneself', p. 46.
44 Ibid., p. 48.

much wider range of issues'.[45] One instance of this is his engagement with social class within the novel, which uses Don Quixote's adventures through early seventeenth-century Spain, and his untimely obsession with chivalry, to document a rapidly changing social landscape in which the feudal configurations of rank and wealth had been eroded, leading to the emergence of newly cashed-up (and newly ennobled) classes while the power base of the gentry declined. Don Quixote's chivalric *idée fixe* is presented not simply as a mad personal quirk, but as a cultural attachment with a social-ideological valency. In this respect the novel becomes a perfect demonstration of Phiddian's contention that 'parody nearly always turns into satire' because it 'works on fundamental assumptions about the nonreferentiality of language' – in this case the chivalric idiom's self-cannibalising reiterations – 'but it normally does so cannily, knowing that language *does* connect with the world, mimesis, and intention, however messily'. While, says Phiddian, 'pure parody which bombinates endlessly in the void of textuality is at least imaginable[,] parody nearly always admits referential impurity'.[46] Ife puts it beautifully when he describes the ageing, impoverished hidalgo, his head full of anachronistic romance, riding 'out into a world in which rich farmers put their sons through university and dukes and duchesses have transformed their castles into chateaux where they pass the time playing effete masquerades'.[47] Chivalry is shown to be Don Quixote's delusional ballast against this changing world; yet, conversely, it is also a discursive currency that continues to circulate among the recently gentrified as well as those involved in Spain's colonial project. Diana de Armas Wilson's assertion that 'Cervantes replies to the New World encounter ... by slyly aligning Don Quixote with the conquistador mentality' points not only to Don Quixote's conceptualisation of his knightly victories using the language of conquest (including promising Sancho an island, like those given to colonists in America), but also to the fact that those Spaniards in America actually doing the conquering were not averse to seeing themselves within the framework of chivalric heroism.[48] This use of Don Quixote's engagements with his social milieu shows that Cervantes's narrative objectivity should not, as Close warns, be mistaken for neutrality, but should be seen, rather, as a shrewd satiric device that renders further commentary redundant.[49]

The book's cultural and geographical canvas is so large that many have found it difficult to nominate a central object of satire. Auerbach's argument

---

[45] Ife, 'The Historical and Social Context', p. 28.

[46] Phiddian, 'Are Parody and Deconstruction Secretly the Same Thing?' p. 691.

[47] Ife, 'The Historical and Social Context', p. 29.

[48] Diana de Armas Wilson, 'Cervantes and the New World', in *The Cambridge Companion to Cervantes*, pp. 206–25 (p. 217).

[49] A. J. Close, *Cervantes: Don Quixote* (Cambridge: Cambridge University Press, 1990), p. 21.

that 'the element of contemporary satire and criticism is very weak' is based on the idea that a satiric position 'must be consistent and methodical if it is to be taken seriously', which cannot happen in a novel whose dilatory narrative works chiefly 'to present Spanish life in its color and fullness'.[50] Although later scholars have not necessarily accepted his verdict that the novel's satire is weak, there is more general agreement on the difficulty of identifying the novel's 'core' object of social satire, such that John Jay Allen has boldly claimed that 'Don Quixote abounds in subtle, perceptive, devastating satire, compounding ironies and deflating presumption and pretension, but it is not a satire.'[51] Others might respond that its critique of chivalry is essentially satiric, although its reformist intent is somewhat muted. In the end, though, the joke is on medievalism, which, the novel suggests, is risible in itself as well as in its choice of object, the idea of which is absurd. Its very premise attracts laughter. But the novel can never fully separate itself from medievalism, for while it scrutinises the anachronistic incongruity which is the tacit condition of all comic medievalist practice, it also uses it. Taking a lead from Cervantes, the chapters that follow will examine both medieval and medievalist texts, to see how the Middle Ages have been laughed at, in and with; and there might even be a few laughs along the way.

---

[50] Auerbach, *Mimesis*, p. 345.

[51] John J. Allen, 'The Transformation of Satire in Don Quixote: "Dine With Us As An Equal" in Juvenal and Cervantes', in *Ingeniosa Invención: Essays on Golden Age Spanish Literature for Geoffrey L. Stagg in Honor of His Eighty-Fifth Birthday*, ed. Ellen Anderson and Amy Williamson (Newark, DE: Juan de la Cuesta Press, 1999), pp. 1–7 (pp. 6–7).

II

OLDIES BUT GOODIES: COMIC RECOVERY

2

Scraping the Rust from the Joking Bard: Chaucer in the Age of Wit

IN 1694, THE YOUNG JOSEPH ADDISON, later a playwright, essayist and notorious strander of prepositions, published 'An Account of the Greatest English Poets' in the fourth part of John Dryden's *Miscellany Poems*. A verse account of the visitation of the Muses ('the Tuneful Nine') to writers of 'British Rhimes' past and present, it nominates Geoffrey Chaucer as the first great poet in the English tradition:

> Long had our dull Fore-fathers slept Supine,
> Nor felt the Raptures of the Tuneful Nine;
> Till *Chaucer* first, a merry *Bard*, arose;
> And many a Story told in Rhime and Prose.
> But Age has Rusted what the Poet writ,
> Worn out his language, and obscur'd his Wit:
> In vain he jests in his unpolish'd strain
> And tries to make his Readers laugh in vain.[1]

Despite alighting only briefly on Chaucer's encounter with the Muses, Addison's account is densely packed rhetorically and conceptually. In a few lines it discloses much about the conflicted way in which the late medieval poet was regarded, both as a comic writer and as an early English writer, in the 'long eighteenth century', a period spanning the late seventeenth century through to the end of the eighteenth. It contains a number of conceptual contradictions which, as will be explored throughout this chapter, reflect the variable nature

---

[1] Joseph Addison, 'An Account of the Greatest English Poets', [in] *The Annual Miscellany for the Year 1694* (Printed by R. E. for Jacob Tonson, 1694), pp. 317–18, in Caroline Spurgeon, *Five Hundred Years of Chaucer Criticism and Allusion, 1357–1900* (New York: Russell & Russell, 1960), vol. I, p. 266.

of Chaucer reception throughout the so-called 'Age of Wit'. First, Chaucer is acknowledged by Addison to be fundamentally comic – he is a 'merry Bard' who 'jests', has 'Wit' (a word not reducible to the comic impulse yet also not easily separable from it) and 'tries to make his Readers laugh' – and yet he fails to amuse. Addison's final repetition of 'in vain' is quite insistent that Chaucer cannot elicit modern laughter. Moreover, although Chaucer's 'many tales' have survived, guaranteeing his status as poetic forefather, his work is lost to modern readers, hopelessly 'worn out' and 'obscur'd' by Age's inexorable erosion of language. It is true that Addison's poem does not consign only Chaucer to obsolescence: Edmund Spenser's 'Mystick Tale' likewise does not bear up under modern scrutiny, Abraham Cowley's 'Wit in its Excess' is deemed regrettable and even Milton's 'clean Current' of verse belies its 'odious bottom'. But Addison's avowal of Chaucerian archaism, appearing a few years before the publication of Dryden's agenda-setting 'polishing' modernisation of Chaucer's verse in his *Fables Ancient and Modern* (1700), is especially telling in the link it makes between the time-boundedness of Chaucer's comedy and that of his language. It is because Chaucer can no longer be understood that he can no longer be found funny.

The metaphor of 'rusted' and 'unpolish'd' verse that dominates Addison's stanza would prove to be persistent in the Chaucer reception of this period, such that Age can, after many repetitions, still be found rusting Chaucer almost ninety years later in 1782, in William Hayley's *An Essay on Epic Poetry in Five Epistles to the Revd. Mr. Mason*:

> See, on a party-colour'd steed of fire,
> With Humour at his side, his trusty Squire,
> Gay CHAUCER leads – in form a Knight of old,
> And his strong armour is of steel and gold;
> But o'er it Age a cruel rust has spread,
> And made the brilliant metals dark as lead.[2]

In Hayley's hands the metallurgical conceit gives the strong impression of being an *idée reçu* which is itself somewhat rusted; there is an assumption that the reader will, by dint of long exposure, immediately identify Chaucer's corroded 'armour' and unspecified 'metals' as references to his language, even though, as I will discuss, Chaucer's English was by that time undergoing something of a rehabilitation. Notwithstanding its recycling of Addison's metaphor, Hayley's account falls into an alternative tradition wherein the Chaucerian comic impulse is seen to have a life quite separate from the poet's language. Here, it rides robustly alongside Chaucer as a 'trusty

---

    2   William Hayley, 'An Essay on Epic Poetry in Five Epistles to the Revd. Mr. Mason, with Notes', Epist. iii (1782), p. 63, in Spurgeon, *Five Hundred Years*, p. 466.

squire', ready to serve its tarnished (but still 'gay') master. That the squire is called 'Humour', rather than Addison's 'Wit', reveals the variable lexicon to which writers resorted across this period to convey their understanding of the nature, function and value of Chaucerian levity.

This is the first of two chapters that, rather than examining comic representations of the Middle Ages, instead focus on ways in which the medieval period has come to be associated in the post-medieval world with comedy and humour. These chapters examine two very different ways in which medieval comic precedents have been reanimated as a way to understand comic forms and practices that are strongly aligned with notions of modernity and progress. I will concentrate first on tracing the diverse and ambivalent ways in which readers and writers in the long eighteenth century invested heavily in an idea of Chaucer as a 'joking bard' (to cite Samuel Cobb's reworking of Addison's term), and will explore how their preoccupation with Chaucerian jocularity intersected with attempts to retrieve a lost comic tradition or, conversely, to identify a continuous presence of wit in English culture and beyond. The documents gathered together by Derek Brewer, Betsy Bowden, Christopher Cannon, and especially Caroline Spurgeon in her volumes detailing Chaucer reception across five centuries, have demonstrated exhaustively that the period spanning the late seventeenth and eighteenth centuries in England witnessed nothing short of an avalanche of engagement with Chaucer's legacy, which comprised a robust (if sometimes highly reiterative) culture of commentary, as well as modernisation, imitation, Chaucer continuation and vital developments in the editing of the poet's works. Within this feverish culture of recovery, one can isolate two central, and intertwined, genealogical impulses: the linguistic and the comic. While the eighteenth-century assessment of Chaucer's linguistic legacy has received considerable scholarly attention, I wish to suggest that the less-examined recovery of the Joking Bard took place in tandem with this, and hence needs to be examined in the context of the period's widespread and varying evaluation of his role in the development of the English language.

Examining how this dual comic–linguistic legacy was variously formulated has conceptual as well as historical significance because it offers a telling instance of how perceptions of 'the comic Middle Ages' can feed into a highly ambivalent mode of medievalism. For while on the one hand Chaucer's medievalness was, for his seventeenth- and eighteenth-century readers, the basis of his claim not only to linguistic primacy but also to comic 'naturalness', it was also – indeed, often simultaneously – regarded with consternation by many of these same readers, who blamed it for his inaccessible language, his 'uneven' versification and, significantly, his comic crudity. The case of Chaucer in the Age of Wit also casts particular light on the role of this kind of comic medievalist recovery in unsettling the categories of historical periodisation. In more deliberate instances, this was reflected in direct claims, and even demonstrations, that the Chaucerian comic legacy continued to thrive, either unadulterated or in updated form. Elsewhere, however, the unsettling was more inadvertent. Despite the widespread commitment to a progressive narrative in which the licentious and benighted Middle Ages had been surpassed by the refined and enlightened present, many engaged, despite themselves, in a performative querying of distinctions between the pre-modern and the modern, by exposing the importance of the Middle Ages for modernity's self-understanding. As this discussion will show, even when comic medievalist texts rest on, and aim to reinforce, the divisions of historical periodisation, they in fact compel us to reassess and displace any easy assumptions that comic tastes and practices divide the modern from the medieval. As will become clear, the Age of Wit laughed not just at the Middle Ages, but also with them, and in them.

Chaucer's solicitation of laughter has been a vital consideration in his reception throughout most subsequent ages. This reception has, in turn, attracted scholarly analysis: among others, Jean Jost devotes a chapter of her edited collection, *Chaucer's Humor* (1994) to examining this reception history, although only four pages of this chapter are devoted to the eighteenth century.[3] Caroline Spurgeon's discussion of 'jovial Chaucer' in *Five Hundred Years of Chaucer Criticism and Allusion, 1357–1900* is more exhaustive: she not only nominates it as one of the four key responses to Chaucer, but spends more time on it than the other three.[4] Spurgeon's survey approach to reception has in recent years been supplemented by critical examinations such as Steve Ellis's *Chaucer at Large: The Poet in the Modern Imagination* (2000) and Kathleen Forni's recent *Chaucer's Afterlife: Adaptations in Recent Popular Culture* (2013), both of which discuss interpretations, continuations and imitations of comic Chaucer. Stephanie Trigg's *Congenial Souls: Reading Chaucer from Medieval to Postmodern* (2002) has complemented these popular cultural analyses by noting comic substrata in the long history of Chaucer scholarship, including scholars' 'customary identification with its genial author'.[5] Jost argues that commentary on Chaucerian wit in the long eighteenth century is not exegetically significant because it is too brief and uncritical, predating the nineteenth-century 'critically perceptive evaluation of Chaucerian comedy'.[6] I argue, conversely, that this historical stage in Chaucer's comic reception is especially noteworthy not just due to its acceler-

3   Jean E. Jost, ed., *Chaucer's Humor: Critical Essays* (New York: Garland, 1994), pp. 8–11.

4   Spurgeon, *Five Hundred Years*, vol. I, pp. xcvi–c, cxxxv–cxxxix.

5   Steve Ellis, *Chaucer at Large: The Poet in the Modern Imagination* (Minneapolis: University of Minnesota Press, 2000); Kathleen Forni, *Chaucer's Afterlife: Adaptations in Recent Popular Culture* (Jefferson, NC: McFarland & Company, Inc., 2013); Stephanie Trigg, *Congenial Souls: Reading Chaucer from Medieval to Postmodern* (Minneapolis: University of Minnesota Press, 2002), p. 205.

6   Jost, *Chaucer's Humor*, pp. xxxvii–xxxviii.

ated interest in the poet, but also because of its renowned preoccupation with comic forms, tastes and practices as indexes not only of individual morality but of historical development and even national character. Indeed, *contra* Jost, it is possible to see the sometimes epigrammatic style of this period's commentary as enacting rather than obscuring its arguments about Chaucerian wit; for in the same way that the years between 1650 and the latter part of the eighteenth century have collectively attracted a range of epithets that consolidate their relationship to modernity, including the Age of Reason and the Age of Enlightenment, the characterisation of this period in Britain as the Age of Wit suggests a culture that placed a premium on a sophisticated, and distinctively modern, form of comic apprehension and expression.

Some time ago, in his book *The Age of Wit*, D. Judson Milburn described this period in Britain, and most particularly in London culture, as 'renowned for levity'[7] and 'distinguished by brilliant conversation and scintillating literary accomplishment in satire, in humorous raillery, and in spirited criticism.'[8] Epitomised in the cultural imaginary by the Augustan literary figures Alexander Pope, Jonathan Swift and John Gay, and their satiric associates in the Scriblerus club, this culture's fetishising of wit was both intensive and far-reaching, not only sustaining the vigorous exercise of wit but also subjecting it to thoroughgoing (and repetitive) appraisal. At its most quotidian level, wit was regarded as a personal attribute, the display of which conferred intellectual and, importantly, social prestige on its possessor. Charles Sedley's *An Essay on Entertainments* (1702), for instance, advises that supper guests, if they wish to be thought elegant, should aspire to be 'facetious, witty, and agreeable', avoiding contentious and grave topics in favour of discoursing on 'pleasant, cheerful, and delightful subjects'.[9] Lest the image of a vibrant metropolitan culture, whose epicentres were the salon and coffeehouse, makes wit seem frivolous, a closer look at Sedley's deceptively straightforward advice reveals that wit encompassed not just the social and fashionable, but also the cognitive and the rhetorical, being used, as Roger D. Lund points out, 'to describe both a faculty of mind and properties of discourse'.[10] It was a key criterion for the evaluation of speech and of literary texts, and was exhaustively anatomised within contemporary philosophy, with philosophers such as John Locke, Thomas Hobbes, the Earl of Shaftesbury and others variously mapping its relationship to the attributes of reason, judgement, imagination and fancy. In their philosophical accounts Locke and Hobbes attempt to quarantine Reason and Judgement from wit, which provoked in

---

7   D. Judson Milburn, *The Age of Wit: 1650–1750* (New York: The Macmillan Company, 1966), p. 187.
8   Ibid., p. 18.
9   Ibid., p. 229.
10   Roger D. Lund, 'Wit, Judgement, and the Misprisions of Similitude', *Journal of the History of Ideas* 65 (2004), 53–75 (p. 53).

them a Platonic suspicion due to its use of 'similitude', which was regarded as a pleasing but potentially misleading exploitation of resemblances, the most meretricious iteration of which is the pun.

In spite of – or, arguably, because of – the seemingly innumerable attempts to parse the term and police its usage, Milburn says wit 'continued to acquire an even greater variety of meanings in the seventeenth and eighteenth centuries', such that it became more and more diffuse in its modalities (which ranged from seriousness through to levity), its connotations and its applications:

> the ingenious neoclassical couplet of John Dryden and Alexander Pope, the vituperations against man and the misery of his reason of Jonathan Swift, the sophisticated correspondence of Lady Mary Wortley Montagu, the fatuous histrionics of Etherege's Sir Fopling Flutter, the libellous and obscene broadsides hawked in every street, the nonsense whispered in milady's ear by a pretentious coxcomb, the Nicker's nocturnal pastime of throwing halfpennies through glass windows – all passed for wit. Little wonder that wit became, almost literally, all things to all people.[11]

This view has been reiterated more recently by Lund, who observes '[w]hile the writers of the later seventeenth and early eighteenth centuries were convinced that they were living in an age of wit, they seemed far less certain as to what this might mean'.[12] The text that is, with justification, cited most frequently by scholars as evidence of wit's blurred conceptual edges is Pope's *Essay on Criticism* (1709/11). Despite the aphoristic seductiveness of its famous couplet, 'True Wit is Nature to Advantage drest, / What oft was Thought, but ne'er so well Exprest',[13] in fact the poem's formulation of wit proves far more elusive. Sometimes, in phrases such as 'sprightly wit', it loosely evokes mirth; in some places an author's wit, which appears to be a synonym for rhetorical ornament, is both parallel and opposing term to the critic's reason; elsewhere it is clearly, though uneasily, related to judgement ('*Wit* and *Judgment* often are at strife, / Tho' meant each other's Aid, like *Man* and *Wife*').[14] This, along with poem's oscillation between approving and pejorative uses of the word, is not a reflection of slipshod thinking on Pope's part. Rather, so native has the term become to the cultural vernacular of the time, his usage of it is essentially idiomatic, operating on an implicit understanding of his audience's practical awareness of the conceptual elasticity of the word, but also its parameters. The mobility of this term meant, then, that it circulated in a

---

[11]   Milburn, *The Age of Wit*, p. 19.
[12]   Lund, 'Wit, Judgement', p. 53.
[13]   Alexander Pope, 'An Essay On Criticism', in *Poems of Alexander Pope*, vol. I, ed. E. Audra and Aubrey Williams (London: Methuen and Co., 1961), ll. 297–8, pp. 272–3.
[14]   Ibid., ll. 82–3, p. 248.

semantic field which encompassed entertainment, aesthetics and morality: depending on the occasion and the commentator, wit could be (or fail to be) amusing, it could aspire to be agreeable and beautiful or it could express (or betray) sense and truth. Nevertheless, it kept the closest and most persistent company with the lexicon of mirth, including satire, raillery, comedy and humour. This last term had in the late seventeenth century exceeded its centuries-old grounding in humoral physiology, coming initially to designate 'character' and thereafter increasingly to operate as a synonym of wit, despite what Milburn calls 'confused' and ultimately unconvincing attempts by authors such as Dryden and Thomas Shadwell to differentiate the two phenomena.[15] The conceptual overlap in humour's and wit's significations of comic impulses, while not exact, was established enough for Shaftesbury to use the terms interchangeably as early as 1709 in his epistolary treatise *Sensus Communis: An Essay on the Freedom of Wit and Humour*.

Given the formidable complexity of wit, it is not my aim here to offer a comprehensive account of how it was understood and practised at this time, so much as to sketch out the hectic range of philosophical and cultural assumptions about wit and humour that shaped the reception of comic Chaucer in this period. So tenaciously was the poet associated with wit, humour and their synonyms across the period that by 1762 Thomas Warton felt the need to correct the common misconception that Chaucer's 'strokes of humour' are 'his sole talent'.[16] The persistence of this view into the late eighteenth century is suggested by the fact that twenty years later his brother Joseph revives this defence, using *The Knight's Tale* to assert Chaucer's talent for 'the pathetic and the sublime' against the 'prevailing prejudice' 'that [his] excellence lay in his manner of treating light and ridiculous subjects'.[17] Despite the implied unanimity about Chaucer's non-serious brilliance, however, the nature and value (both literary and cultural) of his wit remained far from settled questions across the entire period. When discussing the reception of Chaucer in her *Eighteenth-Century Modernizations from The Canterbury Tales*, Betsy Bowden queries the tidy 'evolutionary' arc traced by Caroline Spurgeon, wherein the presentist prejudices reflected in early modernisations were eventually supplanted by rational textualist approaches epitomised by Thomas Tyrwhitt's 1775 edition, which in turn presaged nineteenth-century positivist codicology.[18] Bowden's emphasis on the continued 'interpretive diversity' of the poet's reception across the Age of Wit is certainly borne out

---

[15] Milburn, *The Age of Wit*, p. 202.

[16] Thomas Warton, 'Observations on the Fairy Queen of Spenser', 2nd edn, i (1762), p. 197, in Spurgeon, *Five Hundred Years*, p. 423.

[17] Joseph Warton, 'An Essay on the Genius and Writings of Pope', 4th edn, i. vii (1782), p. 352, in Spurgeon, *Five Hundred Years*, p. 470.

[18] Betsy Bowden, ed., *Eighteenth-Century Modernizations from The Canterbury Tales* (Cambridge: D. S. Brewer, 1991), p. xi.

in the reception of his mirth, which on the whole resists any urge to order it developmentally. Rather, it redeploys an arresting but restricted series of tropes somewhat repetitively to buttress an increasingly recognisable set of positions.

As the two examples that opened this chapter indicate, one of the favoured tropes was metallurgical; together with metaphors of currency and jewels (Dryden's 'rough diamond' being the most famous), these tropes presented Chaucerian wit as a precious substance whose bright surface is obscured by the patina of age. Others made the same point using sartorial metaphors. Although in 1715 Samuel Croxall revels in Chaucer's antique costume, saying 'all in a Kirtle of green Silk Aray'd / With gleeful smile his merry Lesson play'd',[19] he was more commonly portrayed as a merry gentleman unfashionably arrayed. John Dart conveys the majority opinion in his 1718 preface to *The Complaint of the Black Knight, from Chaucer*, fearing that Chaucer 'seems a very unfashionable courtier'[20] to modern readers. Unsurprisingly, given the Enlightenment context, metaphors of gloom and illumination were also plentiful: while many commentators saw his wit as struggling to break through the 'gothic cloud' of his antiquity, the pseudonymous 'Astrophil', writes in 1740: '*Chaucer* rose, the *Phœbus* of our isle, / And bid bright art on downward ages smile.'[21] Some of the bleaker tropes included those in which Chaucer's wit has been shrouded and interred, as well as metaphors of wreckage, with Walter Harte's 1727 image of 'sprightly Chaucer' as now 'one mingled heap of ruin' being among the most pessimistic.[22]

Despite their performative use of witty similitude, these accounts' extensively documented attraction to metaphor suggests that eighteenth-century appraisals of Chaucer's wit do not on the whole engage in overt philosophical rumination on wit in general or Chaucerian wit in particular. Nevertheless, as philosopher Michèle le Doeuff has argued in *The Philosophical Imaginary*, imagery functions simultaneously to mask and to disclose conceptual confusion or 'the points of tension ... of an intellectual venture',[23] and this case is no exception, as commentators used metaphor to fix in place, however temporarily, the slippery notion of Chaucerian wit. The word 'wit' is, furthermore, not rigorously defined by them, but instead collocated loosely with an

---

[19] Samuel Croxall, 'The Vision, a Poem' (1715), pp. 14–15, in Spurgeon, *Five Hundred Years*, p. 337.

[20] John Dart, 'The Complaint of the Black Knight, from Chaucer', *Preface* (1718), in Spurgeon, *Five Hundred Years*, p. 346.

[21] Astrophil, *pseud.*, 'In Praise of Chaucer, Father of English Poetry', *The Gentleman's Magazine* x (January 1740), p. 31, in Spurgeon, *Five Hundred Years*, p. 387.

[22] Walter Harte, 'To a Young Lady, with Mr Fenton's *Miscellany*, and *Notes Upon the Sixth Thebaid of Statius*', in *Poems on Several Occasions* (London: Bernard Lintot, 1727), pp. 97–8, in Spurgeon, *Five Hundred Years*, p. 369.

[23] Michèle Le Doeuff, *The Philosophical Imaginary*, trans. Colin Gordon (London: Athlone, 1989), p. 3.

extensive and oft-invoked lexicon of mirth associated with the poet. With the recurrent use of the avuncular tag 'Old Chaucer', Chaucer is spoken of as witty, sprightly, lively, merry, jolly, gleeful, mirthful, genial, facetious, gay, cheerful, cheery, frolic (used adjectivally), blithesome and jocose; he is said to have archness and vivacity, and to engage in satyr, mirth, drollery, waggery, jest, joking, raillery and pleasantry, all of which attracted loud laughter. Despite their location of wit within a generalised vocabulary of non-seriousness, these commentaries' frequent and varying alignment of Chaucer's wit with the faculties of 'sense', 'judgement', 'fancy' and 'imagination' situates their assessment of it within the proliferating debates of the time about what constitutes wit and, indeed, where wit can be said to be located. He is also described as having, and using, humour: as early as 1737 Elizabeth Cooper is among those already claiming he engages in 'acutest Raillery, with the most insinuating Humour'.[24]

The repeated emphasis on Chaucer's wit also had, as I have suggested, a somewhat overlooked genealogical impetus. One of the most explicit statements of this is John Oldmixon's 1712 contextualisation of Chaucer's writings within what he regards to be a 'thirst after Wit in all Ages'.[25] Oldmixon's remark reflects the humanistic ideal of the 'Republic of Wit', which Milburn argues was revived and thrived for at least a century beyond the second half of the sixteenth century. The ideal of this 'timeless community of cultivated minds … from all ages'[26] was to preserve 'a continuing freedom of the spirit of wit and learning to attack the opposing Gothic forces in society'.[27] The fact that the 'Joking Bard' had unarguably been formed by his medieval milieu was no excuse for leaving him stranded there, estranged from the company of his fellow wits. Indeed, the very act of discussing Chaucer was an exercise in wit according to Sedley's *Essay on Entertainments*: among the conversation topics he recommends are 'Beauty, Painting, Musick, Poetry, and writers of the past and present Age; whereby we may at once improve and refresh our Wits'.[28] While others did not declare their genealogical intent, the desire to situate Chaucer within a longer history of the permutations and the continuities of wit across time is implicit in their practice. George Ogle, for instance, locates Chaucer within a tradition going back to classical comedy by naming him alongside Terence, Plautus and Aristophanes (1739). Although these classical associations suggest that his wit and humour

---

[24] Elizabeth Cooper, 'The Muses Library; Or a Series of English Poetry from the Saxons to the Reign of King Charles II', Preface (1737), p. viii, in Spurgeon, *Five Hundred Years*, pp. 378–9.

[25] John Oldmixon, 'Reflections on Dr Swift's Letter to the Earl of Oxford about the English Tongue' (c. 1712), pp. 24–5, in Spurgeon, *Five Hundred Years*, pp. 322–3.

[26] Milburn, *The Age of Wit*, p. 186.

[27] Ibid., p. 187.

[28] Ibid., p. 229.

were not thought of as uniquely English, they often appear strikingly close to (and arguably influenced by) the notion of gentle raillery and 'free' wit famously outlined in Shaftesbury's *Sensus Communis*. It is true that in this treatise Shaftesbury declines to focus his account on national formations, and, furthermore, does not single England out as a crucible of free wit; in fact, he cites Thomas Hobbes's distrust of satire as an instance of an illiberal English response to the remedial powers of comic critique (indeed, Shaftesbury would go on the following year to coin the term 'Republic of Wits' in his essay *Soliliquy: or, Advice to an Author*). Nevertheless, an ethnocentric inflection within his formulation of wit is arguably revealed when he defines it against the buffonic humour of the Italians, which he regards as a symptom of their enslavement:

> 'tis the only manner in which the poor cramp'd wretches can discharge a free thought. We must yield to 'em the superiority of this sort of wit. For what wonder is it that we, who have more of liberty, have less dexterity in that egregious way of raillery and ridicule?[29]

This more ethnocentric approach to wit and humour made its way into Chaucer reception in such texts as Thomas Warton's *Observations on the Faerie Queene of Spenser* (1754), where, as cited earlier, he famously declared Chaucer an originator of English humour: 'the first who gave the English nation, in its own language, an idea of HUMOUR.'[30] John Hughes, anticipating the metaphorics of the nineteenth century, compared him in 1715 to an 'old British Oak' and praised the deep-rooted 'native strength' he shared with his successor Spenser.[31] This sense of the poet's Englishness is reinforced, moreover, in the numerous pen-portraits of him from this period, such as that written by Thomas Hearne in 1711, where he features as a plump rosy blond of benign yet grave physiognomy.[32] Lest this seem ethnically non-specific, George Sewell narrows down the interpretive possibilities with the declaration in 1718 that 'Our Bard ... if from Picture we may trace, / Had Strength, and Vigour, and an English Face.'[33] It also crops up in other more biographically oriented genres, such as Thomas Brown's amusing 1704

[29] Lord Shaftesbury, 'Sensus Communis: An Essay on the Freedom of Wit and Humour', in *Characteristicks of Men, Manners, Opinions, Times*, 3 vols, vol. I (publisher unknown, 1744), pp. 49–135 (p. 63).

[30] Thomas Warton, 'Observations on the Faerie Queene of Spenser' (1754), p. 228, in Spurgeon, *Five Hundred Years*, p. 410.

[31] John Hughes, 'Works of Edmund Spenser', [in] *Life*, I (Published by Mr Hughes, 1715), pp. xxvi, in Spurgeon, *Five Hundred Years*, p. 340.

[32] Thomas Hearne, 'Extracts from his Diary', April 28 (Sat) 1711, [in] *Remarks and Collections of Thomas Hearne*, ed. C. E. Doble, iii (Oxford Hist. Soc., 1711), p. 155, in Spurgeon, *Five Hundred Years*, p. 315.

[33] George Sewell, 'The Proclamation of Cupid, or, a Defence of Women, a Poem from Chaucer', *Pamphlet* (London 1718), in Spurgeon, *Five Hundred Years*, pp. 347–8.

Letters from the Dead to the Living, which imagines a comic dialogue between Dryden and Chaucer 'in one of the coffee-houses of hell'. In this dialogue, Chaucer in the guise of a modern Wit draws on the period's ethnic typing by taking exception at having been compared to Ovid by Dryden (in the latter's *Fables Ancient and Modern*), admonishing 'there is no more resemblance between us ... than there is between a Jolly well complexion'd Englishman and a black hair'd thin-gutted Italian'.[34]

A similar oscillation between the ethnocentric and the transcultural exists in the frequent descriptions of Chaucer as a satirist, of which only selected examples can be mentioned here: for Joseph Warton, Chaucer 'takes every opportunity of satyrizing the follies of his age', while John Hughes says he 'study'd Humour, was an excellent Satirist, and a lively but rough Painter of the Manners of that rude age in which he liv'd'.[35] As was repeatedly underlined in commentaries, as well as via the period's numerous modernisations of the Canterbury pilgrims' Prologues and Chaucer's General Prologue, his satirical genius was believed to reside in his characterisation and social portraiture, a point which is literalised in John Bancks's 1738 description of him as 'the Hogarth of his age'.[36] In an age renowned for its regard for and practice of satire, this was the highest praise. George Ogle was among those who emphasised the breadth and universality of Chaucer's satiric portraiture, regarding him as 'a Man perfectly conversant in the Turns and Foibles of human Nature'; others, including Charles Dodd in *The Church History of England from the Year 1500 to the Year 1688* (1737) saw his anticlericalism as a historically specific, pre-modern Catholic mode of satire that allowed him to 'tak[e] all occasions to lessen the power of churchmen, and ridicule their character'.[37]

On the whole, this satiric genealogy is not as rigorously tied to a national or ethnic English heritage; rather Chaucer is placed within a lineage of genteel satire that reaches back to Horace and travels forward to Pope. In a period that elsewhere dramatised antagonism between the ancients and moderns (treated satirically in Jonathan Swift's 1704 *Battle of the Books*), he was evoked as a bridging figure between continental antiquity and English modernity, linguistically antique, Horatian in impetus, yet engaging in a liberal satire that appeals in a thoroughly modern (that is, Augustan) way. He is accorded citizenship in a specifically satiric Republic of Wit that includes not only Horace, but also Persius and even Juvenal, though the Horatian compari-

---

34 Thomas Brown, 'Letters from the Dead to the Living', [in] *The Works of Mr Thomas Brown*, ed. James Drake, ii (1707), p. 207, in Spurgeon, *Five Hundred Years*, p. 291.

35 Hughes, 'Works of Edmund Spenser', p. 340.

36 John Bancks, 'Miscellaneous Works in Verse and Prose of John Bancks', vol. I (1738), p. 88, in Spurgeon, *Five Hundred Years*, p. 383.

37 Charles Dodd, 'The Church History of England from the Year 1688' (Brussels, 1737), p. 369, in Spurgeon, *Five Hundred Years*, pp. 379–80.

sons are most common. This extends to a notion of him as a transhistorical satiric parodist who predates Cervantes. It is in 1762 that 'The Tale of Sir Thopas' is identified as a satire of chivalric tales for the first time. Describing the parodic tail-rhyme romance as 'a sort of prelude to the adventures of Don Quixot', in *Letters on Chivalry and Romance*, Richard Hurd argues that Chaucer 'discerned the absurdity of the old romances' and produced Sir Thopas as 'a manifest banter on these books' that 'ridiculed them with incomparable spirit'.[38] This reading of 'Sir Thopas' is reprised almost verbatim three years later in Percy's *Reliques of Ancient English Poetry*, and again in Thomas Warton's 1774 *History of English Poetry*, although Warton specified that Chaucer's intention was 'to ridicule the frivolous descriptions and other tedious impertinencies' of inferior romance, 'not to degrade in general or expose a mode of fabling' that also included superior examples, such as his own.

Yet despite his atemporal cosmopolitanism, he was also registered as being an identifiably English satirist. Among others, James Thomson's description of Chaucer's work as '*native* Manners-painting Verse' (my emphasis) was among numerous contemporary accounts that nominated both Chaucer and his satiric subjects as indigenous 'forefathers'.[39] Thomas Warton, despite elsewhere emphasising the poet's cosmopolitanism, refers to the Canterbury pilgrims as 'our ancestors', insisting that as satiric types 'the figures are all British, and bear no suspicious signatures of classical, Italian, or French imitation'.[40] The genteel and courteous liberality of his social satire is emphasised in John Dart's largely imaginative biographical account (revised by William Thomas) which appeared in John Urry's edition of Chaucer's works (1721–2). This biography suggests that the Ricardian court, with its 'perpetual Mirth, Tilts, and Tournaments', was the perfect environment for a poet of Chaucer's 'learning, wit, amorous disposition, gay humour, and gallantry' to produce proto-Shaftesburyesque satire.[41] But Dart's vision of Chaucer living at ease within a joyful and gracious milieu (surely inauspicious conditions for the production of satire) was a minority one. It is far more common to find Chaucer singled out among his late medieval English peers and immediate successors, especially Gower, Lydgate and Hoccleve, as uniquely successful as an antique English satirist. These others occasionally earn the qualified admiration of their descendants, but there is no suggestion that together

[38]   Richard Hurd, 'Letters on Chivalry and Romance', *Letter vii* (1762), pp. 107–8, in Spurgeon, *Five Hundred Years*, p. 422.

[39]   James Thomson, 'Summer', in *The Works of James Thomson, in Four Volumes Complete*, i (London: A. Millar 1757), pp. 49–116 (p. 108).

[40]   Thomas Warton, 'The History of English Poetry', i (1774), p. 435, in Spurgeon, *Five Hundred Years*, p. 440.

[41]   John Dart, 'Life of Chaucer', revised by William Thomas, in *Geoffrey Chaucer, the Critical Heritage*, vol. I, ed. Derek Brewer (New York: Routledge, 1995), p. 177.

with Chaucer they hold up a collective satiric mirror to their society. So his witty and satiric outlook, even if it was somehow essentially English, was, contradictorily, also exceptional rather than representative of a flourishing late medieval comic culture.

The deeply contradictory nature of Chaucer's reception is thrown into further relief by the fact that while he was considered an urbane satirist who stood outside his time, there was at the same time recurrent commentary expressing discomfort with what was taken to be the typically medieval crudity of his humour. The references to satire engage in a downplaying of any ribaldry in Chaucer's work, but others made much of Chaucer's bawdy humour as being his essence as a medieval writer. Again, reading across the entire period, a cluster of synonyms emerges describing his work as a reflection of his era's taste: both are coarse, crude, indelicate, depraved, vulgar, obscene, indecent, uncouth and are filled with ribaldry, licentiousness, barbarism, 'profaneness' and immodesty. It is difficult not to register the irony of the period that produced verse such as the Earl of Rochester's libertine 'Fair Chloris in a Pigsty Lay' (c.1680) and Jonathan Swift's abject 'The Lady's Dressing Room' (1732), and novels such as Daniel Defoe's risqué *Moll Flanders* (1722) and John Cleland's pornographic *Fanny Hill* (1748) defining itself against the profanity of late medieval society. Nevertheless, Chaucer's commentary of the time abounds with confident assertions contrasting the refinement of the present with, in Daniel Defoe's words, 'the impoliteness of the age [Chaucer] lived in'.[42] Decades of commentary linking Chaucerian obscenity specifically to his putative 'merriness' are summed up pithily by William Cowper, in *Anti-Thelyphthora* (1781):

> what old Chaucer's merry page befits,
> The chaster muse of modern days omits.
> Suffice it then in decent terms to say,
> She saw – and turn'd her rosy cheek away.[43]

They build to a pitch in the 1791 anonymous comment in that after perusing Chaucer's work, 'I am induced to think … that [medieval people's] general intercourse was as totally destitute of polish, as their entertainments of elegance or their castles of convenience'.[44] Even the small minority who defended Chaucerian bawdy still associated his crudeness specifically with his medievalness. While Thomas Gray conceded in 1760 that Chaucer's satire

---

[42] Daniel Defoe, letter to *Mist's Weekly Journal* 69 (5 April 1718), in Brewer, *Geoffrey Chaucer*, p. 174.

[43] William Cowper, 'Anti-Thelyphthora, A Tale in Verse' (1781), [in] *The Life and Works of William Cowper*, ed. Robert Southey, 8 vols, 1853–55, v (1854), p. 91, in Spurgeon, *Five Hundred Years*, p. 459.

[44] Bowden, *Eighteenth-Century Modernizations*, p. 168.

could appear 'stale and unfashionable' to contemporary readers, he argued this should 'lead us to consider the fading and transitory nature of wit in general', a sentiment echoed in Horace Walpole's statement in 1768 that 'for all the divinity of wit, it grows out of fashion like a fardingale'.[45] Few others were prepared to entertain such historical relativism, however, with its implicit threat to their progressivist conviction that their own time was the acme of wit and that Chaucer's humour is vulgar and in need of refinement.

For all the widespread acknowledgement, then, of Chaucer's significance as a comic and satiric precursor, the commentary culture of the long eighteenth century was beset with an ambivalence toward his historical milieu that spanned the critical spectrum. Those who admired him as a satirist sought incongruously to downplay his medievalness even while invoking him as an early English precursor; for those offended by his comic content, he was the apotheosis of medieval impropriety. While this generalised ambivalence, condescension and even hostility toward the Middle Ages might invite us to regard this retrieval of Chaucerian humour as in fact an instance of comic *anti*-medievalism, it is actually yet another instance where an appreciation of, and attempt to retrieve, medieval comic culture contends against a simultaneous ridiculing of the Middle Ages. This reaffirms the necessity, as argued in this book's introduction, for an inclusive understanding of comic medievalism. It is especially pressing in this case, since despite the frequent recourse to notions of Chaucer's uncouth cultural backdrop, the word 'medieval' does not appear in commentaries on his wit. Instead, the word that is regularly used to characterise the medieval is 'Gothic'. Jonathan Brody Kramnick argues that the long eighteenth century's dialectic of preservation and supersession vis-à-vis the past 'is exhibited with perhaps no greater salience than in the trajectory of the word Gothic as it made its way from a term of abuse for older English culture to the consummate expression of that culture's value'.[46] In the case of Chaucer reception, the word's use does not follow the neat rehabilitative trajectory described by Kramnick; at the end of the century it is still being used to evoke the benighted and coarse infancy of English (or, for some, British) culture, although one does also encounter uses that connote a charming antiquity. The paradoxical portrayal of Chaucer, moreover, in which he both transcends and embodies this variable Gothic, is symptomatic of the contradictions that attend medievalism as a multi-temporal phenomenon. As such, this can be described as a medievalism that does not speak its name.

45 Horace Walpole, 'Letter to George Montagu', *Strawberry Hill*, 15 April 1768, [in] *Letters of Horace Walpole*, ed. Mrs Paget Toynbee, vii (1904), p. 180, in Spurgeon, *Five Hundred Years*, p. 431.

46 Jonathan Brody Kramnick, 'The Making of the English Canon', *PMLA* 112 (1997), 1087–101 (p. 1093).

Views about Chaucer's ribaldry, ranging from mild distaste to deep aversion, intersected with the belief that Chaucer's work could only find new audiences if their comic content was 'polished' and, if necessary, censored in order to be brought into line with contemporary comic tastes. The agenda for this was set in Dryden's discussion of his decisions both to edit and paraphrase sections of individual tales, omitting 'what I judg'd ... not of Dignity enough to appear in the Company of better Thoughts', and to avoid the fabliaux altogether, 'confining my Choice to such Tales of Chaucer as savour nothing of Immodesty', were undertaken so as not to 'offend against Good Manners'.[47] In *Literary Offerings in the Temple of Fame: A Vision* (1753), George Colman the elder presents Dryden's custodianship of Chaucer's legacy in terms of Chaucer sacrificing up his 'obscenity' to Dryden's sanitising touch so that his name would 'descend spotless and unsullied to posterity'. This 'rendering tasteful' of Chaucer's wit takes an amusingly different turn in John Gay's inclusion of the poet as a character in his Drury Lane romantic comedy *The Wife of Bath: A Comedy* (1713). Here Gay turns Chaucer into a peculiar combination of the urbane gentleman-wit with 'good sense, breeding, and civility'[48] and a jocular, slightly plump, version of the Restoration swain, who employs various ruses, including disguising himself as an astrologer called Doctor Astrolabe (just one of numerous flat-footed references to Chaucer's *oeuvre*) in order to win the hand of Lady Myrtilla. His status as romantic hero is confirmed by the fact that he was played by Drury Lane heart-throb Robert Wilks.[49] The Wife herself, played by comic actress Margaret Bicknell, has been turned into an earthy and jolly matchmaker figure who, while endearing herself to all, is still amorous, paraphrases snatches from her Chaucerian Prologue and schemes to snare her sixth husband. Despite a strong cast, good music and backing from the Drury Lane management, the play itself had a fate that Calhoun Winton describes as 'dismal' and a 'mystery',[50] being performed only twice; but the rights to the manuscript were bought, and it survives today, although as a somewhat underestimated text in the comic afterlife of Chaucer.

A fascinatingly contradictory (and very famous) example of Chaucer-polishing is found in the juvenilia of Gay's friend Alexander Pope. Pope's decision to modernise 'The Merchant's Tale' and 'The Wife of Bath's Prologue'

---

[47] John Dryden, 'Fables Ancient and Modern, Translated into Verse from Homer, Ovid, Boccace & Chaucer: With Original Poems', 1700, in *Dryden's Works*, ed. Sir W. Scott, revised G. Saintsbury, 1882–93, *Preface*, xi (1855), pp. 208–44, in Spurgeon, *Five Hundred Years*, p. 279.

[48] John Gay, '*The Wife of Bath: A Comedy* (1713 version), Gently Modernized by Ross G. Arthur' (Cambridge, Ontario: In Parenthesis Publications Restoration Drama Series, 2001), p. 5.

[49] Calhoun Winton, *John Gay and the London Theatre* (Lexington: University of Kentucky Press, 1993), pp. 30–1.

[50] Ibid., p. 38.

is not only in defiance of Dryden, but possibly also, according to Geoffrey Tillotson, influenced by adaptations of 'The Merchant's Tale' in early eighteenth-century comic novels.[51] His ambivalence about the bawdy nature of Chaucer's comic narratives, which he had read in Speght's 1598 edition, is evident in the notable differences between these modernisations and his untitled Chaucer imitation. The former deploy euphemism, as well as suppression and open disavowal of the Prologue's and Tale's obscene comedy. The Wife's chuckling and vulgar recollection 'As help me God, I laughe whan I thynke / How pitously a-nyght I made hem swynke!'[52] becomes the much primmer 'the three were old, but rich and fond beside, / And toil'd most piteously to please their Bride'.[53] The most striking obscenity in the Wife's Prologue, the Wife's complaint about monogamy,

> What eyleth yow to grucche thus and grone?
> Is it for ye wolde have my queynte alone?
> Wy, taak it al! Lo, have it every deel!
> Peter! I shrewe yow, but ye love it weel;
> For if I wolde selle my *bele chose*,
> I koude walke as fressh as is a rose
> But I wol kepe it for youre owene tooth
> Ye be to blame, by God! I sey yow sooth.[54]

is softened substantially by Pope, so that it reads:

> Fye, 'tis unmanly thus to sigh and groan;
> What? Would you have me to your self alone?
> Why take me love! Take all and ev'ry part!
> Here's your Revenge! You love it at your Heart.
> Wou'd I vouchsafe to sell what Nature gave,
> You little think what Custom I cou'd have!
> But see! I'm all your own – nay hold – for Shame!
> What means my Dear – indeed – you are to blame.[55]

While the theme of prostitution is more strongly evoked in Pope's use of the word 'custom', underlining the Wife's dubious morality, the line 'have me to yourself alone' and 'what nature gave', this adaptation is conspicuous for its exclusion of the slang vaginal term 'qweynte' and its euphemistic synonym

[51]   Geoffrey Tillotson, 'Introduction', in *Poems of Alexander Pope*, vol. II, 3rd edn, ed. Geoffrey Tillotson (London: Methuen and Co., 1962), p. 7.

[52]   Geoffrey Chaucer, 'The Wife of Bath's Prologue', in *The Riverside Chaucer*, ed. Larry D. Benson, 3rd edn (Oxford: Oxford University Press, 1987), ll. 201–2, p. 107. All future line and page references to Chaucer are to this edition.

[53]   Alexander Pope, 'The Wife of Bath Her Prologue', in *Poems* ii, ll. 58–9, p. 59.

[54]   Chaucer, 'The Wife of Bath's Prologue', ll. 443–50, p. 111.

[55]   Pope, 'The Wife of Bath', ii. 197–204, p. 66.

'*bele chose*'. 'January and May', in shying away from mention of sexual intimacy, truncates the long and funny consummation scene in 'The Merchant's
Tale', including the memorable image of post-coital January's 'slakke nekke'
quivering as he sings. Its version of the tale's notorious 'tree scene', moreover,
is more circumlocutory. Chaucer's famously frank account,

> up she gooth.
> Ladyes, I prey yow that ye be nat wrooth;
> I kan nat glose, I am a rude man –
> And sodeynly anon this Damyan
> Gan pullen up the smok, and in he throng.[56]

is rendered such that Damyan's penetration of May is decorous to the point
of invisibility:

> 'Tis Truth I tell, tho' not in Phrase refin'd;
> Tho' blunt my Tale, yet honest is my Mind.
> What Feats the Lady in the Tree might do,
> I pass, as Gambols never known to you:
> But sure it was a merrier Fit she swore,
> Than in her Life she ever felt before.[57]

His imaginative imitation of Chaucer is, by contrast, a sophomoric effort
which, in the words of Derek Brewer, is 'more bawdy than anything Chaucer
himself actually wrote'.[58] This twenty-six-line faux-Chaucerian poem is a
priapic farce in which a boy, John, hides a stolen duck in his trousers to
conceal it from his aunt and young female cousins. His ruse is undone after
the duck 'tickl[ing] his Erse Roote', causes him to burst his flies, and then
thrusts its neck out of the boy's front, emitting a quack that makes one of
his cousins think his 'yerde can talke'.[59] The poem's narrative ribaldry is
compounded by what could be described as a lexical 'return of the repressed'
in which a number of words and phrases excised from his modernised
Chaucer reappear. The elated post-coital January, described by Chaucer as
'ful of ragerye' (l. 1847), resurfaces in Pope's opening statement 'Women ben
ful of Ragerie' (l. 1); in the following line, 'Yet swinken nat sans Secresie' (l.
2), the Wife's censored 'swynke' reappears. Later, 'tickleth his Erse Roote'
(18) combines the Wife's recollection 'tickleth me about myn herte roote' (l.
471) with 'ers' (l. 3810) from 'The Miller's Tale'. Alison's famous laugh from

---

56 Geoffrey Chaucer, 'The Merchant's Tale', in *Riverside Chaucer*, ll. 2349–53, p. 167.
57 Pope, 'January and May', *Poems* ii, ll. 742–7, p. 51.
58 Brewer, *Geoffrey Chaucer, the Critical Heritage*, p. 172.
59 Pope, 'Imitation of English Poets: Chaucer', in *Poems* vi, ed. Norman Ault and John
Butt, pp. 41–2 (p. 42).

the latter tale echoes unmistakably in the '*te-he*' of the ladies who witness John's humiliation (l. 21). The source for 'yerde' is harder to determine since its appearance in Chaucer is not especially phallic, although there has been some debate about its meaning,[60] but again it constitutes a very frank and determined use on Pope's part of medieval genital terminology.

Another, much later, complex case comes from the anonymous 1791 moderniser of *The Miller's Tale*, who, in an opening 'Address to the Reader', condemns 'the gross indecency of Chaucer's humour' as [a] 'so great drawback from his sterling merit, that his warmest admirers must confess it to be an insurmountable objection to him being a general favourite'. It goes on:

> [S]o interwoven is the tenor of these stories with indecency, that no subterfuge may be devised, by which that blot may be absolutely obliterated. This is the case with that tale, which I have endeavoured to paraphrase: the point of the whole turns on a circumstance, which no circumlocution or guarded expression can convey delicately to the reader's mind, since it is itself indecent.[61]

This high-handed denunciation seems on closer inspection, however, to have a subtler, more self-serving – and arguably more amusing – agenda, especially when the accompanying modernisation is taken into account. In the modernised 'grope' scene between Nicholas and Alison, the lines

> Beneath her stays he thrust his letcherous arm –
> Fast round her supple loins one hand he prest,
> And with the other grasp'd her heaving breast[62]

replace Chaucer's blunt and specific 'qweynte' (l. 3276) with the coyer and more general 'loins', but make up for this by adding a breast fondle not found in Chaucer, but very probably based on John Smith's 1713 modernisation. Similarly, the modernised version of the infamous 'window scene' operates on a basis of scatological equivalence. The lines:

---

[60] Lee Patterson, *Chaucer and the Subject of History* (Madison, WI: The University of Wisconsin Press, 1991), pp. 364–5, n. 88.

[61] Bowden, *Eighteenth-Century Modernizations*, p. 169. For a discussion of the 'legendary smuttiness' of Chaucer's texts in the later context of the United States, where it is the 'defining feature of his reputation' and a site through which public concerns about obscenity, decency, censorship and tolerance have been deliberated, see George Shuffelton, 'Chaucerian Obscenity in the Court of Public Opinion', *The Chaucer Review* 47 (2012), 1–24 (p. 1).

[62] Anon., 'The Miller's Tale from Chaucer', in Bowden, *Eighteenth-Century Modernisations*, ll. 86–8, p. 171.

> [a]t the wyndow out she putte hir hole
> And Absolon, him fil no bet ne wers
> But with his mouth he kiste hir naked ers

become more modest and yet more synaesthetically grotesque when rendered as

> Stooping forward thro' the casement far
> She thrust against his lips her buttocks bare;
> And Absalom, before he smoak'd the jest,
> Ev'n on her bum a luscious kiss imprest.[63]

Chaucer's use of 'mouth' and 'hole' is undeniably not only more obscene than the relatively demure 'buttocks' and even 'bum', but also, as Elaine Hansen and Susan Signe Morrison have remarked, more comprehensively scatological in its reference both to the proximity of the anus and the vagina, and to the relationship between these nether-orifices and the mouth.[64] This convergence of orifices is arguably more pronounced in John Smith's 'Absolon … kiss'd her full sav'rily – twixt Wind and Water', a phrase that is both euphemistic and curiously vivid, especially as it is followed by the synaesthesic evocation of him wiping away 'the Savour / of Olid Salts, and Ammoniack flavour' left from the kiss.[65] But the 1791 moderniser goes some way to closing the scatological gap with Chaucer by describing the kiss as 'luscious', and by the use of the now archaic verb 'to smoak', which according to the *OED* affords the opportunity to pun on 'suspect' and 'smell'.[66] Comparing representations of Nicholas's fart in the second window scene, moreover, the scatological scales are again finely balanced. Nicholas's 'ers' has in modernisation become his more euphemistic 'nether side', and Chaucer's image of Nicholas hanging out of the window 'to the haunche-bon' is, like his portrayal of Alison's 'hole', more graphically anal. Nicholas's backside notwithstanding, his excretory urges are given more attention by his moderniser, as Chaucer's brief 'Nicholas was risen for to pisse' (l. 3798) is replaced by a lengthier description of the clerk's distended bowels:

---

[63] Chaucer, 'Miller's Tale', ll. 3732–4, p. 75; 'The Miller's Tale', in Bowden, *Eighteenth-Century Modernisations*, ll. 504–7, p. 175

[64] Elaine Tuttle Hansen, *Chaucer and the Fictions of Gender* (Berkeley: University of California Press, 1992), p. 226, n. 29; Susan Signe Morrison, *Excrement in the Late Middle Ages: Sacred Filth and Fecopoetics* (New York: Palgrave Macmillan, 2008).

[65] John Smith, 'The Miller's Tale', in Bowden, *Eighteenth-Century Modernisations*, ll. 682, 690–1, p. 29.

[66] Smoke (v.), OED Online, March 2013. Oxford University Press (accessed 28 May 2013).

> But Nicholas, who wish'd the joke to share,
> Of wind a treasure in his bowels bare,
> And (straining, lest too soon the storm should burst)
> His brawny buttocks thro' the window thrust.

Furthermore, Chaucer's 'Nicholas anon leet fle a fart / As greet as it had been a thunder-dent' arguably lacks some the excremental force of the moderniser's 'Nicholas at once discharg'd the load, / Like peals of thunder from a bursting cloud.'[67] What becomes apparent, then, is that the 1791 moderniser's censure of the irredeemably obscene nature of Chaucer's humour functions not just as an apologia for the tale to come, but in fact ingeniously licenses the continuation, or in the case of Nicholas's bowels the amplification, of this obscenity in the modernisation. These examples alert us to the fact that the polishing was a rather more mixed affair than is often acknowledged; while there certainly were some genuine attempts at refinement, in other cases writers flattered their readers' perceptions of their age as witty and polite in order to smuggle in outrageous content.

For many, Chaucer's comic crudity went hand in hand with his superannuated English. Within the proliferating commentary culture of the time, Chaucer's inaccessible language is an unavoidable leitmotif. This recognition of him as an early English writer was central to the practice of English canon formation which, as Richard Terry, Christopher Cannon and Philip Connell have shown, had begun in around the sixteenth century but which gained significant momentum in the eighteenth. Within this tradition, which intersected with the development of linguistic antiquarianism, Chaucer is nominated as the language's originary figure: again, gathering together the principal descriptions scattered throughout the commentaries, he is the English language's Bard, its Homer, its Ennius, its font, its well, its morning star. In some cases he is presented, in the wake of Spenser's 'well of English undefil'd', as the exemplar of pure English: Samuel Croxall, for instance, hailed him as the 'parent of Britannic Lays'.[68] In many other cases, however, this insistence on the poet's linguistic primacy did not rest on nativist arguments for linguistic purity. Rather, having stripped nature of the 'Gothic' garb she had worn in Anglo-Saxon literature, and dressed her instead in cosmopolitan robes, he was credited as the 'great adorner' of English, a trope that had begun with Lydgate's *Troy Book* (1412–20) and was repeated throughout the eighteenth century with a frequency that borders on the compulsive. Across the century commentators reiterated, in most cases virtually unchanged, an account in which Chaucer 'polished' English through

---

[67] Chaucer, 'Miller's Tale', ll. 3806–7, p. 76; 'The Miller's Tale', in Bowden, *Eighteenth-Century Modernisations*, ll. 564–7, 573–4, p. 175.

[68] Croxall, 'The Vision', in Spurgeon, *Five Hundred Years*, p. 337.

his introduction of Italian and Provençal borrowings. Despite the regular decrying of his metrical irregularity (a criticism which in any case was challenged from the 1730s on by Thomas Morell, Thomas Gray and Thomas Tyrwhitt), Chaucer was celebrated virtually ubiquitously in the eighteenth century (with Dr Johnson being an unsurprising exception) as having 'made the English language' as it was then known.

This proclamation of Chaucer's linguistic primacy had a contradictory status in the evaluation of him as humourist. Even for those Augustans who were enamoured of Chaucer's wit, and did not believe it to be crude, it was, ironically, his use of English – the language he was deemed to have 'made' – that presented a serious obstacle to their enjoyment of him. The very thing that made him such a valuable object of study to the antiquarians was regarded, as I indicated at the outset of this chapter, as an unnecessary, indeed, unwelcome accretion of rusticity that obscured, indeed compromised, the genius of his wit. This widespread conviction generated a (now-familiar) rich and oft-replenished stock of tropes in which his language was described as, among other things, a rusted coin, a clouded mirror, a gothic cloud, a gothic ruin, an old coat and a dungheap concealing comic pearls. In a funereal turn, his wit was described as 'buried' or 'embalmed' within his language. For many he is a victim of the 'Gothic' stage of English with which he was forced to grapple. For others, especially those of a more neoclassical bent, he is the victim not just of the early vernacular in which he wrote, but of English itself, which, unlike the unchanging solidity of Greek and Latin, is presented as inherently unstable. In his poem 'Of English Verse', for instance, Edmund Waller describes English as 'a daily changing tongue', suggesting that 'Poets that lasting marble seek / Must carve in Latin or in Greek.'[69] This sentiment is echoed in Theophilus Cibber's remark, in *The Lives of the Poets of Great Britain and Ireland* (1753), that one cannot read Chaucer or Langland 'without lamenting the unhappiness of a fluctuating language, that buries in its ruins even genius itself'.[70] As Cannon points out, this notion of Chaucer as 'haunted by an implacable linguistic change' began in the sixteenth century, as seen in Speght's inclusion of a glossary in his 1598 edition of the poet's collected works.[71] By the early eighteenth century, however, this notion of linguistic alienation had gained the status of truism, unanimously accepted by antiquarians and humourists alike. In a well-known remark in *An Essay on Criticism* Pope suggests that this 'failing language' eventually strips all poets of their fame, relativising Chaucer's obsolescence by predicting 'what

---

[69] Edmund Waller, *The Works of Edmund Waller in Verse and Prose* (London: Published by Mr Elijah Fenton, 1744), p. 147.

[70] Theophilus Cibber, 'Langland, in *The Lives of the Poets of Great Britain and Ireland* (1753), I (Teddington, Middlesex: The Echo Library, 2007), pp. 16–17.

[71] Christopher Cannon, 'The Myth of Origin and the Making of Chaucer's Wit', *Speculum* 71 (1996), 646–75 (p. 649).

now Chaucer is, shall Dryden be';[72] but others believed that the Age of Wit was a period in which English had reached an optimal level of refinement, elegance and moral force. Addison follows his vehement denial of Chaucer's relevance (cited at the opening of this chapter) with ardent praise for contemporary poets, including not only Dryden but also Waller who, while less remembered today, was lauded for 'smoother Numbers and softer Verse' than in other eras.

In tandem with those who aimed to render Chaucer's obscene comedy more genteel, there were those who were believed Chaucerian wit could be retrieved via linguistic modernisation, which had the power, according to Andrew Jackson in 1750, to 'rescue ... the living from the dead'.[73] Interestingly, this linguistic modernisation project mobilised the identical metaphors used in Chaucer's linguistic canonisation, but in reverse: just as he adorned the English language with cosmopolitan sophistication, so must he now be adorned with modern clarity and elegance; just as he was once the polisher of the rustic tongue, so must his own rusty surface now be polished; and, in an intriguing historical transposition, just as his verse once stripped nature of her pre-conquest Gothic robes, so must his own Gothic garb come off, so that, no longer the unfashionable courtier, he can now make the acquaintance of the polite world.

In so doing, however, the promoters of Chaucerian modernisation, both comic and linguistic, subscribed to what John Sitter has perceptively described as an eighteenth-century 'mentalist' approach to wit founded on a Platonic 'dualism of thought and language', which argues that 'wit' resides in the mind of the author in a way that can be detached from the product of that mind. This detachment was central, Sitter argues, to Dryden's famous distinction in *Annus Mirabilis* (1667) between 'wit writing' and 'wit written', a distinction which also underpins the definition of 'paraphrase' in his *Preface Concerning Ovid's Epistles* as '[t]ranslation with Latitude, where the Author is kept in view by the Translator, so as never to be lost, but his words are not so strictly follow'd as his sense'.[74] Sitter argues that 'Most of the late seventeenth- and eighteenth-century attempts to ennoble wit involve a move similar to Dryden's and led to the same problem', which is a notion of native wit as 'imagination or genius ... which in its loftier identity has no visible connection with writing'.[75] This belief in Chaucer's ineffable yet durable wit was reit-

72   Pope, *An Essay on Criticism*, l. 483, p. 293.

73   Andrew Jackson, 'Matrimonial Scenes; Consisting of [...] all Modernised from Chaucer', (1750), in Spurgeon, *Five Hundred Years*, p. 401.

74   John Dryden, 'Preface Concerning Ovid's Epistles', in *The Poems of John Dryden*, ed. and intro by John Sargeaunt (London and New York: Oxford University Press, 1913), p. 509.

75   John Sitter, *Arguments of Augustan Wit* (Cambridge: Cambridge University Press, 1991), p. 81.

erated across the eighteenth century by his modernisers and their supporters. Thinking about this aspect of Chaucerian reception via Dryden's distinctions helps explain the taste for characterising the 'true', witty Chaucer by way of biographies and pen-portraits of his person rather than by his writing; for in these portraits we are given the image of the 'wit writing' while his witty but rusty verse can be sidestepped. This distinction is, in fact, one that sits at the heart of much comic medievalism, and indeed is genealogically significant to medievalism in general, which has, as I have argued elsewhere, continued in some quarters to harbour a persistent Platonist belief – or at least hope – that an elusive but identifiable medieval 'essence' can be preserved irrespective of changes made to the medieval text or object in post-medieval contexts.[76]

There is a clear ethical position attached to this outwardly aesthetic debate, for Chaucer's modernisers not only believed modernisation would, in the words of Hugh Dalrymple, '[Chaucer's] name to ages far remote transmit', but saw themselves as rescuing the poet's intrinsic worth, his wit, from those who simply 'venerated' him for his antiquity. The declared anti-antiquarianism of Chaucer's modernisers is in many ways unsurprising, given the well-known lampooning of scholarly pedantry among the age's most famous wits and scholars, especially the Scriblerians. Arguably the best-known expression of this is in Pope's *The Dunciad* (1743), in its satire of 'Wormius', identified as medievalist Thomas Hearne:

> But who is he, in closet close y-pent,
> Of sober face, with learned dust besprent?'
> Right well mine eyes arede the myster wight,
> On parchement scraps y-fed, and Wormius hight.
> To future ages may thy dullness last,
> As thou preserv'st the dullness of the past![77]

Studded with pseudo-Middle English archaisms, this sly parodic satire is nevertheless complicated by the fact that *The Dunciad*, as Pat Rogers has pointed out, itself 'employs' pedantry as well as just parodying it'.[78] Fairly bristling with notes and other scholarly apparatus, it offers 'a rhetorical gesture of solidarity with the goals of antiquarian study, even as it assails the foolish extremes to which acolytes of the subject might go'.[79] Elsewhere, Pope is less ambiguous, likening antiquarian fascination with aged verse, and Chaucerian verse in particular, to the perverse valuing of the rust over

---

[76] Louise D'Arcens, 'Deconstruction and the Medieval Indefinite Article: The Undecidable Medievalism of Brian Helgeland's *A Knight's Tale*', *Parergon* 25 (2008), 80–98.

[77] Pope, *The Dunciad* in four books, in *Poems* vol. v, ed. James Sutherland, III, 189–90, p. 329.

[78] Pat Rogers, *Essays on Pope* (Cambridge: Cambridge University Press, 1993), p. 243.

[79] Ibid., p. 258.

the gold in an antique coin.[80] Interestingly, for Pope the worst excesses of the antiquarians are captured in their fetishising of age at the expense of polite humour, as he presents them as 'learning Chaucer's worst ribaldry by rote'.[81] Pope's censure is mild, however, compared to the abject description of Vicesimus Knox, who in 1779 described linguistic antiquarianism as 'like raking in a dung hill for pearls';[82] Knox's comments are, according to Ritchie Robertson, part of longer post-Scriblerian anti-antiquarian strain of commentary which continued to hold that the survival of earlier writings should depend on them being made accessible to modern readers.[83]

It is a matter of record today that the modernisation of Chaucer's writing did not meet with approval among readers, usually devotees of emerging philological practices, for whom Chaucer's humour and language were intertwined. This move to recover, anatomise and preserve Chaucer's language was not yet the increasingly scientistic, professionalised philological study that was to come in the nineteenth century, but a linguistic antiquarianism that was its precursor. While it gained real and agenda-setting momentum around the time of Thomas Tyrwhitt's 1775 edition, support for this approach had been building for some decades. As early as 1700 Dryden recounts that the Earl of Leicester had objected to Dryden's own modernisation project, protesting 'that there is a certain Veneration due to [Chaucer's] old Language; and that it is little less than Profanation and Sacrilege to alter it'.[84] As early as 1706, William Harrison, in *Woodstock Park: A Poem*, defends Chaucer as an 'inimitable Bard', and in a politely wry couplet claims that Dryden '[t]ook wond'rous pains to do the author wrong, / And set to modern time his ancient song', continuing, 'Cadence, and sound, which we so prize and use, / Ill suit the majesty of Chaucer's Muse.'[85]

Although a minority opinion at that point, this sentiment can still be found seventy years later, in Thomas Warton's evaluation of Pope's modernisation of *The House of Fame*. With what Kramnick calls Warton's 'preference for Gothic and sublime difficulty over beautiful and sociable ease',[86] he praises Pope's 'usual elegance of diction and harmony of versification', but argues that the Augustan Wit has 'misrepresented' Chaucer's story and that

---

[80]   Alexander Pope, 'The Second Book of the Epistles of Horace' (1737), in Spurgeon, *Five Hundred Years*, p. 383.

[81]   Pope, 'Epistles of Horace', in Spurgeon, *Five Hundred Years*, p. 383.

[82]   Vicesimus Knox, 'On the Old English Poets,' *Essay 39* [in] Essays Moral and Literary, 2nd edn, i (London, 1779), pp. 292–3, in Spurgeon, *Five Hundred Years*, pp. 457–8.

[83]   Ritchie Robertson, *Mock-Epic Poetry from Pope to Heine* (Oxford, New York: Oxford University Press, 2009).

[84]   Dryden, 'Fables Ancient and Modern', in Spurgeon, *Five Hundred Years*, p. 281.

[85]   William Harrison, 'Woodstock Park, a Poem' (1706), [in] *A Collection of Poems by Several Hands*, ed. R. Dodsley, v (1758), pp. 192–3, in Spurgeon, *Five Hundred Years*, p. 293.

[86]   Kramnick, 'The Making of the English Canon', p. 1093.

his attempts to correct its 'extravagancies by new refinements ... did not consider that extravagancies are essential to a poem of such a structure, and even constitute its beauties'.[87] Using the favoured architectural metaphor of recovery, he described modernisation as like 'giving Corinthian columns to a Gothic palace'; a practice which, despite the evocation of classical grandeur, is presented as insensitively and anachronistically modern. Thomas Warton, Oxford's Professor of Poetry and one of the staunchest opponents of modernisation, had already been pursuing this theme since 1754, when he argued that 'nothing has more contributed to [Chaucer] being little looked into, than the convenient opportunity of reading him with facility in modern imitations. Thus when translation ... becomes substituted as the means of attaining the knowledge of any difficult or antient author, the original not only begins to be neglected and excluded as less easy, but also to be despised as less ornamental and elegant'.[88]

Warton's comment is significant for revealing a central tension in the work of the early reception of Chaucer's wit, which bears repeating, though hopefully it is evident by now: that is, whether they believed their role to be excavation and preservation of Chaucerian wit, or conversely to be polishing it up so it shines through its medieval rusticity and obscurity, it is clear that they are deeply dependent on his medieval, 'gothic' foundation to define their modernity. This is particularly worth stating in the case of the 'polishers', whose constant depictions of Chaucer as rusted currency served to reassure them of the new-mintedness of their own verse. Whether Chaucer's audience in the Age of Wit admired or ridiculed him for his medievalness, all, at bottom, needed it to be who they were.

---

[87] Ibid.
[88] Thomas Warton, 'Observations on the Faerie Queen', in Spurgeon, *Five Hundred Years*, p. 409.

3

Medievalist Farce as Anti-Totalitarian Weapon: Dario Fo as Modern *Giullare*

WHEN CONSIDERING THE POST-MEDIEVAL REANIMATION of comic modes as a form of 'comic medievalism', one of the thornier issues to negotiate is how the various modern adaptors actually view 'the medieval' – or, alternatively, constructions such as the 'gothic', or even the 'old', which operate analogously with 'the medieval' – and, in particular, whether they are well disposed toward the Middle Ages' comic culture. In the Enlightenment, when Chaucer was regarded as a 'merry' precursor of modern wit, this was, until later in the eighteenth century, largely at the expense of seeing him as medieval; he was, rather, exceptional to his times, ineffably proto-modern, and it was this that made him retrievable. Those comic aspects that could not be assimilated to the modern canons of good taste were regarded as unseemly reminders of an abject 'gothic' pre-modernity that required excision or revision. Laughing in the Middle Ages, through embracing the elements of his work deemed to bequeath a continuous comic legacy, in many cases could not be divorced from the ridicule directed at his cultural milieu. In the case of the retrieval to be examined in this chapter, the Italian playwright and performer Dario Fo's adoption of the performance persona of the medieval *giullare*, the ambivalence toward the medieval takes a somewhat different, more pointedly historical-dialectical form. For Fo, the Middle Ages in general, and the Italian Middle Ages in particular, are interpreted as hostile to, and prohibitive of, mirthful expression, yet also explosively fertile in comic expression, harbouring a vibrant strain of popular culture that was hardly resistant to repression and hence survives into the present. As will be discussed, he attributes this contradiction to a tension between 'official' culture and a vibrant comic culture of the people which was perceived to be – and, in Fo's view, indeed was – a threat to what can be described as the 'feudal–ecclesiastical complex'. In the case of Fo, one of the most vital questions is what medieval comic culture can be understood to offer the modern in the way of precedents. In the case of many texts to be examined throughout this book, the Middle Ages are held up overtly or covertly as a kind of funhouse mirror to the modern, creating an image which, whether grotesquely or benignly distorted, still serves as a point of, and for, reflection. Fo, however, takes things further, laughing with the Middle Ages by developing a highly politicised conception of medieval comic practice that in turn serves as a model for a modern performance-driven form of social activism. The admiration he has garnered with this singular use of history to address urgent contemporary problems, and the dangerous opprobrium that has included arrests, censorship, intimidation and violence toward his family, together offer testimony to the potency of his brand of comic medievalist activism.

Before moving on to Fo's work, it is helpful to contextualise his concept of medieval comic culture within the broader frame of the modern reha-bilitation of popular culture, which has long harboured a latent medievalist impulse. Among the cluster of competing definitions of the word 'popular' over which scholars have wrestled,[1] there has been one that has taken a longi-tudinal approach, perceiving 'popular culture' to be the authentic expression and repository of 'the people', *il popolo* or *das Volk*, who have been under-stood as a historical category. According to the practitioners of this approach, the customs and traditions of these 'popular classes' have endured across the centuries despite their non-participation in 'official culture'. The culture associated with 'the people' is deemed popular in the sense that it is produced by them and for their own consumption, expressing their interests and their aesthetics. I am calling this a 'medievalist impulse' of popular cultural theory because, as cultural theorists and medievalists have separately argued, its emergence in the nineteenth century is inextricably bound up with the philological, literary and material recovery of medieval culture. James Hall argues that the perception of an 'unofficial' medieval culture had preceded the nineteenth century, but the late eighteenth and nineteenth centuries were distinctive for their celebratory recovery of the culture of the people, a culture regarded both as enduring yet fragile to loss under modernity.[2] In the hands of the 'medievalist left' of the Victorian period, epitomised by socialist William Morris, this delight in medieval popular culture took the form of a nostalgic-utopian belief in the superiority of the unalienated labour of the harmonious preindustrial world.

---

[1]   Raymond Williams, *Keywords* (London: Fontana, 1983), p. 237.

[2]   See James Hall, 'Introduction', in *Understanding Popular Culture: Europe from the Middle Ages to the Nineteenth Century*, ed. Steven L. Kaplan (New York: Mouton, 1984), pp. 5–18 (pp. 7–10); Perry Meisel, *The Myth of Popular Culture from Dante to Dylan* (Chichester, UK: Blackwell, 2010), p. 10; R. Howard Bloch and Stephen G. Nichols, eds, *Medievalism and the Modernist Temper* (Baltimore, MD: Johns Hopkins University Press, 1996).

A later, profoundly influential reclamation of folk culture, on which I wish to concentrate, re-emerged in the 1920s and '30s in the writings of the political philosopher and foundational figure of the Italian Communist Party, Antonio Gramsci. It is difficult to overstate the significance of Gramsci's notion of power to modern and postmodern formulations of the relationship between dominant, official culture and the culture of the oppressed. In *Popular Culture: Production and Consumption*, C. Lee Harrington and Denise D. Bielby claim, among others, that 'when … Gramsci's work became available in English in the 1970s, Cultural Studies' focus was redefined.'[3] His theory of hegemonic power, which accounted for social inequity in cultural and ideological rather than simply economic terms, was instrumental in shaping twentieth-century left-wing historiography and social theory, and, later, such adjacent fields as subaltern studies and certain versions of feminist studies. This concept, which has entered the general academic vocabulary, is nicely summarised by Daniel Strinati:

> Dominant groups in society, including fundamentally but not exclusively the ruling class, maintain their dominance by securing the 'spontaneous consent' of subordinate groups, including the working class, through the negotiated construction of a political and ideological consensus which incorporates both dominant and dominated groups.[4]

The value system of the dominant group is not imposed by force, but by being naturalised as transparently and self-evidently 'right', so that those disadvantaged or devalued under this system nevertheless identify with it and internalise its norms. This consensus, however, can be resisted through the subordinate group's assertion of its own values, desires and customs. Situating Gramscian theory in a lineage of 'medievalist' formulations of popular culture might initially seem counter-intuitive, not least because Gramsci does not speak comprehensively or at length about the Middle Ages in his work. But in his best-known work, the *Prison Notebooks*, he does develop an explicitly historical account in which a hegemonic medieval culture, buttressed by the relationship between the Catholic Church and the feudal order, was contested by a resilient folk culture characterised by ribald buffoonery and anti-authoritarianism.[5] Furthermore, his recourse to the category of 'the people' and his defence of their culture has a strong implicit relationship to the older romantic and leftist move to restore the dignity of long-abiding

3   C. Lee Harrington and Denise D. Bielby, eds, *Popular Culture: Production and Consumption* (Maldon, MA: Blackwell Publishers, 2000), p. 4.

4   Dominic Strinati, *An Introduction to Theories of Popular Culture*, 2nd edn (London: Routledge, 2004), pp. 147–8.

5   See John Fulton, 'Religion and Politics in Gramsci: An Introduction', *Sociological Analysis* 48 (1987), 197–216 (pp. 209–10).

but suppressed folk cultures. What distinguishes the Gramscian acknowledgement of folk culture from nineteenth-century formulations is that its reliance on Marxist-Hegelian assumptions of class antagonism within the medieval social field, and on a belief in the efficacy of folk resistance under conditions of oppression.

Gramsci is a particularly important figure to consider in relation to Fo, who, as a fellow Italian, did not need to wait until the 1970s to adopt the philosopher's conceptual framework. It has become a critical commonplace to note the Gramscian frame of Fo's ideology; but, with the exception of Antonio Scuderi's work, the particularly medievalist inflection of the Fo–Gramsci relationship is generally overlooked. The influence of Gramsci's historical thesis on Fo is most clearly expressed in the play *The Worker Knows 300 Words, the Boss Knows 1,000 – That's Why He's the Boss* (1969), where Gramsci's ghost appears, urging workers to recover their proud folk traditions which have been covered up or expropriated by the Church, the aristocracy and, more recently, the bourgeoisie. Yet the text on which I will be focusing, Dario Fo's 1969 medievalist play cycle *Mistero Buffo* (trans. Comic Mysteries) has been described by Fo scholar Tom Behan as the 'purest and most famous exposition' of 'Gramsci's interest in working-class and popular culture'.[6] *Mistero Buffo* is among the most fully developed examples of a post-medieval humorous text that models itself explicitly on medieval comic precedents, in this case the mystery play cycles of the European Middle Ages. In addition to its enduring appeal to audiences numbering in their millions in the four decades since its first performance, and its translation into numerous languages, *Mistero Buffo* deserves a prominent place in a study on comic medievalism because among the writers, playwrights and filmmakers treated in this book Fo is arguably the most knowledgeable and reflective about how his play operates as a modern reworking of what he takes to be 'medieval comic culture', and how this can be applied within his contemporary context. In this cycle of virtuoso monologues, Fo, as radical left-wing agitator, satirist and master of the farce tradition, explicitly develops a profile for himself as the descendent of a popular tradition of subversive medieval performance, serving up truth to power by way of an intensely physical comedy that laughs heartily with the Middle Ages.

Born in 1926, Fo is one of Italy's most famous performers and playwrights, satirists and activists. As a young man he began to move into the world of performance, working in improvisatory theatre. Alongside his involvement in live theatre, in the early 1950s he also performed satiric monologues on radio, until his show was cancelled after its treatment of biblical tales offended both religious and secular powers. In 1954 he married the

---

6   Tom Behan, 'The Megaphone of the Movement: Dario Fo and the Working Class 1968–70', *Journal of European Studies* 30 (2000), 251–70 (p. 253).

actress Franca Rame, who had come from a theatrical family known for its deep knowledge of Italian performance traditions, and who has been Fo's collaborator for more than five decades. Their performances in the 1950s became increasingly controversial, appealing to audiences but attracting the opprobrium of Church and government, to the point that they had trouble securing performance spaces. In the 1960s, Fo, who had also been writing film screenplays, moved into television, writing and directing a show featuring ordinary people's lives, before falling out with the studio, again due to attempts to control his content. Apart from an acclaimed television performance of *Mistero Buffo* in 1977 (which nevertheless upset the Vatican), Fo has generally remained in theatre, spending the last forty-plus years engaging in topical satiric performances as a kind of theatrical activism. Despite his turbulent relationship with the authorities, Fo received the ultimate official endorsement in 1997, when he became the recipient of the Nobel Prize for Literature. Critics of Fo's Nobel Prize argued that he was a performer rather than a literary writer, but he found many prepared to defend his services to a vibrant and engaged creative culture.[7] Since the time of his Nobel Prize, Fo has also had, in 2006, an unsuccessful tilt at being elected Mayor of Milan; but, as will become clear, it is his performing, writing and teaching that forms the abiding basis of his authority as an activist, with his medievalist theatre occupying a particular, cherished place.

The content of Fo's plays marks him as a fearless critic of social injustice of all kinds, from police corruption (*Accidental Death of an Anarchist* (1970)) civil disobedience actions of the working poor (*Can't Pay? Won't Pay!* (1974)) and workplace inequities (*The Boss's Funeral* (1969–70), *The Worker Knows 300 Words, the Boss Knows 1,000 – That's Why He's the Boss* (1969)). His satire is specific rather than general, focusing on topical events, creating what he has famously described as a 'throwaway theatre', which is not intended for posterity, instead functioning as 'the people's spoken and dramatised newspaper'.[8] From 1968 and throughout the 1970s he wrote his plays to convey counter-information to working-class audiences, many of whom had not been theatre-goers before they encountered him. He reached these audiences through his use of unconventional performance spaces, such as occupied factories during strike actions, football stadiums and so on. Fo is unapologetic about the consciousness-raising nature of his plays, many of which were followed by 'third acts' – symposia in which the audience's

---

[7]   Andrew Gumbel, 'Nobel Prize: Dario Fo, the Showman, Wins Nobel Literature Prize', *The Independent*, 10 October 1997, http://www.independent.co.uk/news/nobel-prize-dario-fo-the-showman-wins-nobel-literature-prize-1234928.html (accessed 17 November 2011).

[8]   Domenico Maceri, 'Dario Fo: Jester of the Working Class', *World Literature Today* 72 (1998), 9–14 (p. 10); Susan Cowan, 'Dario Fo's Throw-away Theatre', *The Drama Review* 19 (1975), 102–13.

sense of appalled hilarity was shaped into militant action – but he is a firm believer in humour as a tool of consciousness raising. Unlike drama in the tragic mode which, he argued, can only rouse an impotent indignation in the audience, grotesque satire based on grotesque injustice 'was the element that … permits … the popular actor, the folk player, to scratch people's consciousness, to leave them with a taste of something burned and bitter', which would in turn compel them to engage in activism.[9]

For someone as avowedly and urgently engaged with the present moment as Fo has always been, the epithet most strongly associated with him is, surprisingly, overtly medievalist: he is widely lauded as 'the people's court jester'. The Nobel Academy's statement about Fo's award situated this persona at the heart of his practice, describing him as one 'who emulates the jesters of the Middle Ages in scourging authority and upholding the dignity of the downtrodden'.[10] The 'jester' epithet alludes to Fo's much-quoted explanation about why, in 1968, he and Rame formed the Communist Party-affiliated company La Nuova Scena (The New Scene)[11] after abandoning the commercial theatrical circuit attended by middle-class and educated audiences: he proclaimed that '[w]e were fed up with being the court jesters to the bourgeoisie, on whom our criticism worked like an alka-selzer, so we decided to become the court jesters of the proletariat',[12] in order to foment political indigestion. This self-fashioning as 'jester' in turn developed out of Fo's researches into the early history of European theatre and more specifically into disappearing traditions of Italian oral performance. Fo claims to have developed this antiquarian impulse as a child, as a result of listening to the tales told by the local vendors, craftsmen and fishermen of Lake Maggiore. He took these tales to be a valuable living repository of folk orality, and memorised them.[13] This historicism can be seen in pre-*Mistero Buffo* performances, such as *Ci ragiono e canto* (*I think and then I sing*), a 1966 performance organised by Fo emerging out of a collaboration with ethnomusicologists, aimed at retrieving and reanimating the popular song traditions of Italy.[14] His research into medieval performance traditions, which involved much primary research,

---

   [9]   Dario Fo, 'Mistero Buffo', in *Plays: 1*, trans. Ed Emery, intro. Stuart Hood (London: Methuen, 1992), p. 7.
   [10]   Nobel Prize Website, 'The Nobel Prize in Literature 1997: Awarded to Dario Fo', http://www.nobelprize.org/nobel_prizes/literature/laureates/1997/ (accessed 17 November 2011).
   [11]   Fo generally had an uneasy relationship with the PCI (Italian Communist Party), and Nueva Scena soon attracted criticism from the Party. This led Fo and Rame to form the independent left-wing company La Commune in 1969.
   [12]   Tom Behan, *Dario Fo: Revolutionary Theatre* (London: Pluto, 2000), p. 8.
   [13]   Antonio Scuderi, 'Dario Fo and Oral Tradition: Creating a Thematic Context', *Oral Tradition* 15 (2000), 26–38 (p. 27).
   [14]   Pina Piccolo, 'Dario Fo's giullarate: Dialogic Parables in the Service of the Oppressed', *Italica* 65 (1988), 131–43 (p. 132).

and was particularly influenced by Paolo Toschi's 1955 anthropological study *The Origins of Italian Theatre*,[15] had begun well over a decade before the appearance of *Mistero Buffo*.[16] This research also led him, perhaps unsurprisingly, to the work of Marxist Annales-school historian Marc Bloch, whom he also names in *Mistero Buffo* as a communist martyr,[17] as well as to Arnold Hauser's 1951 *Social History of Art*, which argues for the interaction between artistic production and the social order.[18]

Out of these researches, which he documents in his prologues to the plays of *Mistero Buffo* and later in *The Tricks of the Trade* (1988, trans. 1991), he resurrects the crucial figure of the *giullare*, the peripatetic medieval performer who gave one-man performances (*giullarate*) in town squares, inns and marketplaces, through which he exposed the pretensions and abuses of the powerful, both religious and secular. The *giullare*'s preferred performance mode in his mockery of power was farce, delivered either in a range of regional dialects, medieval and modern, or in a rapid-fire sub-semantic patois called *grammelot*, a performance language designed both to communicate across regional linguistic divides and to evade charges of treason or blasphemy brought about by the subversive content of the performance. Despite Fo being aligned by scholars with the Italian mime tradition of the *commedia dell'arte*, especially the anarchic figure of the *zanni*, he is careful to distinguish the socially dangerous farce of the *giullare*, who he claims was frequently persecuted and who he takes as his model, from the more innocuous clowning of his successors, the *commedia dell'arte*, which Fo believed to have been more fully co-opted into official culture, performing in the courts of the aristocracy.[19]

Although earlier in this chapter I described Fo as an inheritor of medieval performance culture, his recourse to the *giullare* is arguably closer to a deliberate, politically motivated revival of the techniques and social function of what Fo regards as a lost predecessor. While the *giullare* turns up in different guises in many Fo plays, *Mistero Buffo* contains his most sustained meditation on medieval resistance humour. Although he later went on to distinguish between the more seditious *giullares* and those who were 'reac-

[15] Antonio Scuderi, *Dario Fo: Framing, Festival, and the Folkloric Imagination* (Lanham, MD: Lexington Books, 2011), pp. 5–6.

[16] In an interview in 1978, Fo points to an earlier contact with medieval traditions when he mentions that his 1953 satiric play *The Finger in the Eye* was 'based on a story whose origins go back to the goliard tradition'. See Luigi Ballerini, Giuseppe Risso and others, 'Dario Fo Explains: An Interview', *The Drama Review* 22 (1978), 33–48 (p. 36).

[17] Fo, *Mistero Buffo*, p. 4.

[18] Dario Fo, *The Tricks of the Trade*, trans. Joe Farrell, ed. Stuart Hood (New York: Routledge, 1991), p. 85.

[19] A. Richard Sogliuzzo, 'Dario Fo: Puppets for a Proletarian Revolution', *Drama Review* 16 (1972), 71–7; Tony Mitchell, *Dario Fo: People's Court Jester*, 2nd edn (London: Methuen, 1986), pp. 11–12.

tionaries and conservatives',[20] in *Mistero Buffo* the defiant scatology of the *giullare* is shown, through the historical slide-show discussions punctuating the productions coupled with Fo's own re-enactment of the *giullare's* art, to be part of a larger visual and performance culture of rowdy cacophony and grotesquery, which reaches its apotheosis in the socially inversive community performances of carnival. The playlist in *Mistero Buffo* is as follows:

The Zanni's Grammelot (with the Flagellants' Laude)

The Slaughter of the Innocents

The Morality Play of the Blind Man and the Cripple

The Marriage at Cana

The Birth of the Jongleur (Giullare)

The Birth of the Villeyn

The Resurrection of Lazarus

Boniface VIII

Death and the Fool

Mary Hears of the Sentence Imposed on her Son

The Fool at the Foot of the Cross, Laying a Wager

Mary at the Foot of the Cross

In order to support his rendition of the medieval 'comic mysteries', in the opening discussion of each play Fo presents himself as a theatrical archaeologist, trawling through codexes, unearthing manuscripts in archaic dialects and translating them, and re-examining frescos and mosaics for fragmentary evidence of the medieval performance culture that has so gripped him. This scholarly persona has, however, attracted controversy, with critics noting that while he 'appeal[ed] to the authority of historical documentation' to lend weight to his revivalist project, he in fact crossed into the terrain of creative medievalism, 'fabricat[ing] his sources and his facts'.[21] This included, according to Joseph Farrell, creating visual images by 'an unknown master from the Dark Ages' when he could not unearth sufficient visual evidence.[22] In his introduction to the entire cycle, Fo presents the medieval mystery plays as organs of official narrative in need of rewriting either to expose

20 Fo, *The Tricks of the Trade*, p. 85.

21 Antonio Scuderi, 'Unmasking the Holy Jester Dario Fo', *Theatre Journal* 55 (2003), 275–90 (p. 279).

22 Joseph Farrell, *Dario Fo and Franca Rame: Harlequins of the Revolution* (London: Methuen, 2001), p. 89. Tony Mitchell also notes that when developing *The Obscene Fable* (*Il fabulazzo osceno*), a later addition to *Mistero Buffo* based on a Provençal tale, Fo was unable to locate source materials and so added his own additions 'which convey a popular spirit of bawdry and earthy humour similar to that of Boccaccio, but with more political bite', *Dario Fo: People's Court Jester*, p. 30.

the dynamics of aristocratic and ecclesiastical power, or to dramatise the perspective of the proletarian witnesses to the Christian story. For example, the play 'The Birth of the Jongleur', in which a peasant-*giullare* tells of how he was stripped of his land, family and dignity by the local lord, dramatises, à la Gramsci, the violent collusion between ecclesiastical and aristocratic interests.[23] In the play 'The Raising of Lazarus' the audience witnesses the offstage miracle indirectly, through the amazed 'real-time' reports of lower-class onlookers, while in 'The Marriage at Cana' a rustic drunkard relates how he not only witnessed Jesus turning water into wine, but is still intoxicated from the Dionysian 'bender' that took place as a result, and in which Jesus was a key participant.[24] Despite the fact that these are rewritings of the medieval sources, Fo is insistent that these performances are not his own invention; he introduces the entire cycle with the declaration that they are, rather, re-enactments of Comic Mysteries from the Middle Ages, describing them as 'grotesque performance[s] ... invented by the people'.[25]

And yet despite his claims to be reviving original medieval performances, his plays also function as audacious continuations of the counter-informational *giullare* tradition. This is perhaps best exemplified in the play 'The Birth of the Villeyn', a skit about medieval social rank and the division of labour, in which Fo segues seamlessly from a sketch based on selections from the thirteenth-century poem *Nativitas rusticorum et qualiter debent tractari* by the poet and *giullare* Matazone da Caligano, in which the first peasant is created by a donkey's fart, to a highly topical discussion of the Italian firm Ducati's policy of restricting the toilet breaks of the assembly-line workers at its Bologna plant. He takes up the mantle of medieval comic anticlericalism in his play Boniface VIII, an excoriating satire on pontifical arrogance and greed; the play's material is assembled from a patchwork of medieval sources named and unnamed, but the script is his own; so he becomes a medieval *giullare* in action.[26]

Despite beginning with sometimes quite detailed historical prefaces, which link his researches to the ideological thrust of the scene to come, Fo's mysteries are dominated by vigorous physical and aural (rather than straightforwardly verbal) humour, featuring mime, farce and clowning – all forms that Fo gathers under the heading of *teatro minore* or *teatro popolare*, 'the theatre of the people', performance traditions he claims have been denigrated by bourgeois 'literary theatre'.[27] Fo's skit on the Ducati toilet policy, for instance, involves an elaborate and hilarious mime of attempting to relieve

---

23 Fo, *Mistero Buffo*, p. 50.
24 Ibid., pp. 37–45.
25 Ibid., p. 1.
26 Ibid., pp. 71–84.
27 Fo, *Tricks of the Trade*, pp. 3–4, 84.

himself in accordance with the company's impossible regulations, while the play on Boniface VIII derives much of its comedy from the physical enactment of grotesque corpulence, pomp and narcissism. In the latter play, Fo evokes Boniface's excesses of dress and vanity (and hence those of the papacy, medieval and modern) without props or costumes of any kind, using gesture and sound alone. In this, he claims, he subscribes to Soviet director Vsevolod Meyerhold's pronouncement that a skilled performer of the people's arts could create situation through gesture and hence did not need props.[28]

There is no doubt that Fo's historicised praxis is largely the product of his research into pre-modern performance traditions. But this interest also dovetails with his ideological and political commitments as a radical left-wing activist. In fact, as his reference to Meyerhold indicates, he can be seen as part of a larger far-left and anarchic modernist trend notable for its commitment to an image of medieval anti-authoritarian folk culture. Fo's play's title conspicuously evokes this broader left-modernist lineage by referring directly to Soviet poet–playwright Vladimir Mayakovsky's 1918 play *Mystery-Bouffe*, written in celebration of the Bolshevik Revolution. And Fo's debt does not end with the title; for the earlier play also draws on the mystery play tradition, adapting the narrative of medieval Noah's Flood plays to represent the 'flood' of the Revolution that will wash away the bourgeois world order and replace it with a workers' utopia in the form of an electrified city. Instead of pairing animals, Mayakovsky pairs seven of the 'unclean' (workers) with seven 'clean' characters who represent bourgeois capitalism.[29] Fo's allusion to Mayakovsky is intriguing in that by the time Fo is writing *Mistero Buffo*, Mayakovky's legacy had become posthumously tainted by his official rehabilitation by Stalin, and Fo by this stage had definitely rejected the Party's doctrinaire ideology. This might partly account for why Mayakovsky is not named as a source by Fo, despite the fact that the Russian appears in the same year as a character in *The Worker Knows 300 Words*. Perhaps Fo is evoking the pre-Stalin Mayakovsky, whose early enthusiasm for the Bolshevik Revolution led him to deploy the utopianism and religious semiotics of the medieval mysteries in the service of the new order. It is this gesture that has led Sharon Abramovich-Lehavi to characterise Mayakovsky's play as 'sac/religious', because it 'simultaneously negate[s] the Bible's religious power and authority and use[s] that very same power as an energetic force for creating a meaningful experience'.[30] Despite *Mystery-Bouffe*'s instrumentalisation of pre-modern Christian tradition, Robert Russell refers to it as 'the seminal

[28] Cited in Ballerini et al., 'Dario Fo Explains', p. 43.

[29] Vladimir Mayakovsky, 'Mystery Bouffe', trans. Dorian Rottenberg, in *Classic Soviet Plays*, ed. and intro. Alla Mikhailova (Moscow: Progress Publisher, 1979), pp. 95–172.

[30] Sharon Abramovich-Lehavi, '"The End": Mythical Futures in Avant-Garde Mystery Plays', *Theatre Research International* 34 (2009), 116–23 (p. 118).

work of the Civil War period',[31] drawing on the inherent power of the mystery play form, with its eschatological approach to time, to capture a Bolshevik utopian perspective.[32] Fo was, in turn, drawn to Mayakovsky's commitment to reanimating pre-modern popular culture, with its subversive potential to expose and comically dispose of the ruling classes and their abuses.

The other Soviet writer whose Middle Ages bears a striking resemblance to Fo's is Mikhail Bakhtin's, as developed in his famous *Rabelais and his World*, originally titled *Rabelais and Folk Culture of the Middle Ages and Renaissance*. Bakhtin's formulation of subversive pre-modern folk culture, which has had an enormous influence on the field of cultural studies, and in particular on that field's perception of the social dynamics of 'low' and 'high culture', is so familiar now as to obviate extensive discussion; but it is only right that he should be mentioned here, given his commitment to the notion of the carnivalesque as the socially inversive 'expression of folk consciousness',[33] and for bequeathing us his very full articulation of the excessive and regenerative power of the Dionysian grotesque body, whose 'apertures or convexities, or ... various ramifications and offshoots: the open mouth, the genital organs, the breasts, the phallus, the potbelly, the nose', challenge the authority and integrity of the sealed Apollonian body.[34] The huge impact of Bakhtin's book has produced a received and tacitly perpetuated notion of medieval popular culture as deeply corporeal and visceral, stylistically most commonly expressed in the register of scatology, and ideologically anti-authoritarian, due to its status as an expression of a broadly defined 'folk' culture. There has been a tendency among critics to describe any and all visions of subversive bodily humour as Bakhtinian; and while the impact of Bakhtin's notions of carnival and the grotesque body on the Western intellectual scene justifies this as a heuristic gesture, it wrongly imputes a Bakhtinian impetus to texts such as Fo's which in fact developed their theses of pre-modern popular culture through a Gramscian–Toschian prism, and hence independently of Bakhtin. While Antonio Scuderi has recently pointed to the enriching influence of Bakhtin on Fo's refinement of his approach to pre-modern carnival culture,[35] *Mistero Buffo* is best thought of as accidentally Bakhtinian. I wish to suggest that Bakhtin is less the critical frame through which to understand Fo's work than a strikingly sympatico thinker whose formulation of a subversive medieval comic folk culture was, like Fo's, a historicised expres-

[31] Robert Russell, 'The Arts and the Russian Civil War', *Journal of European Studies* 20 (1990), 219–40 (p. 225).

[32] See James Von Geldern, *Bolshevik Festivals 1917–30* (Berkeley: University of California Press, 1993), pp. 48–53.

[33] Mikhael Bakhtin, *Rabelais and his World*, trans. Hélène Iswolsky (Bloomington: Indiana University Press, 1984), p. 7.

[34] Ibid., p. 26.

[35] Scuderi, *Dario Fo: Framing, Festival*, pp. 5–6.

sion of his rejection of totalitarian rule. Given the context for Bakhtin's text, the totalitarianisms he addressed were the monstrous twins of Nazism and Stalinism, while Fo's evil twins in *Mistero Buffo* are industrial capitalism and the 'soft' hegemonic manipulations of Western consumer culture.

As indicated at the beginning of this chapter, the leftist writer closer to home, to whom Fo's version of medieval culture owes arguably its most profound debt, was Gramsci. In addition to his historicised conception of Gramscian hegemony, Fo's formulation of the restless *giullare*, and of himself as latter-day jester of the people, owes much to Gramsci's concept of the organic intellectual, whose alignment with and emergence out of a specific class or community can potentially produce counter-hegemonic information in both serious and satiric form. Fo's argument that the *giullare* was 'born from the people', taking his anger from the people 'in order to be able to give it back to them … in order that the people should gain greater awareness of their own condition',[36] clearly casts this figure as an activist in the mould of Gramsci's desired intellectual of the working class. Also in the spirit of Gramsci, Fo inserts the *giullare*, a secular figure, into a larger company of organic intellectuals and 'holy fools' within a vibrant scene of medieval Italian 'Christian socialism' *avant la lettre*. These include heretics and reformist activists such as Joachim de Fiore, Gherardo Segarelli and Fra Dolcino, as well as Franciscans, all of whom were, Fo stresses, not simply anticlerical radicals but, importantly, charismatic speakers and peripatetic performers – in his words, 'extraordinary m[e]n of the theatre'.[37] In doing so he continues Gramsci's perception of St Francis as 'a comet in the Catholic firmament', who restored practical religion to the common people along with his fraternity until the Church 'immunised' them by making them into 'a simple monastic order at its service'.[38]

In his notion of the Franciscans as 'men of the theatre' Fo may also have in mind Roberto Rossellini's charming 1950 film *Francesco, Giullare di Dio*. Although the English translation, *The Flowers of St Francis*, takes its title from Rossellini's source text, the enduringly popular late fourteenth-century florilegium, *Fioretti di San Francesco*, in the process it loses the notion of Francis as a charismatic and light-hearted holy fool.[39] The film itself restores this persona, however, through its many scenes in which Francis's religious discourse is delivered with a light smile playing across his lips, a point also noted by Peter Doebler, who points out that Francis's dominant expression is

---

36 Fo, *Mistero Buffo*, p. 1
37 Ibid., p. 71.
38 Antonio Gramsci, *Letters from Prison*, ed. Frank Rosengarten, trans. Raymond Rosenthal (New York: Columbia University Press, 1994), pp. 318–19.
39 *The Flowers of St Francis*, dir. Roberto Rossellini (Cineriz, Rizzoli Film, 1950).

one of visible amusement.[40] The film's true *giullare*, however, is the holy fool Fra Ginepro (Brother Juniper), who is at the centre of a number of the film's episodes, and to whom Rossellini and his co-writer Federico Fellini devote an extraordinary and quite long scene of silent physical comedy, in which he is tossed around by the menacing followers of the tyrant Nicolaio (played by the legendary comic actor Aldo Fabrizi) until he eventually subdues Nicolaio with his humility. The film's frequent middle- and long-distance framing of bucolic scenes in which Francis and his followers (played by a group of young monks rather than professional actors) run around like dizzy schoolboys, or gather flowers for St Clare's visit, emphasises the youth and joyfulness of Francis and his first followers, and tempers the scenes of their extreme privation with bursts of physical liberation. Francis's highly physical performance of piety is conveyed in wordless scenes such as a deeply uncomfortable one in which he doggedly trails a solitary leper until he can embrace the man, who pushes him off and staggers away. This scene, though compelling, is one of two that appear to express some ambivalence toward the extremity of the early Franciscans' piety, the other being when Brother Ginepro cuts the trotter off a neighbour's pig, without the neighbour's permission, so he can make soup for a sick brother. It is only at the end of Rossellini's film that Francis and his brethren set out to preach to the world, so in many respects this is a more private Francis than Fo's or Gramsci's; but the sense of Francis as amused witness and charismatic communicator, both verbally and bodily, is present throughout. Speaking of the 'light' spirituality of the Franciscans, Rossellini says:

> my film wants to focus on the merrier aspect of the Fransciscan experience, on the playfulness, the 'perfect delight,' the freedom that the spirit finds in poverty and in an absolute detachment from material things … I believe that certain aspects of primitive Franciscanism could best satisfy the deepest aspirations and needs of a humanity that, enslaved by its greed and having totally forgotten the Povarello's lesson, has also lost its joy of life.[41]

Although the film's politics are somewhat muted compared with the overt engagement with power structures found in Fo's plays, Rossellini's approach to the subject makes a link between the performance of silliness, anti-materialism and the refusal of nihilism.

---

[40] Peter Doebler, 'Screening the Silly: The Christian Iconography of Roberto Rossellini's *Francesco, Giullare di Dio*', *Journal of Religion in Film* 15 (2011), http://www.unomaha.edu/jrf/Vol15.no1/Doebler_ScreeningSilly.html (accessed 17 November 2011).

[41] Roberto Rossellini, 'The Message of The Flowers of St. Francis', in *My Method: Writings and Interviews*, ed. Adriano Apra, trans. Annapaola Cancogni (New York: Marsilio Publishers, 1992), pp. 31–2.

A preoccupation with St Francis both as medieval forerunner of modern dissidents and as the medieval giullare *par excellence* has continued late into Fo's career, resurfacing three decades after *Mistero Buffo* in his 1999 performance *Francis, the Holy Jester (Lu santo jullàre Françesco)*, a collection of five comic monologues based on the life of St Francis. In this *giullarata*, based on a different set of biographical tales about Francis from those used in Rossellini's film, Fo returns to many of the techniques of *Mistero Buffo*, using historical prologues, a mixture of regional Italian dialects and grammelot (which he calls the 'passe-partout of communication'), and song in order to reproduce what he claims are the suppressed 'harangues' of Francis which have only been recovered by recent scholarship.[42] Conducted, according to contemporary witnesses, in the style of vigorous public declamation, *modus concionandi*, rather than in the graver sermonising *modus praedicandi*, these harangues exhorted listeners by employing the full gamut of histrionic technique.[43] Although, according to rhetorical handbooks such as the *Rhetorica novissima* of Boncompagno da Signa, these harangues were above all dramatic rather than simply comic, and could involve rousing gestures and forceful vocalisation, Fo interprets them as virtuosic displays of clowning that featured pantomime, comic re-enactment, telling gags, facial antics and silly walks.[44]

As part of 'The Tirade of Francis at Bologna, 15th August 1222', for instance, Fo in the persona of Francis (though, as with *Mistero Buffo*, not in costume) offers a performative critique of Bologna's conflict with its neighbour Imola in the form of farcical skits in which he pretends to be soldiers returning with missing limbs and eyes, including one who has to use his feet to shake hands because both of his hands have been severed in battle.[45] Viewers familiar with Fo's oeuvre would recognise in this not only echoes of *Mistero Buffo*, but also a reprise of his hell-raising maniac from *Accidental Death of an Anarchist*, whose antics, involving an imaginary glass eye and a false hand, expose the Milan police's assassination of a left-wing detainee. Even more farcical is a scatological scene in 'Francis Goes to the Pope in Rome' where Francis, having preached to a sty of pigs on Pope Innocent III's orders, returns to the papal palace and splatters mud and pigshit everywhere as he spins around joyfully, exulted by his own humiliation.[46] Both scenes, along with many others across all five monologues, present Francis's buffoonery as a spontaneous yet brilliant strategy for exposing, demystifying and poten-

---

[42] Dario Fo, *Francis, The Holy Jester*, trans. Mario Pirovano (London: Beautiful Books, 2009), pp. v–x.

[43] Raoul Manselli, *St. Francis of Assisi* (Chicago: Franciscan Herald Press, 1988), p. 184; Scuderi, *Dario Fo: Framing, Festival*, p. 114.

[44] Manselli, *St. Francis*, pp. 184–5.

[45] Fo, *Francis, the Holy Jester*, pp. 9–11.

[46] Ibid., p. 58.

Figure 1. The joy of Francis and his brothers at the acceptance of their Rule, by Dario Fo, *Francis, the Holy Jester*, January 2014 performance.

tially dismantling unjust power structures. One scene, however, discloses a potential strain in Fo's utilisation of Francis as an exemplum of dissidence. In the final monologue, 'Francis is Going to Die', the gravely ill Francis is unable to bathe in the soothing warm waters of Bagna Rapo because the local lord has appropriated the public springwaters as his own. When Francis's brethren decry this 'roguery' and call for the people to rise up, Francis sidesteps the question of privatisation and discourages them from 'start[ing] a war over a splutter of warm water'.[47] As Scuderi has also noted, Francis's pacifism leads Fo to execute 'a delicate balancing act' in which he depicts the saint as inspiring political action but not himself, especially in his mature years, engaging in revolt.[48] He is instead presented as a comic lightning rod for the political consciousness of others.

This more recent work again introduces Fo the scholar of medieval culture as a counterpart, or even sponsor, of Fo the medievalist buffoon. This time, however, although he signals his debt to contemporary medievalist scholarship, and his familiarity with medieval documents, he also declares his freedom from the dictates of history. On the one hand he cites the biography *Francis of Assisi: A Life* by Chiara Frugoni as an 'absolutely fundamental' source for his interpretation of Francis, crediting it with informing him that Francis's moniker 'God's jester' (*joculator domini*) was the saint's own bold invention, and with bringing to his attention the suppressed biographical tradition that reveals Francis's distinctive, showmanlike style of preaching.[49] He also alludes to Bonaventura's and Tommaso da Celano's biographies of Francis, as well as medieval anti-buffonic edicts such as the 1220 'Contra Joculatores Obloquentes'. On the other hand, he uses the gaps in the historical record to grant himself interpretive licence, saying to his audience 'I have boldly allowed myself to reconstruct the stories in the narrative from reports of witnesses and contemporary chronicles.'[50] In a further act of rhetorical chutzpah, he presents his performances as pre-empting future historical discovery, saying 'when the full record surfaces … you'll be able to say "I've heard it all already!"'[51] In more recent years this piece has been performed by Fo's appointed successor Mario Pirovano, a self-trained actor who translated *Francis* into English and is now custodian of the Fo-Rame legacy, continuing the transhistorical legacy of comic protest performance.

Fascinatingly, Fo was not the only Italian Marxist artist engaging creatively with medieval dissident culture in 1960s Italy. At around the same time that Fo was creating *Mistero Buffo*, the radical left-wing Italian filmmaker Pier Paolo Pasolini's concern for those systemically excluded from prosperous,

---

47 Ibid., p. 68.
48 Scuderi, *Dario Fo: Framing, Festival*, p. 111.
49 Fo, *Francis, the Holy Jester*, pp. v–vi.
50 Ibid., p. x.
51 Ibid., p. x.

bourgeois Italy – what Fabio Vighi calls his defence of 'the sacredness of the sub-proletariat'[52] – led him, like Fo, back through time to an exploration of the fringe-dwellers of pre-modern Italy. In the first of his medievalist films, *The Hawks and the Sparrows* (*Uccellini e Uccellacci*), released in 1966, two characters of the modern Italian underclasses are transformed into buffoonish Franciscan friars, who unsuccessfully preach to the hawks not to attack the sparrows.[53] Again, the peripatetic anti-materialism of the Franciscan tradition, as outlined by Gramsci, is suggested as both precursor and parallel to the anti-bourgeois lives of what Vighi, borrowing on the terminology of Giorgio Agamben's account of stateless persons, characterises as the picaresque 'homo sacer' figures of Pasolini's modern Italy.[54] *The Hawks and the Sparrows* was followed by Pasolini's Trilogy of Life, which contains his versions of *The Decameron*, *The Canterbury Tales* and *The Arabian Nights*, released just two, three and five years respectively after *Mistero Buffo*'s first performance. In the first two of these films, Pasolini selects episodes from these famous late medieval frame tales which enable him either to celebrate the irrepressible sexual jouissance and the scatological grotesquery of medieval corporeal existence (*The Decameron*), or, in a more Gramscian vein, to dramatise the struggle between medieval people's transgressive natural appetites and the ecclesiastical–feudal regimes that seek to subject these bodies to surveillance, repression and punishment (*The Canterbury Tales*).[55]

The ideological and aesthetic parallels between Fo's and Pasolini's returns to the popular culture of the Middle Ages is surprisingly underexplored. This critical silence might partly be due to the animus Pasolini nursed toward Fo. This was most virulently expressed in 1973 when Pasolini denounced Fo as 'a plague for Italian theatre' immediately after Fo had been arrested for refusing the police access to one of his performances.[56] Less virulent but more revealing of the basis of Pasolini's hostility is his 1968 'Manifesto for a New Theatre', which is replete with oblique but damning references to 'Gesture or Scream Theatre', in which the 'screaming actor of bourgeois anti-bourgeois theatre' desecrates the word in favour of physical theatre.[57] His debunking of this theatre's 'ideology of the rebirth of a primitive, originary theatre, carried out as a propitiatory, or better, orgiastic rite' strikes at

---

[52] Fabio Vighi, 'Pasolini and Exclusion: Žižek, Agamben, and the Modern Sub-Proletariat', *Theory, Culture and Society* 20 (2003), 99–121 (p. 100).

[53] *Uccellacci e Uccellini*, dir. Pier Paolo Pasolini (Water Bearer Films, 1966).

[54] Vighi, 'Pasolini and Exclusion', pp. 105–10.

[55] *The Decameron*, dir. Pier Paolo Pasolini (MGM, 1971), *Canterbury Tales*, dir. Pier Paolo Pasolini (Image Entertainment, 1972).

[56] Joseph Farrell and Antonio Scuderi, eds, *Dario Fo: Stage, Text and Tradition* (Carbondale: Southern Illinois University Press, 2000), p. 13.

[57] Pier Paolo Pasolini, 'Manifesto for a New Theatre', trans. Thomas Simpson, *PAJ: A Journal of Performance and Art* 29 (2007), 126–38 (p. 134).

the heart of Fo's medievalist revival.[58] Fo, in his turn, would go on several years later to comment on his critics' rejection of his use of gesture and noise. In Fo's rejoinder, Pasolini, though never explicitly named, is aligned with the 'prevailing opinion' of bourgeois culture, perhaps a reference to Pasolini's endorsement of the intellectual bourgeoisie as his ideal audience in his Manifesto.[59] That the aversion was mutual, and that Pasolini's 'Manifesto' was central to it, is implied two decades later in Joseph Farrell's passing comment that 'Fo had little patience with aspiring drama writers, for example Pier Paolo Pasolini, who were capable of producing nothing more than "literature".'[60] By the time of his attack on Fo, Pasolini, a long-term Gramscian, had not only already admitted he could no longer hold faith with Gramsci, but was in the process of formulating his 'Abjuration of the Trilogy of Life', which appeared in 1975. In this abjuration he declared the impossibility of representing a 'beloved past', and of presenting an idealised medieval sexual vitality under the auspices of what Pasquale Verdicchio calls 'the revolutionary power of sub-proletarian bodies',[61] believing this belonged to a naïve and now-redundant political programme.[62] This might explain in part his contempt for Fo, whose faith in medieval popular resistance remains undimmed. Indeed the animality of the bodies in Pasolini's funny but unsettling *Canterbury Tales*, and their ultimate failure to withstand the violent forces of ecclesiastical oppression, suggest his faith in the buffonic Middle Ages was waning even as he was presenting them. Interestingly, Pasolini claimed this was an effect of Chaucer's own ambivalent humour, in which raw vital buffoonery is overwhelmed by 'the bourgeois phenomena of irony and self-irony, the sign of a guilty conscience'.[63] So Chaucer is for Pasolini both the apotheosis and the swansong of medieval folk humour. In many respects this conforms with what Bruce Holsinger and Ethan Knapp have described as the Marxian view of the later Middle Ages as the cusp of pre-capitalist and capitalist society.[64] Despite their opposing views, it is highly significant that these two artists, very conscious of one another's works, were engaged in an indirect dialogue about the past, present and future through their adjacent yet discrepant views of the grotesque comedy of the Middle Ages, and as such they certainly merit more critical comparison than they have so far received.

[58]   Ibid.

[59]   See Ballerini et al., 'Dario Fo Explains', p. 39.

[60]   Fo, *Tricks of the Trade*, p. 6.

[61]   In Pier Paolo Pasolini, *The Savage Father*, trans. Pasquale Verdicchio (Toronto: Guernica, 1999), p. 54.

[62]   Naomi Greene, *Pier Paolo Pasolini: Cinema as Heresy* (Princeton, NJ: Princeton University Press, 1990), pp. 196–7.

[63]   Ibid., p. 191.

[64]   Bruce Holsinger and Ethan Knapp, 'The Marxist Premodern', *Journal of Medieval and Early Modern Studies* 34 (2004), 463–71 (pp. 463–4).

Another conspicuous yet under-recognised connection is that between Fo's theatre and Umberto Eco's monastic murder mystery *The Name of the Rose*. While Eco's text is not comic medievalism per se, it is, as I indicated in the introduction to this book, a medievalist novel that is deeply preoccupied with the role of laughter and the comic impulse in medieval religious life. Scuderi has briefly noted a thematic resonance between the two,[65] but I would argue that the connection is deeper than this. Eco's novel is not readily assimilable to the Gramscian-medievalist position adopted by his compatriots Fo and Pasolini; nevertheless, his portrayal of medieval subversive laughter is, I would suggest, a later instance of the defence of a long tradition of Italian mirth being used as a form of commentary on the period known as the 'Years of Lead', the years of political turmoil that had prevailed in Italy from the late 1960s into the 1980s, characterised by unstable government, official corruption, summary justice and internal terrorism at both extremes of the political spectrum. The link between Eco's novel and this leftist comic medievalism is unmistakable, although temporally and geographically displaced, and Eco's novel adopts an ideologically more moderate position. Eco's novel does not bear evidence of the direct influence of Fo or Pasolini, and, given Eco's training as a medievalist, it is not inconceivable that he thought of writing on medieval subversive laughter independently of them, though their high profiles militate against this theory. It is, however, significant that Eco, as frame narrator, opens his novel by stating that the manuscript of Adso's account of the sinister abbey came into his hands during the Prague Spring of 1968, as this locates the recovery of Adso's tale in a moment of popular resistance analogous to the Italian 'hot Autumn' protests of 1969–70 that motivated Pasolini's and Fo's comic medievalism.[66] Without resorting to identifying *roman à clef*-style parallels between, for instance, members of the Red Brigades of the 1970s and the leaders of the militant Franciscan offshoots depicted by Eco, or between contemporary centre-leftists and the novel's moderate dissident William of Baskerville, it is not labouring the novel's historical analogy too hard to see the novel as, to quote Charles Klopp, 'a disapproving commentary on political fanaticism during the preceding decade in Italy (both on the part of the establishment and by those contesting that establishment by violent means)'.[67] Nor is it drawing too long a bow to read its representation of a schismatic papacy and oppressive inquisitorial powers (with their authority to arrest, interrogate and

---

[65] Scuderi, *Dario Fo: Framing, Festival*, p. 109.

[66] Umberto Eco, *The Name of the Rose*, trans. William Weaver (London: Vintage Books, 1998), p. 1. For a wide-ranging and deep account of medievalism in contemporary Italian politics, see Tommaso Di Carpegna Falconieri, *Medioevo militante: La politica di oggi alla prese con barbari e crociati* (Turin: Einaudi, 2011).

[67] Charles Klopp, 'Fiction in Italy since the Years of Lead', *World Literature Today* 79 (2005), 35–8 (p. 36).

execute) as gesturing toward the rapid leadership turnovers and generalised state of exception that had characterised Italian political life throughout the 1970s. There are strong grounds for reading Pasolini's, Fo's and Eco's texts as medievalist bookends to the Years of Lead; however, while Fo's plays and Pasolini's early films optimistically depict folk laughter as resilient, Pasolini's later films and Eco's novel retrospectively muse on its fragility. In 1980s Italy, when the government has just detained leftist activists indiscriminately, Eco looks back to a hostile medieval Church threatened alike by the Franciscan ironist William, the illiterate Dolcinite Salvatore and Aristotle's book about laughter. While it is difficult to offer straightforward proof that Eco's representation of ecclesiastical mirth affected Fo's later work, it is intriguing to consider whether Pope Innocent III's suspicion of Francis because 'I do not like those who smile' in Fo's *Francis, the Holy Jester* carries in it an echo of the words of Eco's venerable Jorge, with his thunderous condemnations of anti-authoritarian laughter.[68] Both playwright and writer, in any case, whether coincidentally or purposefully, certainly traverse enough of the same territory to be taken seriously as dual commentators on the compelling relationship between medievalism, comedy and political resistance.

Dario Fo is, then, crucial both for an examination of the conjunction of comedy and medievalism, and as a key figure in the richly comic vision of pre-modern popular culture fostered within leftist modernism. With his distinctive and highly lauded combination of reverence for repressed but enduring popular cultural forms, his winking use of scholarly authority and his bravura grasp of physical performance traditions dating back to the Middle Ages, he has brought to millions of people a (re)vision of the Middle Ages that, as well as being radical and extremely funny, invites his audience to share in the laughter with a past that is long gone yet abidingly present.

---

[68] Fo, *Francis, the Holy Jester*, p. 47.

III

HIT AND MYTH: PERFORMING AND PARODYING MEDIEVALISM

4

Pre-Modern Camp and Faerie Legshows: Travestying the Middle Ages on the Nineteenth-Century Stage

ERUSING THE FRONT MATTER OF THE LIBRETTO to *Whittington, Junior,*
and his Sensation Cat, an 'Original Civic Burlesque' which premiered
at London's New Royalty Theatre on 23 November 1870, one is struck
by an intriguing contradiction. First, in a blithely ahistorical gesture, the
author Robert Reece waves away the necessity for 'of-the-Period' characterisations, asserting, tongue in cheek, that the demands of 'Burlesque [are]
superior to the dull realities of History'.[1] Decidedly less arch, however, are his
protestations that the production's costumes are 'historical', the appearance
of its auxiliary players 'copied from contemporaneous prints', and its music
'selected ... from rare MSS. of the time of Richard the Second and *Ye Lute*
Players' Manual. N.B. – No Music later than the Fourteenth Century has
been admitted.'[2] Even before venturing into the script itself, with its fusion of
folklore and pantomime, and its dialogue that mixes topical references with
truly excruciating Shakespearian allusion (contemplating Whittington's cat,
for instance, one character asks 'Tabby or not tabby – that is the question'), it
is clear from the outset that for all its populist simplicity, this play is engaged
in a complex self-authorisation that balances comic licence against an appeal
to an almost scholarly historical authenticity.

In this respect Reece's play is completely typical of its genre, and indeed of
the rich comic performance culture of the nineteenth century in which theatrical representations of the Middle Ages featured prominently. Burlesque,
extravaganza, pantomime, harlequinade, comedietta, opéra bouffe, oper-

---

[1] R. Reece, *Whittington, Junior and his Sensation Cat: An Original Civic Burlesque*
(London: T. H. Lacy, 1870), p. 3.
[2] Ibid., p. 2.

etta and fairy spectacle were major forms of popular entertainment in the Victorian period, characterised by a distinctive tension between their ambitious antiquarian representational mode and their relatively facile content and blithe unconcern about the 'medievalness' of their subjects. With their promiscuous looting of the Middle Ages for the purposes of topical humour, these avowedly ephemeral performances countered the high seriousness and portentous stylistics both of 'legitimate' dramatic forms, which they relentlessly parodied, and of such medievalist literary texts as Tennyson's *Idylls of the King* and Scott's *Ivanhoe* as well as popular historical texts. Their participation, moreover, in an international 'traffic' in comic medievalism, which saw them being widely emulated in colonial and former-colonial environments, created a lasting international taste for a burlesque Middle Ages. By examining the representations of medieval history, legend and folklore in a range of comic performances from this period, this chapter aims to determine what they disclose about the production and reception of 'the medieval' in popular comedic performance. The key plays examined here have been selected from the plethora of Victorian performances containing medieval allusions, on the grounds that as well as lampooning the best-known events and legends relating to the Middle Ages (while also parodying the best known legitimate medieval dramas of their own time), they all feature the blend of pedantry and irreverence that is distinctive of their genre. This chapter will, furthermore, explore the question of whether the 'casual medievalism' of these plays is symptomatic, or even paradigmatic, of performative comic adaptations of the Middle Ages.

When considering the comic register that best corresponds with these entertainments, which are avowedly trivial but culturally symptomatic, it is hard to go past the cultural idiom of camp, which, as Kathleen Coyne Kelly and Tison Pugh have also argued, captures perfectly the contradictory, fugitive humour of burlesque medievalism in a range of ways that will be explored in this chapter.[3] Yet to invoke camp, and to situate it within a taxonomy of comic forms, is to set out on unstable critical terrain; for as even its most seasoned theorists avow, camp is much easier to recognise than to analyse. Theorist Fabio Cleto, despite offering arguably the most comprehensive summary of camp's theorisation since the 1950s in his *Queer Aesthetics and the Performing Subject* (1999), concedes that it 'hasn't lost its relentless power to frustrate all efforts to pinpoint it down to stability'.[4] Its elusiveness and constant mobility are reflected in the ongoing critical disa-

---

3   Kelly and Pugh say 'understanding camp as contested critical ground ... also helps us to understand some of the critical difficulties attendant upon defining medievalism'. See 'Introduction', in *Queer Movie Medievalisms*, ed. Kathleen Coyne Kelly and Tison Pugh (Farnham, Surrey: Ashgate, 2009), pp. 1–17 (p. 12).

4   Fabio Cleto, ed., *Queer Aesthetics and the Performing Subject – A Reader* (Ann Arbor: University of Michigan, 1999), p. 2.

greement over whether it is best described as a sensibility (Susan Sontag's favoured term in her watershed essay 'Notes on Camp'), an aesthetic, a style, a taste or, in Cleto's more encompassing formulation, a 'cultural economy',[5] which has ideological and evaluative dimensions as well as aesthetic. Related to this are debates about the extent to which camp is, in Sontag's words, 'a quality discoverable in objects and behaviour of persons',[6] and the extent to which it is engendered by the transformative 'Camp eye' of the observer; or alternatively whether it is what Cleto describes as an operation of 'semiotic destabilisation'[7] based on 'the unavoidable overlapping of subject and object of perception, of read object and reading subject, with the overstructure of preconceptions and pre-understandings that the subject brings to the object'.[8] The critical attempt to grapple with the slipperiness of this term has in turn led numerous theorists to devise disputed hierarchies based on whether phenomena deemed camp are deliberately or inadvertently so, whether they are 'high or 'low' camp,[9] whether they have their origins in homosexual or heterosexual cultures and so on, which have created further instability. Despite the discrepancy of opinion among theorists, there are several criteria for camp which have gained a degree of critical consensus, all of which, as I will go on to demonstrate, correspond closely to the comic theatrical entertainments of the nineteenth century. These are an attraction to artifice and style, 'the love of the exaggerated, the "off", of things-being-what-they-are-not';[10] an embrace of the derivative; a strong kinship with parody, of which it is a sophisticated subgenre; an ambiguous relationship to the emotional registers of both humour and seriousness; and a mutually defining relationship with queer cultural production.

One of the least analysed elements of camp, however, is its intersection with a historicist sensibility. In this chapter I argue that the characteristics identified above are vital to a camp historical outlook that is directly relevant to, and recognisable within, comic medievalism in general, and nineteenth-century burlesque medievalism in particular. It is true that theorists have not completely ignored the idea that camp taste might entertain a distinctive relationship to the past. Sontag has gone furthest in this respect, locating the emergence of this relationship in the eighteenth century, citing such forms as artificial ruins and Gothic novels as evidence that this period not only

5   Ibid.

6   Susan Sontag, 'Notes on Camp', in *Against Interpretation and Other Essays* (New York: Farrar, Strauss & Giroux, 1966), pp. 275–92 (p. 277).

7   Cleto, *Queer Aesthetics*, p. 4.

8   Ibid., p. 11.

9   Christopher Isherwood, *The World in the Evening: A Novel* (London: Methuen, 1954), p. 110.

10   Sontag, 'Notes on Camp', p. 279.

'indefatigably patronized the past'[11] but set the agenda for a paradoxical camp nostalgia that continues up to the present. This ambivalent sensibility is less 'a love of the old as such' than a perception of temporality in which the passage of time 'provides the necessary detachment' to enable a comical engagement with the past at the same time as it 'arouses a necessary sympathy' to form a more sentimental attachment.[12] A paradoxical combination of sympathy and detachment is thus at the core of camp historicism. This element of Sontag's account, however, is not so much explained as evoked through a series of examples; and later theorists, responding to the urgency of delineating camp within a defence of queer culture, have not developed the notion of camp historicism appreciably since Sontag's essay. Despite this relative silence, it should not be lost on scholars of medievalism that a remarkable number of Sontag's examples of camp are, in fact, either medievalist or closely adjacent to medievalism, including Tennyson, Ruskin, Pre-Raphaelite paintings, Aubrey Beardsley drawings, Tiffany lamps, Gothic novels, artificial ruins and nineteenth-century Aestheticism (as well as its offshoot, Art Nouveau). Although Sontag does not appear to recognise or reflect on the spectre of the Middle Ages haunting these camp forms, her account nevertheless gestures toward a definite camp sensibility within medievalism which, as I will elaborate, is most pronounced in the comic theatrical form it took in the nineteenth century.

In many ways it is hardly surprising that theatrical texts and performances might attract the camp label. Although the term's etymological origins have not been unanimously settled, the most widely accepted linguistic forbears, the French *se camper* (to posture boldly) and the Italian *campeggiare* (to stand out, to be conspicuous), both have strongly theatrical and performative resonances. This etymological grounding in conspicuous display was actualised in a uniquely spectacular fashion in nineteenth-century theatre, which, with the detailed magnificence of its scenery, the vastness of its background casts and the sophistication of its stagecraft, invites a reading that emphasises its close correspondence with what Sontag calls 'the hallmark of Camp', that is 'the spirit of extravagance'.[13] In his milestone study of nineteenth-century theatrical aesthetics, *Victorian Spectacular Theatre 1850–1910*, Michael Booth regards this period's taste for pictorial entertainments, which included not only theatre but also such forms as panorama, diorama, cyclorama and stereoscope, as symptomatic of emerging Victorian modernity, which fostered (and prospered from) a growing inclination toward the visual stimulation afforded by metropolitan environments, accelerating habits of conspicuous consumption, a love of sensationalism, a taste for ostentatious detail that

---

11   Ibid., p. 280.
12   Ibid., p. 285.
13   Ibid., p. 283.

was also expressed in domestic interiors, and a fascination with ever more refined technologies of visual representation, illumination and illusionism.[14]

Alongside this appreciation of avowedly modern spectacle – or, according to Booth, 'the other side of the coin'[15] – was a prevailing trend that favoured historical-realist performance in which 'legend and history had to be actualised and made visually familiar and accessible' via the extravagant yet meticulous visual idiom of the day.[16] That this trend intersected with, and owed much to, contemporary archaeological and antiquarian activities is epitomised by Charles Kean's production of Lord Byron's *Sardanapalus* at the Princess's Theatre in 1853, the programme of which acknowledged the debt its dizzyingly grandiose Assyrian sets owed to the archaeological discoveries of Austen Henry Layard, which were now taking imperial pride of place in the British Museum. So potent was the impulse to deploy this aesthetic of amplification to reproduce historical events and locales onstage that Booth describes it as 'one of the most important features of late-eighteenth- and nineteenth-century thought and art',[17] while theatre historian Richard Schoch has characterised the Victorian period as 'a time when the desire to know and possess the past rivalled science as the dominant system of cognition and history as a practice seemed to overtake the whole scope of representational activities'.[18] Although this general culture of historical spectacle ranged across history from ancient Eastern civilisations to eighteenth-century Europe, representations of the Middle Ages held a privileged place within it. Booth describes the historical-realist movement as 'originally medievalist and romantic in character'.[19] Medievalist theatre was, however, not simply part of the larger nineteenth-century antiquarian project: rather, one can argue in agreement with Schoch that theatre was arguably the most successful iteration of medievalist antiquarianism, as it animated and presented – as in literally made present – personages, events and scenes from the Middle Ages.

From an antiquarian perspective, one of the key nineteenth-century theatrical encounters with the Middle Ages was via Shakespearian drama. While much study has been devoted to the prolific phenomenon of nineteenth-century Shakespeare performance, far less has been said about it as a vehicle for the dissemination of theatrical medievalism. But Schoch's assertions that '[o]ne of the inherent complications of Victorian theatrical medievalism was its unavoidable reliance on Renaissance dramatic texts'

---

[14] M. R. Booth, *Victorian Spectacular Theatre 1850–1910* (Boston: Routledge & Kegan Paul, 1981), pp. 4–5.

[15] Ibid., p. 18.

[16] Ibid., p. 14.

[17] Ibid., p. 17.

[18] Richard W. Schoch, *Shakespeare's Victorian Stage: Performing History in the Theatre of Charles Kean* (Cambridge: Cambridge University Press, 1998), p. 1.

[19] Booth, *Victorian Spectacular*, p. 17.

and that '[a] Shakespearian past inevitably ghosts or haunts [Victorian] theatrical representations of the medieval past' emphasise the medievalist substratum of much Shakespearian performance.[20] As indicated above, the best-known Victorian producers of Shakespeare, such as Charles Kean and his company, had built their reputation on their exhaustively researched, grandiose stage sets and fastidiously correct period costumes. Although their antiquarian ambitions extended broadly across history, they arguably reached their apotheosis in the reproduction of the English Middle Ages via Shakespeare's chronicle plays. As dramatisations of English history, Kean's productions of Shakespeare's chronicles were significant for their deployment of an antiquarian aesthetic in the service of a nationalist theatrical pedagogy. These plays were regarded as historical records, and Shakespeare as a vehicle for teaching English history to British and colonial publics. Such was the historical exactness of the Keans's 'upholstered Shakespeare' that Kean, arguably more fêted for his research than his acting, was made a Fellow of the Society of Antiquaries in 1857. Schoch attributes to these performances an ideological purpose in which medievalism is implicated, claiming that the pictorial antiquarianism of nineteenth-century historical drama in England was a recuperative gesture reflective of a modern urban society anxious about its alienation from history: 'a people dispossessed of their own history … are always already struggling to repossess that history in its former totality and unity by rehabilitating the very material things … which are authorized to constitute a national heritage.'[21] Pedagogic Shakespeare needs to be understood as just one part of a larger phenomenon comprised of performances that ranged widely in genre, tone and intent, and in which the medieval past was represented on a sliding scale from antiquarian exactitude to mythic spectacle. The steady stream of medievalist drama being produced and consumed throughout the nineteenth century included, for instance, Gothic dramas such as Matthew Gregory ('Monk') Lewis's *The Castle Spectre and The Tower of Nesle*, and Charles Robert Maturin's *Bertram, or, The Castle of St. Aldobrand*, which tapped into the popular fascination with 'medieval' gloom, horror and irrationality.[22] There were also a considerable number of plays whose action was based on historical events from the Middle Ages, especially the English Middle Ages. To take just two examples, Robert Taylor Conrad's 1835 *Aylmere, or the Kentish Rebellion* was performed in 1855 at the Prince of Wales, Sydney, while John Braham and Thomas Dibdin's Napoleonic wartime 'historical comic opera' *The English Fleet in 1342* was first performed in 1803 at the Theatre Royal, Covent Garden. Given its patriotic message about the

---

[20] Schoch, *Shakespeare's Victorian Stage*, p. 10.
[21] Ibid., p. 12
[22] See Anastasia Nikolopoulou, 'Medievalism and Historicity in the English Gothic Melodrama: Maturin's *Bertram: or, The Castle of St. Aldobrand*', *Poetica* 39/40 (1994), 139–53.

medieval antecedents of contemporary British naval dominance, it is not hard to understand its appeal for both British and colonial audiences, whose lives as settlers had been shaped in so many ways by British seafaring. Other plays, while dramatising episodes from the Middle Ages, were focused more intently on exploring the historical figures at their centre. Apart from the late medieval English and French monarchs depicted in Shakespeare's chronicle plays, which were regularly mounted throughout the late nineteenth and early twentieth centuries, audiences encountered such heroic figures as Joan of Arc and Jack Cade, leader of the 1450 Kentish rebellion, along with a gallery of medieval monarchs and nobles that included Louis XI of France (in Dion Boucicault's play of that name), Richard Coeur de Lion, James III of Scotland, Robert the Bruce, the Merovingian King Chilperic, after whom Hervé named his 1868 operetta, and William the Conqueror's father Robert Duke of Normandy, who was the central character in Giacomo Meyerbeer's much-performed opera *Robert le Diable*. Also prominent were dramas developed out of medieval literary-historical figures such as Robin Hood and King Arthur, Parsifal and William Tell. Audiences were introduced to the most famous author of trecento Florence, Giovanni Boccaccio, through Franz von Suppé's operetta *Boccaccio*, in which the writer is the central character.

There were also numerous plays inspired by nineteenth-century medievalist literature. Among these, three particularly powerful influences can be singled out. The first is Victor Hugo's novel *The Hunchback of Notre Dame* (1831), set in fifteenth-century Paris. Of the many stage derivatives from Hugo's novel, the most performed across Britain, her colonies and North America appears to be a range of plays with the title *Esmeralda*.[23] There were also other, more parodic performances based on the same story, such as Henry Byron's *Esmeralda, or the 'Sensation' Goat!*, and Fredrick Hobson Leslie's *Miss Esmeralda*, which first played at The Gaiety Theatre in October 1887. The second major text to receive multiple stage adaptations was Goethe's poetic masterpiece *Faust*. This was most famously dramatised in operatic form, first in Lutz's 1855 grand opera *Faust and Marguerite*, and soon after in Gounod's 1859 *Faust*, performed repeatedly throughout the 1860s, '70s and '80s. Interestingly, satires of the Faust story were circulating even prior to the operatic treatments, such as William Leman Rede's burletta *The Devil and Dr Faustus* premiering at the New Strand Theatre 31 May 1841. This parodic strain was, moreover, still finding audiences well after the peak of Victorian *Fausto-*

---

[23] The details on these are unclear, but these *Esmeralda*s could variously have been adaptations or selections from, among others, the 1836 opera *La Esmeralda* written by Hugo himself with Louise Bertin, or the 1838 opera *Esmeralda* by Alberto Mazzucato, or the 1844 ballet *La Esmeralda* by Cesare Pugni, or the 1847 opera *Esmeralda* by Alexander Dargomyzhsky, or the 1869 opera *Esmeralda* by Fabio Campana, the 1851 opera *Esmeralda* by Vincenzo Battista, or, as is most likely after 1883, the hugely popular opera *Esmeralda* by A. T. Thomas.

mania; in 1888 the burlesque 'Faust Up To Date', also written by Lutz, was performed by the London Gaiety company. Finally, the medievalist novels of Walter Scott, in particular *Ivanhoe* and his Crusader novels, spawned a small industry of theatrical presentation. *Ivanhoe* gave rise to a rash of theatrical versions, as well as numerous medieval Jewry spin-offs, including W. T. Moncrieff's *The Jewess, or the Council of Constance* and Fromental Halévy's grand opera *La Juive* (both 1835). Scott novels set during the crusades, such as *The Talisman* and *Count Robert of Paris*, also inspired a tenacious fad that led to a number of medievalist-orientalist dramas, such as the spectacle *The Moors of Spain*, performed throughout the 1850s and beyond, George Colman's historical musical drama *The Mountaineers*, about the fifteenth-century siege of Granada, which was repeatedly revived throughout the century, and *Tancredi*, also performed at the Victoria in 1856 and probably adapted from Rossini's admired 1813 opera of the same name.

In many cases audiences encountered representations of medieval societies that were loosely regionalised. Along with the abovementioned English and Hispanic-oriental settings, a loosely conceived 'Italianate' Middle Ages featured particularly in operatic productions: Guiseppe Verdi's medievalist offerings included *I Lombardi*, which Italianised the medieval Crusades genre, *I Vespri Siciliani*, set in thirteenth-century Palermo, *I due Foscari*, set in fifteenth-century Venice, and Suppé's *Boccaccio*, set in fourteenth-century Florence. A loosely 'Ibero-Latinate' Middle Age took the stage in Verdi's *Il Trovatore*, set in fifteenth-century Spain, and Donizetti's *La Favorita*, set in fourteenth-century Castile. And, of course, there was the mytho-Teutonic medievalism of William Vincent Wallace's hugely popular and famously spectacular 1860 opera *Lurline*, and later of Wagner's operas, which were performed worldwide throughout the second half of the century. These productions often followed closely from one another, so that regular theatre-goers in metropolitan centres were frequently bombarded in a short space of time with widely divergent depictions of the medieval era.

As indicated at the opening of this chapter, this antiquarian and historical fascination continued to be strongly present in lighter and more comic medievalist performance in this period. This is particularly the case with the burlesque, which was an enormously popular comic vehicle for presenting medieval legend to modern audiences. It is commonplace for scholars to point to the hectic cross-pollination of comic genres in this period, such that it is often futile to attempt a definitive distinction between such forms as opéra-bouffe, burletta, burlesque, harlequinade or indeed fairy extravaganza, which, with its fairy grottoes and other-worldly *dramatis personae* clearly drew upon the idiom of nineteenth-century romantic medievalism, with its fascination for the folkloric world of faëry.[24] For this reason the term 'medi-

---

[24] Paul Buczkowski's discussion of James Robinson Planché, that father of British

evalist burlesque' is being used here as a general descriptor to refer to a broad range of comic plays whose plots travestied grandiose events and personages from medieval history and legend. Despite their pre-modern settings, these plays featured popular contemporary songs lightly re-purposed to fit the plays' content, and their dialogue was peppered with local and topical references, typically written in rhyming couplets and heavily seasoned with ridiculously laboured puns (helpfully italicised, lest they be missed). William Brough's 'historical burlesque' *Joan of Arc!*, for example, which premiered at the Royal Strand Theatre on 29 March 1869, includes repeated and undeniable allusions to recent interest in the question of women's franchise. Just before Joan enters with her 'party of Amazons', other characters say of her:

> THIBAULT: She's gone, sire, for a soldier. She recites
> Speeches 'bout women's wrongs and women's rights.
> Says women's claims no more can be resisted,
> But to them all must *list*, and so she *listed*.
> KING: Turned a soldier, eh? One comfort then we note,
> A military 'person' cannot vote.[25]

This exchange clearly alludes to the widely publicised (and ultimately unsuccessful) efforts in 1867 of John Stuart Mill, who had been MP for Westminster, to have the wording of the Representation of the People Bill changed from 'man' to 'person', in order to enable women to vote. This theme crops up again in a later speech about Joan:

> LIONEL [She] Brings a troop of young feminine plebeians,
> Which troop, *all she 'uns*, thinks to save *Orleans*!
> They about women's rights and such stuff rage,
> Of women's suff'rings, and of women's suff'rage.[26]

The reference to women fulminating about 'women's sufferings and women's suffrage' echoes many satires in publications such as *Punch*, in which Mills's parliamentary actions and his 1869 essay *The Subjection of Women* are presented as stirring up discontent among women who are otherwise cheerfully submissive (*Punch*, 1 June 1867). Despite this topicality, burlesque's parodic nature made it into a voracious, even predatory, genre, ranging

---

fairy extravaganza, emphasises his heavy reliance on the French tales of Marie-Catherine d'Aulnoy, which he translated into English and made the basis of many of his extravaganzas. Planche's translation of Charles Perrault's fairy tales also expresses the intimate link between fairy extravaganza and the popular antiquarian interest in fairy tales. See Buczkowski, 'J. R. Planché, Frederick Robson, and the Fairy Extravaganza', *Marvels and Tales: Journal of Fairy-Tale Studies* 15 (2001), 42–65.

  25 William Brough, *Joan of Arc! A New and Original Historical Burlesque* (London: T. H. Lacy, 1869), p. 7.

  26 Ibid., p. 13.

widely across history and across cultures for satiric quarry. No historical event or figure, no serious drama, no piece of high literature, was safe from its cannibalising clutches. As such, nineteenth-century audiences were likely to see burlesque treatments of Homeric legend, orientalist tale, the Latin-American *conquista* or even contemporary society rubbing shoulders fairly indiscriminately with medievalist burlesque. Sometimes this cross-historical cannibalising even took place within a single play, as in William Mower Akhurst's adaptation of a burlesque based on the Carolingian romance *Valentine and Orson*.[27] According to the *Argus* review of the play, scenes featuring the château of King Pepin, the Gothic interior of 'The Castle of the Green Knight' and the medieval city of Orléans were interspersed with scenes in an Egyptian temple, a vista of classical Athens, and 'the Frozen Regions', and finally culminated in a tableau featuring an 'equestrian statue' of Melbourne's adopted son, the recently perished explorer Robert O'Hara Burke.[28] Despite the broad historical net cast by burlesque, events and legends from the Middle Ages and their nineteenth-century nostalgic reworkings were deemed particularly ripe for travesty, and were regular targets of the burlesquers' pens. In North American and colonial environments most of these burlesques took the form of minimally localised British hits, although a small number of them can be more readily described as reflective of their local provenances.[29]

Their grounding in both historical parody and contemporary satire bears out Shoch's general contention that burlesques by their very nature implicated themselves in that which lay outside them, including other texts and performances, and their cultural-historical contexts.[30] Schoch, who has spearheaded the recent rehabilitation of this maligned Victorian genre, argues that the burlesques' 'inherently metadramatic' nature – that is, their status as populist comedic plays that travesty recognisable 'legitimate' dramas – makes them uniquely telling instances of popular culture's response to the development of Victorian theatre.[31] This resonates with Booth's earlier statement that '[a]lmost every popular melodrama and opera had received burlesque treatment by the 1880s'.[32] To Schoch's point can be added the argument that they are a particularly apposite genre for treating medievalist themes, for their

[27] *Harlequin Valentine and Orson*, performed at the Theatre Royal, Melbourne, 1861.

[28] *The Argus*, Friday, 27 December 1861.

[29] Louise D'Arcens, *Old Songs in the Timeless Land: Medievalism in Australian Literature 1840–1910* (Turnhout, Belgium: Brepols, 2011); and, Andrew Lynch, 'King Arthur in Marvellous Melbourne: W. M. Akhurst's Burlesque Extravaganzas', *Australian Literary Studies* 26 (2011), 45–57.

[30] Richard W. Schoch, *Not Shakespeare: Bardolatry and Burlesque in the Nineteenth Century* (Cambridge: Cambridge University Press, 2002), p. 30.

[31] Richard W. Schoch, *Victorian Theatrical Burlesques* (Aldershot, UK: Ashgate, 2003), p. xii.

[32] M. R. Booth, *Theatre in the Victorian Age* (Cambridge: Cambridge University Press, 1991), p. 197.

referentiality echoes and reinforces the appropriative impetus at the heart of medievalism. Moreover, they are a perfect demonstration of what Cleto calls camp's 'investment in seriality'. His argument that 'the transgressiveness of camp relies in [*sic*] its privileging of the secondary and the derivative … of serial reproduction over the original, showing that the secondary is always already copy of a copy'[33] can be applied particularly to those plays which reflexively parody nineteenth-century medievalist texts. The *Illustrated London News* review of Henry Byron's *Esmeralda; or the 'Sensation' Goat!* notes that 'the story of the original is carefully followed' except that Hugo's original scenes are 'closely packed … with parodies'.[34] The same publication applauds the 'interesting sprinkle of well-mangled parodies' in Byron's *Ill-Treated Il Trovatore: Or the Mother, the Maiden, & the Musicianer*, a burlesque described by its author as 'founded on a famous though somewhat confusing Opera'. This lampooning of the convoluted plot of *Il Trovatore* was, according to Roberta Montemorra Marvin, typical of the British comic response to Verdi's medievalist opera.[35] In both cases, it is clear that in the experience of nineteenth-century burlesque there is a form of mutual camp recognition between performance and spectator, in which the texts' unapologetic elevation of their comic distortions and even 'corrections' of the 'original' modern medievalist text is precisely what elicits delight from the reviewer.

One medievalist text that can be singled out for its rich serial afterlife in burlesque form is Walter Scott's *Ivanhoe*. Among the many comic treatments of Scott's 1819 novel, Byron's extravaganza *Ivanhoe! In Accordance with the Spirit of the Times*, first performed at the Strand Theatre on 26 December 1862, presents as a telling example. On the one hand, it quotes *Ivanhoe's* character descriptions extensively in its own character notes, and it follows the novel's general plot closely until the final scene, in which dénouement is wedged alongside Christmas tidings and the obligatory 'England's Glory' conclusion. On the other hand, the finale explicitly evokes a flattening camp seriality in which the burlesque iteration equals its literary and performative forebears, as the characters sing 'what oft we've done / with parody and pun / Place Ivanhoe upon a par!'[36] Scott's novel also becomes a reference point for another extravaganza entertainment, the re-enactment tournament at Cremorne Gardens on 8 July 1863. After comparing the 'gorgeous' and meticulously detailed chivalric procession at Cremorne to the sodden fiasco that was the 1839 Eglinton Tournament, where 'the Black Knight was compelled to throw a mackintosh over his armour', the *Illustrated London News* review's

---

33 Cleto, *Queer Aesthetics*, p. 20.

34 *The Illustrated London News*, 5 October 1861, p. 344.

35 Roberta Montemorra Marvin, 'Verdian Opera Burlesqued: A Glimpse into Mid-Victorian Theatrical Culture', *Cambridge Opera Journal* 15 (March 2003), 33–66.

36 Henry J. Byron, *Ivanhoe! In Accordance with the Spirit of the Times – An Extravaganza* (London: T. H. Lacy, 1862), p. 48.

description of the accompanying comic entertainment suggests that *Ivan-hoe*'s endearing jester Wamba has become the byword for medievalesque clowning: 'the intermittent factitiae of a party of jesters, who bethwacked one another with bladders in the most approved Wamba-like manner'. This allu-sion is reiterated in Warwick Wroth's description of the procession in his 1907 *Cremorne and the Later London Gardens* as 'a whole Ivanhoe in motion'.[37]

What the Tournament reveals about these light medievalist entertain-ments is that, notwithstanding their intertextual parodic nature, the writers, performers and stage artists who worked on them clearly revelled in vividly recreating weighty historico-mythic moments from the Middle Ages. As with the melodramatic, sensational and also the 'legitimate' genres discussed earlier, this antiquarian impulse was most visible in the burlesques' use of scenery, costume and staging. Again to cite the restricted sample of burlesques written by Byron and Brough, the libretti indicate that the medievalist *mises-en-scène* were produced by celebrated scenic artists including Albert Callcott, John O'Connor and George Gordon, all of whom had been responsible for exhaus-tively researched scenery in numerous 'legitimate' productions.[38] Similarly, George Augustus Sala's 1869 burlesque *Wat Tyler MP* included extremely elaborate sets that caused *The Times* reviewer to proclaim it (in what, it must be said, are almost ubiquitous terms of praise), 'one of the most costly and elaborate spectacles ever seen at any theatre', lavishing particular praise on its historical exactitude, which, as the Gaiety Theatre manager declared, was as carefully mounted as anything by Charles Kean.[39] A final striking example can be found in the libretto of Edward Fitzball's equestrian spectacle *Robin Hood; or, the Merry Outlaws of Sherwood*, which began its season at Astley's Royal Amphitheatre on 8 October 1860. In conjunction with the hippodra-matic extravagance provided by 'the largest stud of highly-trained horses, ponies, &c., in the world', audiences were treated to scenery with scholarly ambitions, including 'An ancient street in London in the time of Henry the Second', 'a ruin, so ancient as to resemble a vast pile of rocks', 'An arched door, stained glass windows', 'A gothic window' and 'Exterior of Nottingham Castle, the walls and ramparts covered with spectators'.[40] The lavishness of the scenery and 'many noble spectacles' was acknowledged by reviewers, but it is also possible to detect faint disapproval in the comment that it is 'calculated to attract'; the conspicuous silence about the content, moreover, mitigated only by the aloof prediction that 'the drama will probably achieve great popularity', gives the impression that this kind of entertainment, for

---

[37] Warwick Wroth, *Cremorne and the Later London Gardens* (Whitefish, MT: Kessinger Publishing, 2010), p. 15.

[38] Booth, *Victorian Spectacular*, pp. 7, 23.

[39] Ibid., p. 23.

[40] Edward Fitzball, *Robin Hood; or, the Merry Outlaws of Sherwood: A Dramatic Equestrian Spectacle – In Three Acts* (London: T. H. Lacy, 1860), pp. 2, 4, 11, 17–18, 30.

all its physical pretensions to 'research', occasionally achieved a big-budget vacuity parallel to the historical cinematic blockbusters of today.[41]

Acknowledging the mismatch of earnestly reconstructed historical form and frivolous content, evident in so many of these entertainments, is vital to understand their theatrical, ideological, historical and comic valency. It is arguably in this mismatch that the camp potentiality inherent in medievalist theatrical spectacle is most fully and overtly realised, because the 'spirit of extravagance' underpinning their aesthetic is brought into the service of a camp approach to the past that, in Sontag's words, 'emphasiz[es] texture, sensuous surface, and style at the expense of content'. Indeed, for Sontag 'the contrast between silly or extravagant content and rich form'[42] is the distinguishing attribute of camp art. Unlike the 'legitimate' drama, the comic plays' striving for pictorial fidelity, and their meticulous embodiment of the past through costume, gesture and scenery, were significantly and deliberately mitigated by their signature embracing of anachronism (in which, for instance, Joan of Arc could be both a beloved medieval heroine and a shrill Suffragette *avant la lettre*). They sat incongruously at the cusp of antiquarian fetishism and populist anachronism. In harbouring this incongruity, these plays reflected the ambivalence at the heart of both medievalism and camp. Their physical splendour reflected the antiquarian desire to reanimate the nationalist high points of English medieval history, and their fast-and-loose verbal and performative treatment of their material reflected an apparently more irreverent attitude toward this illustrious past.

In an influential argument about the relationship between Victorian pictorial and performative arts, Martin Meisel claims that the pictorialism of nineteenth-century drama as described by Booth and others was not limited to its *mise-en-scène*, but extended rather to the dramaturgy itself.[43] This observation is certainly borne out, indeed epitomised, in the visually and aurally sumptuous pictorialised Shakespeare of Kean and his imitators, with its tendency to organise the plays into a series of highly spectacular tableaux and set-pieces. While Meisel takes melodrama as his example, his argument is also applicable to burlesque, which built spectacle and pictorial elements such as *tableaux vivants* firmly into the development of the plot. To take just one instance, in William Brough's 1863 Christmas extravaganza *King Arthur; or, the Days and Knights of the Round Table*, a stage direction calls for the execution of a 'grand tableau of the round table'.[44] The libretto does not specify the exact nature of this tableau, or of the poses plastique that

[41] *The Illustrated London News*, 1054, 13 October 1860, p. 337.

[42] Sontag, 'Notes on Camp', p. 278.

[43] Martin Miesel, *Realizations: Narrative, Pictorial, and Theatrical Arts in Nineteenth-Century England* (Princeton: Princeton University Press, 1983), p. 39.

[44] Review from *Illustrated London News*, 2 January 1864, p. 706, issue 1210. On *poses plastiques* as a 'sculptural subspecies' of *tableaux vivants*, see Anita Callaway, *Visual*

the reviews suggest were enacted within it, but the dramatic, gestural pictorialism of the poses would seem to reinforce the scenic historicism of the play by situating it within the illustrious painterly and monumental history of European Arthurianism. Yet it would seem that their status is more ambivalent than this; for, as Anita Callaway notes, *tableaux vivants* simultaneously honour and burlesque the artworks they recreate.[45]

Callaway's remark draws out another direct link between burlesque medievalism and camp as a comic mode. It is at this point that my earlier description of camp as a 'comic register' requires some clarification, for part of camp's elusiveness resides in the fact that it exceeds the purely comic. Although at its most conspicuous level, Sontag claims, 'the whole point of camp is to dethrone the serious',[46] or in Cleto's words, to expose 'the crisis of depth, of gravity',[47] reducing camp's complexity to this would not distinguish it from any other mode of comedy. What makes camp distinct is, to use Christopher Isherwood's much-quoted formula in *The World in the Evening*, its capacity to make fun not *of* things, but rather *out of* things, 'expressing what's basically serious to you in terms of fun and artifice and elegance'.[48] To again invoke Sontag, 'camp taste identifies with what it is enjoying. People who share this sensibility are not laughing at the thing they label as "a camp", they're enjoying it. Camp is a tender feeling.'[49] These characterisations of camp's affectionate complicity with its object are in strong accordance with several key scholars' identification of a 'tender' strain within nineteenth-century popular and comic theatre. Booth's observation that 'a mixture of strong pathos and emotions with low and eccentric comedy runs right through Victorian comedy'[50] is echoed by Barry J. Faulk's description of the 'distance and extreme empathic proximity' that together made up the camp esprit of music hall.[51]

This notion of a kind of 'camp complicity' with the Middle Ages should not, however, be taken to mean that the burlesques were devoid of any historical or ideological significance for their audiences. Rather, the medieval period was arguably the most ideologically charged among the earlier societies subjected to burlesque treatment. Those burlesques in particular which featured episodes of medieval English history or mythology were poised uneasily between Victorian imperialist triumphalism and an equally Victorian

Ephemera: Theatrical Art in Nineteenth-century Australia (Sydney: University of NSW Press, 2000), pp. 60–84.
45 Callaway, *Visual Ephemera*, p. 60.
46 Sontag, 'Notes on Camp', p. 288.
47 Cleto, *Queer Aesthetics*, p. 34.
48 Isherwood, *The World in the Evening*, p. 124 (my italics).
49 Sontag, 'Notes on Camp', p. 292.
50 Booth, *Victorian Spectacular*, p. 179.
51 Barry J. Faulk, *Music Hall and Modernity: The Late-Victorian Discovery of Popular Culture* (Athens, OH: Ohio University Press, 2004), p. 56.

throwaway approach to the pre-modern legend and history on which they drew. Their ambivalent use of medieval English source material dramatises a cultural tension in which a nostalgic reiteration of deep historical origins rubs shoulders with exhilaration about, and anticipation of, relentless change under modernity. This is seen mostly clearly in *The Exposition: A Scandinavian Sketch*, by (Charles William) Shirley Brooks, which premiered at the Strand Theatre on 28 April 1851, only days before the opening of the Great Exhibition alluded to in the title. This play's incongruous fusion of Norse gods and metropolitan London presents these as bookends to a progressivist historical narrative in which England has followed a trajectory from pre-modern insularity to the pinnacle of modern cosmopolitanism symbolised by the Crystal Palace which forms the backdrop of the play's second half. The conclusions of *Robin Hood, King Arthur, Ivanhoe* and *Whittington, Junior*, although less overtly concerned with England's economic and cultural dominance, likewise portray an England in which justice, unity and manifest destiny have prevailed over mayhem and discord, supporting Schoch's contention that in the Victorian period "'performing the Middle Ages" was in itself a political event because it strove to construct and express a national identity through the display of historical relics and historical bodies'.[52] As spectacular culminations of the historical and pictorial elements of these plays, all of these final scenes are the most ideologically charged and hence the most culturally revealing. Lest they seem, however, simply to reinforce a banal nationalist-imperialist vision, it is vital to recall the instability that renders the burlesque, in Schoch's words, '[l]ess a site of vulgar didacticism than of playful contestation',[53] that is, a vehicle of political imagination rather than of political statement. Their final grand tableaux and choruses were gorgeous and rousing, but also frequently mock-heroic, both participating in and, by means of parody, querying nationalist aspiration by overtly offering improbable long-historical fantasies of nationhood rather than political blueprints.

Developing further the question of the burlesques' parodic nature, the question of what audiences might have gained from these productions must take into account what cultural awareness they might have brought to their viewing of them. According to some critics the burlesques are notable for their straddling of erudition and popular entertainment. In order for their irreverent treatment to be intelligible, they depended on audiences who were conversant not only with the original texts, events or people being burlesqued, but also earlier performances and productions, which were also often being lampooned. If the audience has no knowledge of that which is being burlesqued, there is no burlesque. As Fotheringham says, '[t]he

---

[52] Schoch, *Shakespeare's Victorian Stage*, p. 116.
[53] Schoch, *Not Shakespeare*, p. 152.

pleasure of viewing in part depended on identifying as many witty borrowings and generic inversions as possible'.[54] And yet Schoch also admits that
much of the burlesques' humour, especially their torrential punning, would
have passed over the original audiences' heads. This raises the question of
whether these plays presumed erudition on the part of their audiences, or
whether they traded rather in knowingness, Peter Bailey's 'select conspiracy of
meaning that animates [an] audience', giving it a 'flattering sense of membership' that reflects its 'own well-tested cultural and social competence'.[55] While
Bailey refers chiefly to music hall, his description could equally describe the
mode of appeal the burlesques made to their audience, especially taking into
account Richard Fotheringham's description of Victorian audiences:

> [a]nyone who considered themselves worldly ... had some notion of
> the characters, the plots, and the key moments in the seminal stories of
> the times, and could follow (or pretend to follow) the intertextual jokes
> which both public gossip and stage burlesque exploited to excess.[56]

Reading the libretti, and bearing in mind that these burlesques generally had
a fairly attenuated relationship to their dramatic and literary precedents, it
would not seem that their level of parody demanded deep erudition from
their audience. The libretti disclose the dramatists' expectations that their
audiences will have some grasp on topical issues, as well as a regular theatre-
goer's competency in Shakespeare's plots and famous speeches; but it appears
that only a general knowledge of medieval and medievalist works is assumed.
This is also borne out in the reviews. These acknowledge the burlesque's logic
of wholesale demolition and flattening camp seriality, in which the medieval
legends and their grandiloquent contemporary appropriations are rendered
equally ridiculous, but nevertheless contain only glancing allusions to medieval history or legend, and even then such allusions are to such ubiquitous
and recent reference-points as Tennyson or Scott. Those audience members
with deeper knowledge might have been invited to detect more subtle notes
of historical parody, but those less familiar need not feel left out of the joke.

Bailey's incisive characterisation of knowingness as 'what everybody
knows, but which some know better than others' applies directly to this
parodic-historical theatre.[57] Burlesque's parodic 'conspiracy of meaning' is,
moreover, intrinsic to its camp historicism, as the audience is invited to revel
in the plays' many-layered derivative status while also being immersed in

54 Richard Fotheringham, ed., *Australian Plays for the Colonial Stage* (St Lucia:
University of Queensland Press, 2006), p. xxvii.
55 Peter Bailey, *Popular Culture and Performance in the Victorian City* (Cambridge:
Cambridge University Press, 1998), p. 137.
56 Fotheringham, *Australian Plays for the Colonial Stage*, p. xxvii.
57 Bailey, *Popular Culture and Performance*, p. 128.

their lush historicist *mise-en-scène*. Bailey not only acknowledges that 'camp has obvious affinities with knowingness,'[58] but, moreover, along with Cleto, Faulk and Andrew Ross, locates the development of camp as an idiom in the theatrical culture of nineteenth-century metropolitan modernity. Faulk's analysis of late Victorian theatre criticism argues that camp was not simply a stage aesthetic but also what Andrew Ross calls 'an operation of taste' shared by dramatists, critics and audiences alike, in which the ephemeral and the inauthentic were appreciated while 'the whole business of taste-making' was ironised.[59] In the case of the medievalist burlesques, this enjoyment is further enriched by an ironising of the business of historical recreation, which, though exquisite, is regarded as densely, even absurdly, mediated by its multiple textual and theatrical precedents.

The camp conspiracy between text and audience is intensified, moreover, by the burlesques' reflexive acknowledgement of their own implication in the production of a comic Middle Ages for popular consumption. Brooks's *The Exposition* is especially striking in this respect. It opens with an exchange between two characters, Author and Spirit of the Times, in which the dejected Author laments a lack of fresh historical and mythic material from which to draw his burlesque (an unwittingly ironic lament considering the genre would remain popular for over three more decades). Having rejected the Arabian Knights, the Genii and Moorish orientalist themes as 'used up', he proclaims resignedly:

> AUT: There's nothing left but the old track to follow,
> With Jupiter, and Juno, and Apollo.
> They'll do again, and every one confesses
> The ladies look so well in classic dresses.[60]

An exchange ensues over Author's lack of historic-mythic imagination and the narrowness of his 'heathenish acquaintance', with Spirit of the Times urging him to become acquainted with an alternative pantheon:

> AUT: Yes, with Roman idols I'm at home.
> SPI: No, England wants no Idol-farce from Rome.
> If you need fables, surely history's mouth
> Tells more than worn-out legends from the South. ...
> AUT: Still, if we take without it, what's the odds?
> SPI: Why don't you try the Scandinavian Gods? ...
> This mythology – if one could work it –
> Does seem a track out of the beaten circuit.

---

[58] Ibid., n. 87.
[59] Faulk, *Music Hall and Modernity*, p. 54.
[60] Shirley Brooks, *The Exposition: A Scandinavian Sketch, Containing As Much Irrelevant Matter As Possible – In One Act* (London: Hailes Lacy, 1851), p. 4.

Offering the ill-informed Author a brief lesson on Saxon England, the Spirit continues

> SPI: These Danes, you see, in olden time, adored
> Gods of their own – a wild, fierce, jolly horde,
> Who drank, sang, quarrelled, bullied, laughed and flirted,
> Much as Greek Gods were pleased to be diverted,
> When to the invader they were forced to give in;
> These gods were worshipped in the Land we Live in.
> Of Grecian gods an English public tires,
> Shew it the jovial idols of its sires.[61]

As discussed earlier, these violent and buffoonish gods of England's medieval past have not been selected solely for their novelty, but are central to the play's triumphalist portrayal of the nation's historical progress. Still, viewers can be amused by the notion that the selection of Norse content is motivated by the commercial imperative of plundering the past for novelty, because it appeals to their sense of cultural competency on more than one level. As seasoned theatre-goers, they can laughingly recognise burlesque's indiscriminate raid on history while also being gratified by the 'insider knowledge' this scene conveys of the professional pressures behind the creation of historical burlesque. Additionally, the scene allows the more historically aware among them to take pride in their knowledge of an Old English pantheon of which the Author character professes ignorance. On a related note, both Reece's *Whittington, Junior* and Brough's *Joan of Arc!* conclude with speeches from their eponymous hero(in)es that again addresses themselves flatteringly to their audience's sense of cultural literacy. These speeches' manifest purpose is to disavow the burlesque genre's responsibility to produce any kind of authentic historical representation:

> DICK: Don't on this nonsense waste a witticism,
> When all burlesque's one great anachronism.
> In spite of complaints from serious sources,
> We still pursue, you see, our fearful courses[62]

and

> JOAN: Do what you like, it won't affect the plot;
> Historians doubt if I were burned or not![63]

[61] Ibid., pp. 4–5.
[62] Reece, *Whittington, Junior and his Sensation Cat*, p. 37.
[63] Brough, *Joan of Arc!* p. 38.

As speech-acts, however, they solicit a three-fold complicity from their audiences, whom they appeal to as sophisticates who are conversant with burlesque's use of anachronism, knowledgeable enough of the play's source material to identify its distortions, and urbane enough to be entertained rather than offended by them. The complex work of interpellation undertaken in these speeches delineates perfectly the camp-historical knowingness that is the *passe-partout* to appreciating medievalist burlesque.

In arguing for camp as a species of Victorian theatrical knowingness, Bailey, like Cleto, identifies its link to Parlary (or 'Polari'), a subcultural argot used in nineteenth-century theatrical circles that also crossed into British homosexual culture.[64] While this link was associative rather than causal, it is worth acknowledging because it discloses the convergence of burlesque, as a camp form, with queer discursive practice. The camp queerness of burlesque is most conspicuous in its extensive use of cross-dressing, a cherished feature it shared with other closely related comic genres such as pantomime and fairy spectacular. Breeches roles, in which young female performers played male roles, and drag roles, in which (usually) older male actors played female roles, were a staple of these performances: to take just two examples, in Brough's *King Arthur*, Arthur, Sir Lancelot and Sir Tristram are all breeches roles, while in Byron's *Ivanhoe!* this is the case with the majority of male characters, including Wilfred of Ivanhoe, Prince John, the Black Knight, De Bracy and Wamba. Conversely, in the first season of Brough's *Joan of Arc!*, Joan was played as a drag role by the comic actor Thomas Thorne, while in *Ivanhoe!* Rebecca's drag portrayal was received as a first cousin to the pantomime dame; as late as 1894, reviews were still singling out male actors' performances of this character as the comic highlight of this much-revived piece.[65]

In describing this variety of historical camp as 'queer', some caution is required, for these performances frequently reinforced hetero-normative representational modes and social values. Breeches roles, to begin with, at one level performed a similar scopophilic function to that of the *corps de ballet* 'fairy transformation' interludes, with their diaphanous, leg-exposing costumes, allowing fuller display of the young female form [see Plate 2]. This fact is brought home by the 1861 *Illustrated London News* review of Byron's *Esmeralda*, which tellingly described the performance of Gringoire by acclaimed comic actress Marie Wilton as 'pert and pretty'.[66]

The drag roles, for their part, played directly to misogynist notions of grotesque femininity, especially of an aged (and in the unfortunate case of Byron's Rebecca, Jewish) variety. *Joan of Arc!* offers a fascinating case in

---

64 Cleto, *Queer Aesthetics*, p. 30.
65 *The Illustrated London News*, 3 November 1894, p. 580.
66 *The Illustrated London News*, 5 October 1861, p. 344.

Figure 2. Miss Maud Boyd as Robin Hood, *The Sketch*
Magazine, 27 December 1893

point, for rather than staging Joan's execution, it punishes her at the end by
forcing her to wear women's clothes, which allowed the male actor playing
Joan to emerge in drag after wearing armour for most of the play. Because
Joan is a young character, the grotesquery is introduced via the costume
itself, which is described as 'very dowdy'.[67] Nevertheless, burlesque cross-
dressing did allow for the staging of some queer spectacle, featuring romantic
pursuits and couplings between same-sex (especially female) bodies. To take
just two examples, Brough's *King Arthur* features a same-sex Arthur-Guin-
evere pairing, while Byron's *Ivanhoe* couples a female Wilfred of Ivanhoe
with a female Rowena. The simultaneously comic and erotic charge of this

<hr />

[67]   Brough, *Joan of Arc!* p. 32.

cross-dressing reflects the particular sexual valency of the medieval past within Victorian burlesque, especially when compared with the representations of the classical era in light entertainments of the same period. While, as Rosemary Barrow has pointed out, popular perceptions of Roman decadence created opportunities to include filmy toga-style costumes and erotic tableaux-vivants based on classical statues, perceptions of medieval religiosity, heroism and romance – the regular quarry of the burlesque writers – meant this period did not readily provide the same titillating fare. By means of cross-dressing, medieval characters' sexuality is introduced yet disavowed. This gesture, which is riotous and domesticating in equal measure, makes sex present but also makes it absurd, even impossible. The camp implications of these transvestic practices go beyond the representation of sexuality, however, for it is through them that the burlesque can truly be said to have travestied the Middle Ages, in the double sense of parodying and queering medieval history and legend in all its serial reiterations. In making Arthur a visually saucy breeches role, for instance, Brough expressly differentiates his character from 'the various legends of "the Blameless King"', in particular, he claims, the bloodless Arthur of 'Tennyson's fanciful "Idylls"'.[68] The signature 'tender' ambivalence of camp is again in evidence, as these irreverent cross-gendered bodies were (Joan's 'dowdy' dress notwithstanding) garbed in gorgeously amplified versions of historical costumes, and their acting, at its best, combined pathos and mischief. A contemporary review of Mrs John Wood's burlesque acting admired 'her sincerity and the genuine comic effect it produced'[69] while a review of the actor Frederick Robson praised his burlesque medievalist-Shakespearian portrayals because 'however extravagant his gestures and articulations, we find that they are odd expressions of a feeling intrinsically serious'.[70]

Responding to critics such as Moe Meyer for whom the word 'queer' is a 'specifically gay formation', Cleto argues that 'queer does not invest just gender, but semiotic structures at large, the signs of domination moving in concert with sexual and non-sexual hierarchies'.[71] One of these larger 'semiotic structures' queered by the burlesques is surely historical representation itself, which, by having camp added to its repertoire, can incorporate a medievalism where longing for the past erupts into a unique kind of loving laughter.

---

[68] Brough, *King Arthur: Or, the Days and Knights of the Round Table* (London: Thomas Hailes Lacy, 1863), p. 2.

[69] Barnard Hewitt, 'Mrs. John Wood and the Lost Art of Burlesque Acting', *Educational Theatre Journal* 13 (1961), 82–5 (p. 85).

[70] Craven Mackie, 'Frederick Robson and the Evolution of Realistic Acting', *Educational Theatre Journal* 23 (May 1971), 160–70 (p. 163).

[71] Cleto, *Queer Aesthetics*, p. 19.

5

Up the Middle Ages: Performing Tradition in Comic Medievalist Cinema

A T THE END OF MICHAEL KIDD's 1958 musical comedy *Merry Andrew*, the amateur archaeologist Andrew Larabee, played with customary hapless charm by Danny Kaye, faces a difficult choice: whether to return to school teaching or pursue his newly discovered facility as a natural clown. His dilemma is resolved when his father reveals that Andrew's clowning skills have an honourable pedigree, having been inherited from a distant ancestor, Thomas Larabee, who had been jester to a king. As the film's title confirms, Andrew's name signals the atavistic return of a lost ancestral line of 'merry-Andrews', buffonic entertainers associated with London's Bartholomew Fair, whose physical clowning and madcap wordplay were, according to an unconfirmed claim by Thomas Hearne in 1735, epitomised in the antics of 'merry' Andrew Borde, humourist and physician to Henry VIII with a posthumous reputation as a kind of Tudor Patch Adams.[1]

By evoking the tradition of the court jester, the film also neatly alludes to a much more recent comic past: only two years earlier Kaye had starred in the well-known musical comedy *The Court Jester*, directed by Melvin Frank and Norman Panama. As with *Merry Andrew*, in this film Kaye's character Hubert Hawkins, despite masquerading as jester to the usurper King Roderick as a part of a plot to restore the kingdom's true heir, finds that he has a unique talent for 'making a fool of [him]self' through cavorting, banter and facial antics, epitomised in the film's famous patter song, 'The Maladjusted Jester'. In addition to showcasing Kaye's virtuosic talent for such tongue-twisters as 'the pellet with the poison's in the vessel with the pestle / the chalice from the palace has the brew that is true', *The Court Jester* is significant for the

---

[1] R. W. Maslen, 'The Afterlife of Andrew Borde', *Studies in Philology* 100 (2003), 463–92 (p. 472).

analogy it draws between contemporary musical comedy and the japes and capers of the medieval court entertainers. Martha Bayless rightly argues that '*The Court Jester* takes its place in a long history of narratives that highlight the potential guile and shiftiness of jesters and entertainers', pointing particularly to the queer liminality of Hubert's serial impersonations and protean identity.[2] It is equally true, however, that Hubert's trickster persona is vital to his mission, as a follower of the rebel the Black Fox, to unseat the usurping ruler and restore order, so as a comedian he is ultimately, and flatteringly, presented as a servant of truth and justice, and his entertainment as a form of selflessness. In 'The Maladjusted Jester', he sings:

> I found out soon that to be a buffoon
> Was a serious thing as a rule
> For a jester's chief employment
> Is to kill himself for your enjoyment
> And a jester unemployed is nobody's fool.[3]

Considering the context of the film's production, these final lines make a coded but charged statement about the relationship between entertainment, truth and freedom. In a period still affected by the widespread Hollywood industry blacklistings resulting from the House Committee on Un-American Activities – indeed, Kaye joined the Committee for the First Amendment in protest against the blacklisting of left-wing entertainers – lyrics referring to 'unemployed' jesters and jesters killing themselves are surely far from incidental. Indeed, placing modern entertainers like Kaye in a historical lineage of socially critical (or 'maladjusted') comedy is an audacious move that makes him and *The Court Jester*'s creators surprising older cousins to Dario Fo. In a chiasmus common to so much comic medievalism, in *The Court Jester* medieval comic performance is made over in the image of modernity (Kaye's vaudevillian shtick is strongly evident, referencing earlier American theatrical tradition as much as medieval jesting), and then nominated as a precedent, or even an origin, to make a point about the comic practices of the cinematic age. So just as Kaye in *Merry Andrew* played an archaeologist-turned-clown, so too his 'jester' films are archaeologies, digging down through performance history to the comic bedrock of salutary medieval buffonic tradition.[4]

---

2   Martha Bayless, 'Danny Kaye and the Fairy Tale of Queerness in *The Court Jester*', in *Queer Movie Medievalisms*, ed. Kathleen Coyne Kelly and Tison Pugh (Farnham, Surrey: Ashgate, 2009), pp. 185–200 (p. 191).

3   Lyrics from the song, 'Maladjusted Jester', words and music by Sylvia Fine, in the movie, *The Court Jester*, dir. M. Frank and N. Panama (Dena Enterprises, 1955).

4   Albrecht Classen, ed., *Laughter in the Middle Ages and Early Modern Times: Epistemology of a Fundamental Human Behavior, its Meaning, and Consequences* (Berlin: de Gruyter, 2010).

This archaeological tendency extends beyond Kaye's filmography, with numerous films grounding their own comedy in perceived long traditions reaching back to the Middle Ages. While others have argued eloquently for medieval films' medium-specific representation of time, I suggest that focusing on the comic films within the larger corpus requires an approach that foregrounds not just their cinematic nature but also their acknowledgement of a deep history of pre- and extra-cinematic (especially comic and musical) performance. As will be seen throughout this chapter, many of these films combine layers of allusion to pre-cinematic performance with witty parodic nods to those contemporary 'straight' medievalist films that had been so instrumental in forming popular views of the Middle Ages. Although the Victorian burlesques were also deeply parodic, cinema has at its disposal both stage and screen source texts from which to draw its humour. *The Court Jester*, for instance, does not just feature medieval jesting, but also makes clear parodic reference to the iconic 1938 *Robin Hood* directed by Michael Curtiz and starring Errol Flynn. A highlight of Hubert's opening song, in which he impersonates his master the Black Fox, is Kaye's affectionate parody of Flynn's boisterous hands-on-hips-head-thrown-back laughter, as he leaps around a sound-stage forest strongly reminiscent of Curtiz's celebrated Technicolor greenwood. Similarly the film's casting of Basil Rathbone cannot but evoke his legendary 1938 performance as Sir Guy of Gisbourne. As Richard Burt has commented in his persuasive account of 'movie schmedievalism', serious film and 'schlocky parody … circulate and contaminate one another'.[5]

These cinematic citations notwithstanding, in this chapter I will excavate the pre-cinematic layers embedded in many films in which the Middle Ages receive comic representation. Moreover, the notion of 'archaeological comedy' in medievalist cinema does not simply apply here to its layering of performance history, but can also be modulated to apply to comic films' anachronistic portrayals of the Middle Ages. Just as an archaeological cross-section is a compacted slice of time in which multiple eras are simultaneously visible, so these films offer comically impossible medieval worlds in which strata not only from multiple 'Middle Ages' but also from pre- and post-medieval eras are densely packed. As will be seen, this is equally, though differently, the case with comedies that are 'entirely' medieval and those whose humour rests on the multi-temporal dissonance created by time-travelling protagonists. Finally, the satire underpinning many of the films to be discussed in this chapter can be described as archaeological in that their anachronistic medieval depictions provide a means to excavate the beliefs and assumptions of modernity – including modernity's assumptions about the Middle Ages. This notion of comic archaeology, then, provides a supple heuristic for

5   Richard Burt, 'Getting Schmedieval: Of Manuscripts and Film Prologues, Paratexts, and Parodies', *Exemplaria* 19 (2007), 217–42 (p. 220).

understanding the unique coalescence of comic method, satiric intent and historical mise-en-scène found in much comic medievalist cinema.

Returning to my first iteration of 'archaeological comedy', another well-known instance can be found in 'Do Aphrodisiacs Work?', the first of the seven sketch-like sequences that make up Woody Allen's 1972 film *Everything You Always Wanted to Know about Sex** (**But Were Afraid to Ask*). Here Allen appears as the unprepossessing court jester who, by dint of his lead-balloon comedy routine and his attempted seduction of the Queen, ends up being beheaded (though this is depicted metonymically, as the severed look-alike head of his fool's bauble falls into the bucket under the chopping block). The film is loosely adapted from David Reuben's 1969 book of the same name, but this medieval sequence is Allen's own creation, and clearly situates his comic *nebbish* (timid loser) persona in a trans-historical lineage of inept comedians. A cross-section of the archaeological layers in Allen's performance reveals not only the medieval jesting of the royal court scene, but also the Shakespearian fool's sexual banter, as well as vaudeville ('seriously, ladies and germs'), and a low-rent variety of Las Vegas stand-up comedy, in which the comedian alludes to his own performance history (Felix's opening 'it's great to be back here at the palace' amusingly evokes Caesar's Palace). Via Allen's unmistakable New York Jewish accent, moreover, Felix's routine also evokes the anti-authoritarian shtick of the *badchen*, the Jewish wedding jester who, like his counterparts in other cultures, was permitted to mock the greed and cruelty of the powerful.[6] This figure is also glimpsed in 'The Maladjusted Jester' as Kaye lapses fleetingly into his famous Russian-American-Jewish accent, but the allusion is more developed in Allen's fool, who mocks the King's taxation of the poor as well as his punitive rule. Felix's routine is not condemned because of its satiric force, but because the King and court find it maddeningly unfunny; his jokes are met with echoing silence, to which he responds with such floundering stand-up ripostes as 'I know you're out there, I can hear you breathing.' In this way, Allen declines to depict the conventional jester of satiric tradition, offering instead its obverse, a failed jester whom he claims as the ancestor of his own brand of neurotic self-deprecating comedy. But there is, of course, a temporal paradox at work here: Felix is a failure as a jester precisely because his trans-temporal comedy, as Cecilia Sayad points out, 'simply does not fit the [medieval] story world' of the film[7] and hence fails to amuse, while his persona, complete with the distinctive bespectacled face under the fool's cap and bells, is unmistakably Allenesque.

6   For a brief outline of some of the forerunners of stand-up in the history of Ashkenazi Jewry, see the entry on Jewish Comedy in the *Encyclopedia of Modern Jewish Culture*, ed. Glenda Abramson, vol. I (London and New York: Routledge, 2005), pp. 252–8 (p. 254).

7   Cecilia Sayad, 'The Auteur as Fool: Bakhtin, Barthes, and the Screen Performances of Woody Allen and Jean-Luc Godard', *Journal of Film and Video* 63 (2011), 21–34 (p. 25).

Unlike *The Court Jester*'s Hubert, whose undeniably Danny Kayesque comedy is nevertheless not marked as anachronistic to the film's diegetic world, it is through Felix simultaneously being (a lame) Woody Allen that he becomes the failed comic 'ancestor' that Allen claims.

An archaeological cross-section of *Monty Python and the Holy Grail* (1975) reveals that it is embedded in a parallel theatrical tradition, owing a conspicuous debt to the Oxbridge review culture out of which the Python ensemble emerged. As documented by J. F. Roberts, the university review genre, in which sketch-based set pieces are strung together along a central thread, brought the Python team success in the UK live comedy circuit and formed the foundation of their early forays into televisual sketch comedy (*Do Not Adjust Your Set, Monty Python's Flying Circus*), a point also noted by Laurie Finke and Martin Shichtman.[8] The success of the film's highly digressive and disjointed narrative structure – a structure it shares with many the films to be discussed here, which tend to be organised into discrete chapters – is also due to Arthurian romance's episodic structure lending itself readily to this style of comic set-piece adaptation. There is also, via the film's grounding in sketch-review genre, a strong inheritance of the popular nineteenth-century entertainment forms discussed in Chapter 4, including the Victorian burlesque and music hall. This is conspicuous in the film's 'Knights of the Round Table' musical number, which is an ingenious parodic mélange combining male chorus-line dancing with a song that fuses 'cheeky' music hall instrumentation and barbershop vocals. The gender-play of the chorus line recalls the drag tradition of burlesque and pantomime, as do the film's other drag characterisations, most notably Terry Jones's as Dennis's mother in the much-loved socialist peasants scene. The Python team's literacy in screen technique drives the musical sequence's increasingly frenetic editing, which both conveys the lunacy of the Camelot knights and telescopes the riotous disorder into which the film will later descend; but its nod to theatrical convention is unmistakable. The inheritance of Victorian burlesque's currency of 'knowingness' also lingers in the film's intensely parodic, indeed meta-parodic, texture, in which canonical and recent texts are lampooned alike. Stephen Wagg locates much of its popularity in its 'collision' of 'high culture' and 'banal mass culture' which creates a comic register that is accessible to audiences in possession of different degrees of erudition.[9] I will

8   J. F. Roberts, *The True History of the Black Adder: The Unadulterated Tale of the Creation of a Comedy Legend* (London: Preface Publishing, 2012); Laurie A. Finke and Martin B. Shichtman, *Cinematic Illuminations: The Middle Ages on Film* (Baltimore, MD: Johns Hopkins University Press, 2010).
    9   Stephen Wagg, 'You've Never Had It So Silly: The Politics of British Satirical Comedy from *Beyond the Fringe* to *Spitting Image*', in *Come on Down? Popular Media*

return to the film's use of parody later, but for now it works as a highly revealing instance of comic medievalist film's archaeological complexity, in which theatre, television and cinema are all sedimented.

Another deeply eclectic historical parody emerging out of the Python camp which owes much to theatrical tradition is Terry Gilliam's *Time Bandits* (1981). In this film the young hero Kevin's bedroom has been invaded by a troupe of time-travelling bandit dwarves who take him back to a number of earlier periods, including the legendary England of Robin Hood. This film offers the amusingly dissonant spectacle of John Cleese's Robin Hood emerging from a grimy, smoky forest scene (complete with outlaws ripping each other's limbs off) dressed in the impeccable Lincoln green tights-and-tunic ensemble of nineteenth-century melodrama and early Hollywood, and speaking in clipped Oxbridge tones. The hint of passive-aggressive menace beneath Robin's bluff joviality, as he pressures other outlaws to hand over their booty to help him in his 'work with The Poor', evokes both Cleese's politely violent Lancelot in *The Holy Grail* and his unforgettable turn as the unctuously spiteful Basil Fawlty in *Fawlty Towers* (1976–9); but his pristine demeanour predominantly recalls previous Robins of the stage and of early screen productions with their stagey 'filmed play' aesthetics. Nineteenth-century sensation drama is also mocked in the scene where the carriage of the wooing couple Michael Palin and Shelley Duvall is ambushed by the film's troupe of bandit dwarves. Despite living in the thirteenth century, they address one another in exaggerated Victorian tones and even end up tied to a tree in approved melodramatic fashion. The humour in these scenes appears, on the surface, to be extremely broad and directed against the Middle Ages, which is presented simultaneously as violent, filthy and yet absurdly effete; more closely examined, its intertextuality makes it more subtle (though, it must be said, quite uneven), as it lampoons not so much the Middle Ages as the preposterous and contradictory ways in which modern perceptions of the past have been formed through popular entertainment.

In some cases, the dance between theatre and cinema is more complex than it initially seems. Andrei Tarkovsky's *Andrei Rublev*, which I mentioned in the introduction to this book, also includes a medieval jester or *skomorokh* in its second chapter, 'Buffoon, 1400'. Tarkovsky's film differs from those discussed above, however, in that it avoids even the parodic inclusion of theatrical stylistics, so its archaeological engagement with medieval comic tradition is undertaken in the service of a meditation on cinematic practice. As a director who has argued against 'composite' quasi-theatrical conceptions of cinema, in which the medium is reduced to 'the straightforward

Culture in Post-War Britain, ed. Dominic Strinati and Stephen Wagg (London: Routledge, 1992), pp. 254–84 (pp. 271–2).

and seductive purpose of recording theatrical performance',[10] he eschews the relatively static camera used in *The Court Jester* and *Everything you Wanted to Know,* using instead, as Haydock has also noted, a mobile, panning camera that strays beyond the jester's performance into the time and space of Russia in 1400.

Despite its spirited depiction of medieval folk entertainment, this scene is among the most difficult to assimilate into a discussion of comic medievalism for several reasons. First, the boisterous hilarity with which it begins, as the peasants enjoy the jester's bawdy anti-authoritarian song and obscene capering, is soon succeeded by the film's characteristically pensive mood as the jester is rounded up, beaten (and, we later learn, tortured) by the local Boyars; so the scene becomes, at most, ironic rather than comic, as the authorities show they are even wickeder than the jester's irreverent joking had implied. Second, while in other films it is possible to identify a relatively straight line of inheritance being drawn between jesters and modern performers (such as Kaye or Allen), the significance of Tarkovsky's *skomorokh* is less easy to determine, because the director's musings on the nature of his art are somewhat gnomic, both on the question of his use of history and on the question of whether this persecuted character, along with the film's eponymous artist, can be seen as allegorical of the Soviet director.

On the latter question, Tarkovsky's comments in Soviet-era interviews are, for understandable reasons, evasive;[11] but these demurrals have not prevented viewers from seeing the jester as analogous to the film-maker under state control. There is, however, another way of considering this comic figure's resonance with Tarkovsky without resorting to allegory, and that is through the film-maker's concept of cinema as a uniquely temporal rather than pictorial art form. Tarkovsky's conviction that cinema's essential and distinguishing capacity is to 'take an impression of time' is expressed through the slow, circular panning visible throughout 'Buffoon, 1400' (although this is subject to minor cutting in some versions). Depictions of history are, for Tarkovsky, driven less by standards of antiquarian accuracy than by an ambition to render history as a 'consequence' of time, which is an ongoing condition of human existence. Answering criticisms of *Andrei Rublev's* historical inaccuracies, he says 'pure direct History, though it doesn't get relegated into the background, dilutes itself in the atmosphere of time'.[12] Far from being abstract and remote, this existential conception of time, in which history is embedded, is experienced subjectively as memory, so that the past is 'the

[10]   Andrei Tarkovsky, *Sculpting in Time: Reflections on the Cinema,* trans. K. Hunter-Blair (Austin: University of Texas Press, 1986, reprinted 2005), pp. 62–3.

[11]   See, for instance, Michael Ciment, Luda Schnitzer and Jean Schnitzer's 1969 interview 'The Artist in Ancient Russia and in the New USSR', in *Andrei Tarkovsky: Interviews,* ed. John Gianvito (Jackson: University Press of Mississippi, 2006), pp. 16–31.

[12]   Gianvito, *Andrei Tarkovsky,* p. 18.

bearer of ... the reality of the present' that 'settles in our soul as an experience placed within time'.[13] Following this, then, the *skomorokh* can be seen
not so much as a historical allegory of the Soviet director, but rather as an
'archaeological' memory figure enfolded into Tarkovsky's subjective experience of himself as a Russian artist, while the folk culture he embodies is at
the core of the film's chthonic evocation of Russia's historic and mythic past.
While his approach to the question of the past differs markedly from that
of Kaye, or indeed of Dario Fo as discussed in Chapter 3, he too is laughing
with the Middle Ages via the figure of the jester.

On a more frivolous note, Mel Brooks's cult comedy *History of the World
Part 1* (1981) is cinematic in that it engages parodically with the genres of
early Hollywood by presenting its Spanish Inquisition sequence in the style
of a Busby Berkeley musical spectacular, complete with monastic chorus lines
and an aquaballet sequence featuring synchronised swimming nuns who rise
up through the water on a giant menorah. We encounter the wincing wordplay of vaudeville stand-up when a monk says of the inquisitor Tomás de
Torquemada, 'do not ask him for mercy; let's face it, you can't Torquemada
anything', as well as Jewish Borscht Belt-style stand-up in a short cameo where
the legendary comic Jackie Mason plays a Jew recounting, in a thick Jewish-
American accent, his torment at the hands of the inquisitors. One especially
playful irony here is that Brooks's all-singing-all-dancing Torquemada is
more successful as a comic entertainer than Brooks's previous incarnation
Comicus, the failed 'stand-up philosopher' of the film's Roman sequence, a
witty slave in the Plautian tradition of the *servus callidus* who manages to
offend the Emperor while performing a routine at Caesar's Palace – in this
case the Las Vegas casino hotel, where the routine was filmed.[14] Of course, the
comedy of the Inquisition sequence is not limited to genre parody; its upbeat
musical routine is vital to its use of a powerful social satire founded on the
incongruity between style and content. Brooks, whose comedy frequently
draws on his Jewish identity, singles out the Inquisition as a medieval flash-
point in the long history of Jewish persecution culminating in the atrocities
of the Holocaust, and as such can be seen as a pre-modern counterpart
to 'Springtime for Hitler', the famous mock-Broadway showstopper Brooks
wrote for *The Producers* (1968), the lyrics of which were partly reprised in
'The Hitler Rap', recorded for the soundtrack of his remake of *To Be or Not to
Be* (1983). The audacious gallows humour of the Inquisition scene, in which
the Jewish captives remain stoically and even comically defiant in the face
of their singing gaolers, works as a jubilant declaration of Jewish survival

---

[13] Ibid., p. 56.
[14] For more on traditional Roman comedy see George E. Duckworth, *The Nature of
Roman Comedy: A Study in Popular Entertainment* (Norman, OK: University of Oklahoma
Press, 1994), pp. 249–53.

after centuries of Christian hostility and oppression, conforming to Woody Allen's succinct formula, quoted at the beginning of this book, that 'comedy is tragedy plus time'.[15]

The collusion of religious violence and social oppression in medieval culture is also central to the comic historical vision and, as I will later argue, to the archaeological satire of Mario Monicelli's *L'armata Brancaleone* (Brancaleone's Army, 1966) and its sequel *Brancaleone alla Crociate* (Brancaleone at the Crusades, 1970), two films deserving of more scholarly attention from medievalists than they have so far received. As the two major historical films in the *commedia all'italiana* that Monicelli was instrumental in shaping, the *Brancaleone* films are quintessential picaresque tales that trace the outlandish exploits of an impoverished knight-errant, Brancaleone di Norcia (played in full declamatory mock-heroic mode by Vittorio Gassman), and his small, scruffy 'army' of misfits, which includes in the first film various brigands and vagrants, an orphan boy, a tiny and wizened Jew and a Byzantine bastard son, and in the second film a blind man, a cripple, a dwarf, a leper (later revealed to be a fugitive princess), a masochistic penitent, a baby and a witch. Under Brancaleone's blustering and chaotic leadership they embark on a range of adventures that includes falsely (and unsuccessfully) claiming a patrimony bequeathed in a stolen document, following a religious zealot, unsuccessfully attempting to collect ransom for a sham hostage, visiting hermits and stylites, settling the quarrel between Pope Gregory VII and Clement III, going to the Holy Land (returning a kidnapped heir to his crusading father while there) and getting into lots of fights along the way.

Lorenzo Codelli notes that theatrical and literary texts were among Monicelli's primary influences. It is not surprising to discover that his taste for the absurd was developed through his early reading of playwright and author Luigi Pirandello and, significantly, of Cervantes. Reviews routinely compare medievalist comedies to *Don Quixote*, especially if those comedies in any way feature an inept knight, but it is no exaggeration to say that Monicelli's films come the closest of any to Cervantes's parodic satire. This is not just because they feature a comically debased, picaresque version of a knight-errant narrative, although it is impossible to watch Brancaleone's constant falls, buffets and gaffes without thinking of Cervantes's hero; and Brancaleone's piecemeal and constantly changing armour, which looks like it has been assembled from the castoffs of warriors from England to medieval Japan, cannot but evoke Don Quixote's rusty paste-board travesty. What is most intangibly but strikingly Cervantean about Monicelli's films are their satiric-parodic register, which modulates in a similarly nuanced way to Cervantes's between laughing

[15] Birgit Wiedl, 'Laughing at the Beast: The Judensau – Anti-Jewish Propaganda and Humor from the Middle Ages to the early Modern Period', in *Laughter in the Middle Ages and Early Modern Times*, ed. Albrecht Classen (Berlin: de Gruyter, 2010), pp. 325–64.

at and laughing in the Middle Ages, and between ridicule and sympathy for their hero, who, as a pitch-perfect burlesque of the romance hero, moves the audience to derision, amusement and tenderness in equal measures. More-over, Monicelli's narrative, while robustly executed, has a finely calibrated emotional structure: just when Brancaleone's stentorian pronouncements on chivalrous conduct threaten to become too absurd, or his exposure of his companions to danger reveals chivalry's violent and delusional underbelly, he either scores a victory or extends kindness to a vulnerable outcast, which restores his innate nobility – until the next mishap.

The film's cast of misfits have been described as presenting 'history from the point of view of the humble people, the little guy'.[16] Although larger historical events find their ways into the films – the Crusades and papal rivalry are two conspicuous ones – their significance plays out on the smaller stage of the characters' lives. Codelli, and Marcia Landy after him, have both identified this tendency as a counter-historical strategy in Monicelli's work.[17] The satiric target of the *Brancaleone* films is first and foremost what Monicelli saw as the apologistic way in which the medieval period has been depicted to the Italian people, and the nationalistic, ethnocentric and Christocentric implications of these representations. He nominated the immaculate look of the Hollywood Middle Ages as his first *bête noire*; Bergman's *The Seventh Seal*, on the other hand, receives a warmly parodic tribute in Brancaleone's encounter with the Grim Reaper, which transmutes the solemnity of the knight's chess game with death into a chaotic sword/scythe duel in the sand dunes of Palestine. The apparently haphazard structure of the *Brancaleone* films, as well as their earthy palette and the realism of their hot and dusty mise-en-scènes, is a clear riposte to the Technicolor Middle Ages of *Robin Hood* and its ilk. Monicelli's critique extended further, moreover, taking aim at academics' airbrushed, 'glossy vision' (*visione patinata*) of the medieval period as refined and highly civilised, and replacing it with an Italian Middle Ages that is hierarchical, barbaric and xenophobic (internally and externally):

> Civilization, truth, and science were on the other side: the side of Islam. That's what the Crusades were all about. We went to occupy places where they were more civilized. Of course, we were repulsed. I wanted to show this was the real Middle Ages in Italy – barbaric and uncivi-lized, savage, grotesque.[18]

---

[16] Deborah Young, 'Poverty, Misery, War and Other Comic Material: An Interview with Mario Monicelli', *Cinéaste* 29 (2004), 36–40 (p. 38).

[17] Lorenzo Codelli, 'Mario Monicelli: 1915–2010', *Positif* 600 (2011), 56–7 (p. 56); Marcia Landy, 'Comedy and Counter-History', in *Historical Comedy on Screen*, ed. Hannu Salmi (Bristol: Intellect Press Ltd, 2011), pp. 177–98 (p. 177).

[18] Young, 'Poverty, Misery, War', pp. 38–9.

The realist impulse underpinning this is evident in Monicelli's use of framing techniques characteristic of Italian neo-realism, in which close-up is eschewed and bodies are embedded in their environments, creating a mise-en-scène that encompasses the characters' life-world. To say, however, that these films simply replace fantasy with social realism would be simplistic. This is especially true of their visual and aural aesthetic, in which brooding, empty landscapes and deserted towns, again inherited from Italian neo-realism, give way to surreal, almost futurist interiors inhabited by a range of cameo characters (often women) in operatically camp costumes designed by Piero Gherardi, costume and design director on a number of Federico Fellini's films, including the oneiric *Juliet of the Spirits* (1965). Some of Monicelli's scenes even reprise the gusting winds that accompany Juliet's visions in Fellini's film. While these stylised environments seem removed from the mimetic Middle Ages outside, in another way they crystallise the film's 'medievalness'. The scene in an Italo-Byzantine palace, for instance, where Brancaleone finds himself being whipped by the sexually frenzied (and very '60s-looking) Lady Theodora, is both anachronistic and essentially medieval according to the film's vision of a world in which cruelty, pain and sacrifice become a perverse form of pleasure. The use, for the dialogue, of a pseudo-archaic, macaronic Italo-Latin of Monicelli's own devising (he says he 'invented an Italian that didn't exist') is in keeping with the films' overall comic strategy of offering 'uno parodia molto vera', that is, a meta-parody in which medieval chivalry and medievalist representation are lampooned by depicting a Middle Ages that is manifestly not real, but nevertheless aims to be true. Monicelli reused this language in his 1984 comedy *Bertoldo, Bertoldino e Cacasenno*, set in ninth-century Veneto. This approach to satiric and parodic truth licenses the creation of a condensed medieval world in which the First Crusade and the Black Death co-exist as temporal indexes of a past epitomised by war and disease.

Landy argues that the *Brancaleone* films are social satires in the archaeological cast described earlier, which 'explore affinities with contemporary cultural and political life'.[19] While Monicelli has explicitly denied that these films satirise contemporary Italy, elsewhere he has admitted that their bottom-up approach to recounting the past corresponds with the socialist perspective that abides across his oeuvre. His displaced satire of the delusional violence of Italian Fascism is subtly present in Brancaleone's occasional maniacal outbursts in which he insists he is 'il Duce' of his band. Characters who have power or authority are presented variously as mercurial, cruel, vengeful, exploitative and arrogant, while warmth and compassion are the preserve of the film's pariah figures, including the Satanist witch Tiburzia, who ultimately sacrifices herself to Death to save Brancaleone. The medieval

---

19   Landy, 'Comedy and Counter-History', pp. 177–98 (p. 181).

Church fares the worst in the films' satire of power, being presented as a chief perpetrator of aggression and intolerance. The modality of this satire is largely comic compression; according to Monicelli, 'it was easy to find farcical situations' (*situazone farsesche*) in medieval Catholic history,[20] and so disparate historical details such as competing claimants to the papacy, religious asceticism and trials of faith are condensed into absurd scenes such as the papal face-off in *Brancaleone alla Crociate* where the dispute is resolved by Brancaleone being forced to walk across hot embers by a stylite who adjudicates the outcome. Elsewhere, the tone is bleak and haunting. Arguably the films' most moving episode is one in *Brancaleone alla Crociate* titled 'The Ballad of Intolerance', in which the itinerant band come across a tree from whose branches dangle dozens of lynched bodies. When Tiburzia, who has the power to speak with hanged people, asks them how they got there, the disembodied voice of one body replies that the village priests and dignitaries rounded them up and killed them for their sins. These 'sins' are mostly trifling and non-violent, ranging from an interest in astronomy to eating salami on a Friday, and even, in the case of one figure, simply being a Jew.

Several speeches in this scene give the lie to Monicelli's claim that these films are not commenting on modern Italy, such that this image of medieval atrocity also resonates with the enormities of the twentieth century. When the band first see the tree in the distance, they mistake the hanging corpses for 'strange fruit' (*strani frutti*), a phrase immediately identified with the doleful song made famous by Billie Holiday about the lynching of African Americans in the modern South. Later, after we learn of the innocent Jew's execution, the voice of another body, claiming to 'see afar' into time, says '[t]ravellers, be glad, the world will not forever be intolerant', and offers a sanguine future vision of peace and equality that can only be taken as chillingly ironic in light of the monstrous intolerance of recent European history, and, more locally, the turbulence of Italy in 1970. The progressivist myth of modern civility is further crushed, this time without irony, when the unsettling voice of an especially ghoulish corpse utters an opposing prophesy: 'you will be as we are'.[21] The use of voiceover for the corpses' speeches in this scene means that their voices float beyond the diegesis, addressing not just the band but history – and, indeed, us.

If the suppleness of the Brancaleone films means that their comic object defies ready capture, blurring in the oscillation between jovial burlesque and mordant social satire, *Monty Python and the Holy Grail* presents an even greater challenge. Without doubt the most exhaustively discussed of all comic medievalist films, it has attained the status of *primus inter pares*,

[20] Mario Monicelli and Andrea Palazzino, 'Il Medioevo di Monicelli: una parodia molto vera', *Babel* 15 (2007), http://babel.revues.org/720 (accessed 30 April 2013).

[21] *Brancaleone alla Crociate*, dir. Mario Monicelli (Fair Film, O.N.C.I.C., 1970).

despite the fact that it is preceded by Monicelli's equally sophisticated historical comedy. The nuances of its engagement with the long Arthurian tradition
have been the subject of insightful scholarship by medievalists in the context
of Arthurian studies and, more recently, in analyses of medievalist cinema
produced by, among others, Haydock, Finke and Shichtman, and Pugh and
Weisl. What earns it such an exalted place in the story of comic medievalist
cinema is its compellingly unstable humour, which either changes target
with lightning quickness, or else hits several targets at once. The breadth
of its sweep has led scholars such as Wagg to argue that the Python team's
comedy is not properly satiric in the sense of offering a focused reformist
critique of folly.[22] This perspective can be, and has been, contested by read-
ings that emphasise the film's meta-medievalist satire of the centuries-long
dissemination and perpetuation of received views about the Middle Ages,
and Arthurian legend as a metonym for the period. Wagg's reservations are
understandable, however, because in order to make its (admittedly fairly
diffuse) satiric point the film uses parody as its primary comic vehicle, and
hence is more legible as a densely archaeological parodic text that not only
spoofs known representations of the Middle Ages but also imagines a few of
its own, such as Terry Gilliam's high-diving cartoon monks or Michael Palin's
anarcho-syndicalist serf.

The film's parodic satire is aimed at both creative and popular historical
modes. Others have discussed its multifaceted mimicry of a whole host of
creative medievalist texts, which reaches from the miraculous heroics of medieval romance (figured through the visual aesthetics of Victorian Arthurianism
and what Finke and Shichtman call cinematic 'hyperviolence')[23] through to
the fetishistically filmed knights of Robert Bresson's *Lancelot du Lac* and the
Nordic solemnity of Ingmar Bergman's *The Seventh Seal* (Haydock). Less
considered, however, is the question of whether the film is actually laughing
at, with or in the Middle Ages. From its parodies of medieval romance, which
on many occasions go well beyond generalised burlesquing, thus disclosing
the Pythons' familiarity with English and possibly French Arthurian literature, it would seem that it is specifically the ideals of heroism and nobility
in the Middle Ages that are being mocked. The oblique but recognisable
lampooning of *Sir Gawain and the Green Knight* is a case in point. The
Castle Anthrax sequence mimics Gawain's gruelling quest through trials and
freezing weather, miraculous sighting of Hautdesert, enforced convalescence
and subsequent chivalric and sexual testing at the hand of Bertilak's wife,
except in this film of the permissive 1970s 'Lady Bertilak' becomes 'four-score
blondes and brunettes aged between sixteen and nineteen-and-a-half' begging
to be spanked, and Gawain's sexual and homosocial resilience contrasts with

---

22   Wagg, 'You've Never Had It So Silly', pp. 272–5.
23   Finke and Shichtman, *Cinematic Illuminations*, p. 59.

Galahad's manifest disappointment at being 'saved' from corruption by his brother knights. More subtly, the 'Trojan rabbit' episode, in which the Round Table knights bungle their attempt to enter the French castle by failing to climb inside the wooden rabbit, offers a deflationary and preposterous allusion to the conventional link drawn between Troy and England in medieval chronicle and, more specifically between Camelot and Troy in the opening and final stanzas of *Sir Gawain and The Green Knight*.

Through the selection of *Gawain* as a text to parody, however, the Pythons engage in a more sophisticated meta-parody: that is, parody based on a text that itself already parodies what it claims to represent. As many commentators have noted, the narrative of *Sir Gawain and the Green Knight*, in particular its mischievous invocation of the 'tipping point' of homosociality into homosexuality in the 'exchange of winnings' pact between Gawain and Bertilak, is one that unsettles or even, to cite Carolyn Dinshaw's argument, 'queers' chivalric literature through a 'denaturalizing parody' of its heteronormative ideals.[24] The Castle Anthrax scene's parodic logic inverts that of the poem, in that it stages the promise of sado-masochistic group sex between the knight and the maidens as the excessive corollary of chivalric heteronormativity, but it relies nevertheless on the *ad absurdum* logic that makes Gawain's narrative so entertaining. As such this scene does not so much laugh straightforwardly at medieval romance as draw on and rework a reflexive impulse already inherent within one of its most sophisticated iterations.

The use of medievalist meta-parody is arguably even more pronounced in the film's 'Sir Robin' episode. In this case it is the idea of chivalric courage that appears to be lampooned, rather than the sexual ethics of knighthood. By featuring a cowardly knight who absconds when confronted by a signally non-threatening giant whose three heads bicker with each other with high-camp indignation, it violates the narrative expectations of medieval knight-errantry tales (expectations which are fulfilled, with perverse relish, by the Black Knight in his encounter with Arthur). The scene also parodies the composition and transmission of such heroic narrative forms as the *chanson de geste* and the romance, by staging the instantaneous transmission of Sir Robin's failure into oral lore through the taunting song of the minstrel who accompanies him. Again, however, these elements borrow directly from medieval literature itself, specifically Chaucer's gleeful parodic demolition of the conventions of chivalric narrative, and their transmission in tail-rhyme, in *The Tale of Sir Thopas*. The camp giant's three heads allude directly to the three heads of the giant Thopas boasts of meeting in Fytte two, while Sir Robin's escape echoes the hasty retreat made by Thopas when confronted by

---

[24] Carolyn Dinshaw, 'A Kiss is Just a Kiss: Heterosexuality and its Consolations in Sir Gawain and the Green Knight', *Diacritics* 24 (1994), 205–26 (p. 216).

the giant Sir Oliphaunt in the first Fytte, with the main difference being that Sir Oliphaunt's stone hurling send-off is replaced by the film-giant's bemused exclamation: 'Oh, he's buggered off!' Sir Robin's minstrel companion calls to mind, furthermore, the minstrels Thopas summons to sing inspiring tales of heroic deed while he is armed. Here again, the film's comedy lies both in its parodic treatment of the medieval source text, and in that text's own parodic treatment of the chivalric encounter.

Holy Grail's satiric-parodic treatment of the popular historical Middle Ages proceeds somewhat differently from the film's own parody of creative texts. This parody is focused, ironically given Jones's later career as a maker of 'jocumentaries' (to be discussed in Chapter 6), on the shooting of a television documentary on King Arthur fronted by 'A Very Famous Historian', whose address to the camera is collapsed into the film itself. Finke and Shichtman describe the anonymous historian as a generalised 'parody of the British academic';[25] but with his horn-rimmed spectacles, bow tie and hand gestures, his resemblance to the historian A. J. P. Taylor, then Fellow of Magdalen College, Oxford, and the first British 'T.V. don', is unmistakable, and obviates the need to name him or even to parody his name. Indeed, the fact that in the book of the film, the actor John Young is listed as 'the historian who isn't A. J. P Taylor at all', while Rita Davies is listed as 'the historian who isn't A. J. P. Taylor (honestly!)'s wife' confirms that the parody is specific.[26] This does not, however, limit the scope of the scene's satire of televisual history. As the historian delivers his speech, a knight on horseback rides seemingly out of the past and cuts his throat, killing him. This revenge attack of 'actual history' on the TV historian, with his unadventurous lecture-style mediation of the past, seems entirely in keeping with Jones's later stated rejection of the academic ownership of historical knowledge, and his belief that a more engaging use of the televisual format could better deliver historical truth to audiences. Lest the knight's assassination of the historian appear to support the fantasy of an unmediated Middle Ages laughing back at its academic and popular appropriations, the playful aporetic logic of this sequence should be acknowledged. The knight rides not out of the past but out of one scene in a fiction film into another, embodying, moreover, a combination of the comic past and what Finke and Shichtman call the close-contact 'hyperviolence' that signifies the medieval within cinematic convention.[27] Here, as Haydock punningly puts it, the satire 'cuts in a number of directions at once',[28] the target of this joke being not just the historian but his subject.

[25] Finke and Shichtman, *Cinematic Illuminations*, p. 57.

[26] Graham Chapman, Terry Jones and others, *Monty Python and the Holy Grail (Book)* (London: Methuen, 1977; repr. 1989, 2002).

[27] Finke and Shichtman, *Cinematic Illuminations*, p. 59.

[28] Nickolas Haydock, *Movie Medievalisms: The Imaginary Middle Ages* (Jefferson, NC: McFarland & Company, Inc., 2008), p. 12.

Other comic films are based less on the paradoxes of historical representation and more on paradoxical notions of medieval oppression, including those of a specifically sexual nature. Comic films made in Britain during the period referred to today as the Sexual Revolution got considerable mileage out of contemporary perceptions of the Middle Ages as an era in which rampant sexual energy endured hand-in-hand with rigorous oppression. Here again the instability of comic medievalism is strongly in evidence, for although these films are at one level ridiculing the benighted sexual discourses of medieval ecclesiastical and aristocratic culture – in particular their misogyny – at another level they are imagining an alternative, progressive Middle Ages, the legacy of which is directly visible in the 'swinging London' out of which they have emerged.

One relatively forgotten bawdy medievalist comedy in which this tension is hilariously evident is 1971's *Up the Chastity Belt*, the second of the camp histories that make up the British *Up* series which includes *Up Pompeii!* (TV series 1969–70; film 1971), and the Great War comedy *Up the Front* (1972), and as such is, as J. F. Roberts has noted, a forerunner of the cross-historical *Blackadder* series of the 1980s.[29] In *Chastity Belt* Frankie Howerd, an icon of twentieth-century British camp comedy, stars as the serf Lurkalot ('because I do'), seller of aphrodisiacs and chastity belts, a character with multiple archaeological strata, being the medieval descendant of Howerd's *Up Pompeii* character Lurcio, who was developed out of the actor's West End turn as the slave Pseudolus in *A Funny Thing Happened on the Way to the Forum*, who was in turn a *servus callidus* in the Plautian tradition. The film's plot is a slipshod mélange of saucy and/or absurd set pieces based predominantly on conventions of post-*Ivanhoe* medievalism: set in the time of King Richard's sojourn at the Crusades, it includes Robin Hood and his men, Prince John and Norman barons with names like Sir Coward de Custard and Sir Braggart de Bombast; it also involves scenes such as Lurkalot fighting in disguise as the Man with No Name, an avatar of Wilfred of Ivanhoe's *Desdichado* diverted through 1960s Spaghetti westerns. Tropes from earlier comic texts, medievalist and otherwise, are recycled: Lurkalot's use of magnets to win his duel recalls the magnetised armour in *The Court Jester*'s joust scene, while the plot in which Lurkalot is actually the lost twin of King Richard draws on doubling and mistaken-identity tropes that reach right back through comic history.

The film's portrait of the Middle Ages mostly concentrates, however, on pre-modern sexual mores, in order to provide a vehicle for its cast, a number of whom were established risqué comics. Eartha Kitt brings her unique growling appeal to her role as King Richard's highly sexed Eastern lover Scheherazade, singing the film's signature tune, 'Give me a Knight

---

[29] Roberts, *The True History of the Black Adder*, pp. 86–9.

for my Nights' (Kitt would appear in another medievalist comedy eighteen years later, playing Freya, a keeper of ancient lore in Terry Jones's rather limp Viking odyssey, *Erik the Viking*). Veteran camp comic Hugh Paddick, who had been half of the comedy duo Julian and Sandy along with *Carry On*'s Kenneth Williams, delivers an extreme (and extremely funny) high-camp Robin Hood who addresses Lurkalot as 'duckie', his speech peppered with the homosexual theatrical slang Polari and double entendres around the themes of night-time swinging and being 'picked up by the Norman soldiers'. Appearing four years after the decriminalisation of male homosexuality in England, the film imagines an English Middle Ages in which queerness is outrageously and unapologetically visible, but situated at the margins in Robin's hedonistic greenwood 'camp'. Lurkalot, candidly addressing the audience in Howerd's trademark fashion, is both bemused commentator on, and knowing participant in, the contradictory sexual culture of medieval England. In one of the film's better-known scenes, he sells a chastity belt to a husband about to go on Crusade, only to turn around promptly and sell spare keys to a jostling crowd of men, thus facilitating both the repression and the expression of sexual desire. The chastity belt as a modern emblem for the medieval control of female sexuality persists in later comedies such as Mel Brooks's *Robin Hood: Men in Tights* (1993), in the visual gag where Maid Marion emerges from her bath clad in metal knickers with an 'Everlast' logo stamped on the waistband.[30] In *Chastity Belt*, however, produced at the height of second-wave feminism, it morphs unexpectedly into a symbol of female resistance: in a scene reaching back to the ancient precedent of Aristophanes' *Lysistrata*, Lurkalot melts down weapons to forge chastity belts for Saladin's harem, so they can take sexual strike action and hence end the Crusades, which are presented in the film as a getaway for bored husbands fuelled by the sexual licentiousness of Richard and Saladin, with interfaith aggression as a flimsy pretext. The very contradictoriness of *Chastity Belt*'s sexual vision of the Middle Ages reflects its libertarian provenance, as it invests in the idea of sex as the quintessential human impulse while also subscribing to a kind of naïf Foucauldianism in which Western medieval sexuality is highly visible discursively while being physically repressed.[31]

The dense temporal compression evident in these films, which as I have noted throughout this book is common in comic medievalism, frequently gathers disparate but conspicuously 'medieval' events and phenomena together to create a setting in which pre-modern alterity is writ large. This kind of intra-epochal anachronism is, furthermore, frequently accompanied

[30] Albrecht Classen, *The Medieval Chastity Belt: A Myth-Making Process* (New York: Palgrave, 2007).

[31] Michel Foucault, *The History of Sexuality vol. 1: An Introduction*, trans. Robert Hurley (New York: Pantheon Books, 1978), pp. 17–35.

by inter-epochal anachronism, in which, most commonly, comedy arises out of the dissonance of the modern entering the medieval mise-en-scène. On most occasions the historical diegesis remains intact, and the modern intrusion is simply aesthetic or idiomatic: the female characters of *The Court Jester* and the *Brancaleone* films conforming to 1950s and '60s standards of beauty, for instance, or Woody Allen's jester's New York-style shtick, or Brian Helgeland's *A Knight's Tale* (2001) showing medieval people singing and dancing to 1970s and '80s rock anthems.[32] Elsewhere, the intrusion constitutes an actual rupture of the diegesis, as is the case with the English Bobbies at the end of *Monty Python and the Holy Grail* who arrive to arrest the knights for killing the Famous Historian. Nowhere is the mutual alterity of modernity and pre-modernity more evident, however, than in time-travel films. Revising Greene's notion of 'creative anachronism' which I discussed in the introduction to this book,[33] these films stage a deliberate and literal collision of epochs which, in Greene's words, 'bring[s] a concrete present into relation with a specific past and play[s] with the distance between them'.[34] While there are films of this genre that are not comic in tone – Vincent Ward's *The Navigator: A Mediaeval Odyssey* (1988) is one example – time travel is a trope that has been exploited repeatedly for its comic potential within cinematic medievalism.

Within the taxonomies of humour theory, the situation-comedy to be had from collapsing the distance between epochs, and dramatising the mutual befuddlement arising from the cross-historical encounter, aligns with notions of incongruity humour in which amusement is generated from the split perspective demanded of the viewer, who in this case needs to move between both modern and medieval worldviews but with the ironic omniscience of one who can see beyond both. The trans-temporality of this scenario has, moreover, as William McMorran has observed, 'obvious satirical possibilities',[35] as the received beliefs and values of the respective periods are made strange and hence opened up to comic scrutiny and possibly even to challenge.

The text that set the template for comic medievalist time travel, and spawned a cinematic tradition in its wake, was, of course, Mark Twain's *A Connecticut Yankee in King Arthur's Court*, in which the hard-nosed Hank Morgan, courtesy of a blow to the head, finds himself back in Camelot in 528. Looking through the many cinematic reiterations of this tale listed in Kevin

---

[32] Louise D'Arcens, 'Deconstruction and the Medieval Indefinite Article: The Undecidable Medievalism of Brian Helgeland's A Knight's Tale', *Parergon* 25 (2008), 80–98.

[33] Thomas M. Greene, 'History and Anachronism', in *Literature and History: Theoretical Problems and Russian Case Studies*, ed. Gary Saul Morson (Stanford: Stanford University Press, 1986), pp. 205–20 (p. 210).

[34] Ibid.

[35] William McMorran, 'Les Visiteurs and the Quixotic Text', *French Cultural Studies* 19 (2008), 159–72 (p. 164).

Harty's *The Reel Middle Ages*,[36] of which only a selection are discussed here, it becomes apparent that despite the many large and small alterations made to the template throughout its history on film, including the social identity of the time traveller and the story's satiric focus, the one factor that is consistent to all versions is that the origin of the time traveller is always contemporary America and the destination is always the Middle Ages, whether it is 528, as in Tay Garnett's 1949 musical comedy of the same name, or 1328, as in Gil Junger's looser 2001 adaptation, *Black Knight*.[37] The twentieth- and twenty-first-century provenance of these films means they are not chiefly motivated by Twain's intention to satirise nineteenth-century romantic medievalism; but they do on the whole reproduce the historical progressivism at the heart of the novel's comic scenario, in which the time traveller's contact with modernity gives him (or her, in the case of the 1998 version *A Knight in Camelot*, starring Whoopi Goldberg) a significant advantage over those encountered in the medieval past, who are still mired in ignorance or, worse, superstition perpetuated by the films' self-interested Merlin figures. In most cases the modern protagonists, despite being quite ordinary people, are granted high status as a result of their contact with amusingly quotidian scientific innovations. In Tay Garnett's 1949 version, Hank Martin (Bing Crosby) astonishes the people of Camelot with his use of a magnifying glass, matches, a paperclip and a magnet, the latter being a trope used repeatedly in medievalist comedies to signify modernity. His unflappable belief in these accessories, and in his own go-ahead ingenuity, keeps him cool even when facing the chopping block. In later versions such as *A Kid in King Arthur's Court* (1995) and *A Knight in Camelot*, a portable CD player, rollerblades and laptop computers all lead to their owners being regarded as powerful wizards by the amazed medieval innocents.

Another repeated trope that marks the superiority of modern America is music. Setting the blueprint, in the 1949 version Hank Martin introduces the court minstrels to Bing Crosby's own trademark big-band sound. Again, a long history of live performance is evoked – the minstrels play music that signifies as 'early' but sounds post-medieval – but unlike the archaeological figure of the modern-medieval jester, the modern musician is a figure of cultural supercession, who shocks and even revolutionises the Arthurian court.[38] This is reprised in *Black Knight*, when the African American time traveller Jamal Walker (Martin Lawrence) gets the court of King Leo to play

---

[36] Kevin J. Harty, *The Reel Middle Ages: American, Western and Eastern European, Middle Eastern and Asian Films about Medieval Europe* (Jefferson, NC: McFarland, 1999, repr. 2006), pp. 89–101.

[37] *A Connecticut Yankee in King Arthur's Court*, dir. Tay Garnett, (Paramount Pictures, 1949); *Black Knight*, dir. Gil Junger (20th Century Fox, 2001).

[38] For a book-length account of this phenomenon, see John Haines, *Music in Films on the Middle Ages: Authenticity vs. Fantasy* (New York and Oxon: Routledge, 2014).

and groove to Sly and the Family Stone's 'Dance to the Music' (a song also used the same year in the animated medievalist comedy, *Shrek*), and again in *A Kid in King Arthur's Court* when the teen protagonist Calvin Fuller (Thomas Ian Nicholas) scandalises the court by blasting hard rock through an improvised mead-horn sound system. The films add ideological advancement to technological progress in their modern protagonists' subscription to democratic rather than autocratic government, their attempts to save medieval women from arranged marriages, and their alienation from ultraviolence. While viewers today might note that the lasso Crosby's Hank prefers to lance and armour implicates him within a modern history of American colonial violence, in the film it is presented as a free-wheeling, efficient and non-violent alternative to the encumbering armour and deadly weapons of his medieval foe.

On the whole, as also noted by Finke and Shichtman, Tay Garnett's adaptation evades the satiric critique of nineteenth-century America implicit in much of Twain's novel.[39] Instead, the insouciant hero Hank, despite himself being a local blacksmith-turned-mechanic, is an unqualified subscriber to the American ideal of entrepreneurialism, which he extols in his opening song 'If You Stub Your Toe on the Moon'. It is difficult to spot any evidence that this film presents modernity as laughable in any way. Other versions, however, are more ambivalent. In what could well be a subtle riposte to Hank's 'Moon' song, Russ Mayberry's 1979 *Unidentified Flying Oddball*, produced in the developmental phase of space shuttle travel, takes a light-hearted swipe at the neo-colonialism of the NASA space programme by having an aeronautical engineer Tom Trimble and his android double (both played by Denis Dugan) land in Camelot as a result of a malfunctioning space mission. Despite the backfiring of a number of Tom's attempted technological interventions in the medieval scene, the film's modern techno-fetishism, featuring jet-packs and the like, ultimately prevails. *Black Knight* opens with the most pointed satire of modernity among all the versions, filtering contemporary America through the lens of the run-down simulacral theme park Medieval World, staffed by poorly paid African Americans living with few prospects in South Central LA. Its hero Jamal is one such employee, who ends up in England in 1328 after falling into the park's littered moat. Ultimately, however, after his return to the present, having gained self-esteem through his restoration of England's usurped queen, he is no longer aimless and arrested, but fully embraces modern entrepreneurialism, repeating his medieval feat by helping his employer Mrs Bostick improve Medieval World so that, as Finke and Shichtman's astute analysis observes, it can attract a 'mainstream' (that is, white) clientele.[40] So while modernity is ridiculed up to a point in these films,

---

39 Finke and Shichtman, *Cinematic Illuminations*, p. 42.
40 Ibid., p. 358.

their narratives eventually retreat into the quasi-satirical comedy of the 'superiority' variety,[41] in which modern values are in the final instance affirmed.

In two other time-travel comedies, Terry Gilliam's *Time Bandits* and Stephen Herek's *Bill & Ted's Excellent Adventure* (1989), the medieval period is only one of several destinations visited by the time traveller; but in both cases it occupies a privileged position. In *Time Bandits*, the hero Kevin's journey into the past is foreshadowed when, the night before his adventure begins, a knight on horseback bursts out of his wardrobe and gallops into a poster of a forest on his wall. The following night, moreover, the wardrobe disgorges a company of dwarves, another all-purpose, ambiguous metonym of the Middle Ages which, apart from embodying the idea of the medieval period as stunted vis-à-vis modernity, simultaneously caters to modern crypto-eugenicist views of the Middle Ages as less genetically 'perfected' and to ideas of medieval society as more tolerant of physical imperfection. The symbolic density of the dwarf figure is such that almost every comedy discussed in this chapter includes at least one. Through both of these tropes, the Middle Ages comes in this film to stand in for 'the past' itself. The medieval also takes on a paradoxical and manifold significance in *Bill and Ted's Excellent Adventure*, in which two high school friends (played by Alex Winter and Keanu Reeves) are gifted with a time machine from the future that allows them to collect people from the past for a history assignment in which they must report what three people from history would think of their home, San Dimas California in 1988. First of all, the friends make three separate visits to distinct medieval contexts: fifteenth-century England, Mongolia in 1209 and France in 1429, thus visiting this epoch more than any other. Conversely, when their time machine takes them forward to the year 2688, they discover that having passed their history assignment (thanks, paradoxically, to the time machine from the future), they are destined to become the revered ancestors of a utopian society seven hundred years into the future; that is, they have the proleptic experience of being the 'medieval' people of the future, an identity reinforced by their repeated alignment, as Lynne Lundquist observes, with oral rather than literate culture.[42] This ingenious, historically relativising plot device means that modernity, far from being the standard against which the past is measured, itself becomes subject to both the bemused appraisal of the past and the knowing judgement of the future. Archaeologically speaking, it is only a medial stratum in the film's playful cross-section of deep time.

Typically for the genre, the film's comedy arises chiefly out of cross-historical misunderstandings, and from the friends' failure to adjust their

---

[41]   Ibid.
[42]   Lynne Lundquist, 'Myth and Illiteracy: Bill and Ted's Explicated Adventures', *Extrapolation* 37 (1996), 212–23.

behaviour or West Coast idiom to suit their historical surrounds, addressing medieval dignitaries as 'royal ugly dudes'. A vital difference between this and the *Connecticut Yankee* films, though, is that the modern characters are more ignorant than their medieval forebears, their only advantage being that they are aware of the posthumous fame of those they are collecting. But as they set out to discover what the historical characters think of 1988 America, the two heroes also form their own opinions about the medieval past, and it is here that their modernity asserts itself through tropes that are remarkably consistent with their *Connecticut Yankee* counterparts. During their time in fifteenth-century England, they fall in love with two 'historical babes' whom they vow to rescue from arranged marriages, and are exposed to medieval ultraviolence, a trope which threatens to return during their kidnapping of Genghis Khan from 1209, and is hinted at in the sword Joan of Arc leaves behind when they collect her from 1429. As becomes apparent in the anarchic scene when the historical characters run amok in the San Dimas mall, it is this violent pre-modern energy that ultimately makes both of these characters unassimilable to modernity: Genghis Khan terrifies onlookers with his brutal beheading of a shop mannequin, while Joan's overzealous hijacking of an aerobics class leads to her arrest. The reassertion of Joan's medieval alterity in this scene is not, however, altogether flattering to modernity, for it suggests that if Joan were a modern woman her legendary passion and energy may well have been domesticated into feminine self-disciplinary regimes. But the notable, indeed conclusive, exceptions to this historical logic are the two historical babes, whose seamless integration into 1988 California (and into the boys' band, Wyld Stallyns) at the film's end suggests they are transferable across historical periods within a continuous narrative of heterosexual coupling. The apparent timelessness of their desires means they are neither objects of modernist ridicule nor ridiculers of modernity, and thus the film's satiric historical relativism is resolved into a sexual and musical universalism made over in the image of the present.

Another reverse time-travel comedy, in which medieval people are transported to the modern world, is Jean-Marie Poiré's *Les Visiteurs* (1993). In this film, the twelfth-century Count Godefroy de Montmirail (Jean Reno) and his squire Jacquouille le Fripouille (Christian Clavier) are mistakenly sent forward from 1123 to 1992, where Godefroy encounters his distant descendant Béatrice, who is a visual throwback to her ancestress, and Godefroy's beloved, Frénégonde. Like *Bill and Ted*, the plot of *Les Visiteurs* is based on a looped temporality, in which medieval characters in the modern present (which is the future of the Middle Ages) must paradoxically intervene in the medieval past in order to guarantee a chain of events that will lead to the present taking place as it does. In this case, Godefroy, having arrived in his own lands but in the late twentieth century (in this respect the film is more literally archaeological, showing the same terrain transformed by time), must get back to the moment in 1123 just before he mistakenly shot Frénégonde's father and hence lost her forever. The fact that the uncannily similar Béatrice exists and has his name reminds the audience that he must ultimately succeed.

The question of the film's comic attitude to the past has been a subject of debate among commentators. William McMorran observes that in the film's opening scene in 1123, Godefroy, King Louis le Gros and King Henry I together violate just about every article of chivalry imaginable, Henry through violence toward a woman, Louis through indulging in illicit sex and Godefroy through enabling Louis's behaviour.[43] Added to this comic deflation of the past is the grotesque portrayal of the displaced medievals. Guy Austin has noted the film's heavy emphasis on the revulsion directed at their excessive bodies, especially that of Jacquouille, whose testicular name and repeated association with excrement align him with the lower bodily stratum celebrated by Mikhail Bakhtin and Georges Bataille.[44] Much of the historical-incongruity comedy intrinsic to the genre is given a scatological inflection, as in the scene where Jacquouille drinks from Béatrice's toilet – a scene that situates the medieval as the abject other of both modern hygiene and technology. Godefroy, on the other hand, represents chivalric hypermasculinity in his unhesitating use of violence. Although this buffonic portrait of an amoral and corporeal Middle Ages can appear anti-medieval, scholars such as Anne Jäckel have discussed the possibility that the film is in fact mobilising a type of bawdy national humour, *l'esprit gaulois*, that Jäckel argues can be traced back to such 'ancestral' texts as the medieval fabliaux.[45] This argument is somewhat tenuous, given the number of medievalist tropes the film shares with numerous non-French (indeed non-European) texts, even though *Les Visiteurs* does take the level of grotesquery to greater depths than most. The broad cultural reach of the film's comic violence and scatology led to it being remade by Poiré for an Anglophone audience as the 2001 *Just Visiting*, set in Chicago.

Its hygienic conveniences notwithstanding, the modern world of *Les Visiteurs* is ridiculed more comprehensively than in any other form of this genre – and, arguably, more pointedly than are the Middle Ages. Modern France is presented as a diminished place dominated by convention and bourgeois complacency – qualities epitomised by Béatrice's unappealing husband, Jean-Pierre the dentist. Even with her atavistic noble features, Béatrice wears a bourgeois ensemble of polo shirt and dress-shorts that belies her noble origins. While, unlike the Los Angeles of *Black Knight*, modern France does boast the material remains of an *in situ* Middle Ages, this past has been thoroughly commodified and bourgeoisified. The conversion of Godefroy's

    43 McMorran, 'Les Visiteurs and the Quixotic Text', pp. 166–7.
    44 Guy Austin, 'Body Comedy and French Cinema: Notes on Les Visiteurs', *Studies in French Cinema* 6 (2006), 43–52 (p. 49).
    45 Anne Jäckel, 'Les Visiteurs: A Popular Form of Cinema for Europe?' in *European Identity in Cinema*, ed. Wendy Everett (Bristol: Intellect, 2005), pp. 41–9.

castle into a hotel run by Jaquouille's descendant, the aspirational Jacquard, has reduced it to a posher, heritage-culture version of *Black Knight*'s kitsch Medieval World. Stumbling into this sterile environment, the two medieval characters, for all their grotesquery, are symbolic of a lost world of passion and human vitality. Godefroy in particular becomes a compelling figure of nostalgic masculinity, in contrast to the ineffectual Jean-Pierre, such that Béatrice is on one occasion drawn to him in a non-ancestral way. Although it is essential to the plot that Godefroy return to medieval France in order to guarantee the modern present, we are left wondering whether this present, with its heritage hotels, Range Rovers and nice crockery, is the one that should have come to be. For this reason, *Les Visiteurs* is the most sustained of all the medievalist time-travel films in its satire of modern life. In its narrative details it is highly specific, but in the broad contours of its comedy and the ambivalence of its archaeological satire, it captures perfectly the hilarity yet also the symptomatic irresolution about the past and about the here-and-now that arise whenever the comic Middle Ages make their way into film.

IV

THAT'S EDUTAINMENT: COMEDY AND HISTORY

6

'The Past is a Different and Fairly Disgusting Country': The Middle Ages in Recent British 'Jocumentary'

THE PHRASE USED IN THE TITLE OF THIS CHAPTER is taken from the back cover blurb of *The Worst Jobs in History*, the book accompanying the 2004 Channel 4 television series of the same name hosted by the actor, presenter and face of popular history in Britain, Tony Robinson (also known as 'Baldrick' in the famous BBC comedy series *Blackadder*, and host of Channel 4's long-running popular archaeology programme *Time Team*). The phrase is not the invention of the book's publishers but is Robinson's own, also featuring on the book's opening page. It is of interest for several reasons. First, and most obviously, it announces the series' comic disposition toward the past; Robinson assumes that audiences will recognise its parodic deflation of L. P. Hartley's terminally overused phrase 'the past is another country' and thereby register from the outset the series' determination to distance itself from the nostalgia and reverence for the past that have (argu-ably wrongly) been attached to Hartley's aphorism.[1] Second, its introduction of the ironically modest modifier 'fairly disgusting' into the famous phrase is noteworthy not only because it forecasts the series' scatological preoccu-pation with the visceral and excremental dimensions of the past (a preoc-cupation also indicated in the promise that Tony will 'get to the bottom (quite literally)' of history), but also because it indicates that Robinson will be passing judgement on the past, exposing the reliance of past societies on the 'disgusting' exploitation of the poor and the vulnerable, whose meagre existence was eked out through humiliating, tedious, unsanitary and even dangerous occupations.

---

[1]   L. P. Hartley, *The Go-Between* (London: Hamish Hamilton, 1953), p. 9.

This chapter examines the representation of the medieval past, and in particular the 'British Middle Ages', in three television series: Robinson's *Worst Jobs in History*, *Medieval Lives*, the eight-part BBC series written and presented by *Monty Python* member-turned public historian Terry Jones, and *Horrible Histories*, the historical sketch-show screened on the BBC's children's channel, CBeebies, based on the hugely successful book series of the same name written by British author Terry Deary and illustrated by Martin Brown. The BBC series, which had just completed its fifth season at the time of writing, is part of a junior historical franchise of gargantuan proportions and viral proliferation: to date the book sales alone have topped twenty-five million books worldwide, of which over half have been in the UK, and the *Daily Telegraph* has described Deary as 'most influential historian in Britain today'.[2] Although he has been credited in a *Books Magazine* review with 'inventing a genre', in fact a number of famous precedents exist, most obviously W. C. Sellar and R. J. Yeatman's 1930 classic parodic history textbook *1066 and All That*, the format of which has clearly been borrowed by Deary and, by extension, the series.[3]

Robinson's and Jones's series, both first screened on free-to-air television to British audiences in 2004 (Robinson's went on to have two series, the second being screened in 2006), are linked by their shared investment in the benefits of combining historical content with comic treatment in an episodic documentary format combining audience address from the charismatic host, costumed re-enactment, expert interview and, in the case of *Medieval Lives*, comic graphics. *Horrible Histories*, which has been screening since 2009, shares this investment, but presents it in a live-action sketch-based format featuring scripted vignettes based on accounts from Deary's book series. Despite differences of format, these shows all fall within the category of 'edutainment'. This term is commonly invoked across a whole range of literatures, from pedagogic theory to analyses of contemporary popular culture, but tends to be frustratingly under-defined, possibly because of its breadth of application. Its clearest (though still rather general) definition is offered by educational theorists David Buckingham and Margaret Scanlon, who describe it as 'a hybrid mix of education and entertainment that relies heavily on visual material, on narrative or game-like formats, and on more informal, less didactic styles of address'.[4] Under this broader rubric, the three series to be discussed here can be clustered under the collective heading of 'historical jocumentary'. Unlike 'mockumentary' in which comedy is derived from the straight-faced application of documentary form to fictitious or outlandish

2   Alice Thomson, 'History As It Bloody Well Was', *Daily Telegraph*, 10 May 2007.

3   W. C. Sellar and R. J. Yeatman, *1066 and All That: A Memorable History of England* (New York: Barnes and Noble, 1993).

4   David Buckingham and Margaret Scanlon, 'Selling Learning: Towards a Political Economy of Edutainment Media', *Media, Culture & Society* 27 (2005), 41–58 (p. 46).

content, I coin the term 'jocumentary' here to characterise those forms which use comic technique while simultaneously appealing to the cultural weight accorded their historical content and, in the case of *Worst Jobs* and *Medieval Lives*, the pedagogic authority vested in television documentary as a genre. In 'packaging' historical content within comedic experience, they operate under the assumption that their content will be communicated more effectively, and to a wider audience.

This assumption is, of course, hardly new: the first-century *Rhetorica ad Herennium* urges the orator to use *imagines agentes* or agent images whose funny, grotesque and shocking nature will appeal to the listener's *affectus* thereby rendering them more eligible for recollection. The continuing influence of this paradigm throughout the Western development of pedagogic, dictaminal and advisory literature, as argued in Mary Carruthers' seminal studies of medieval memorial book culture,[5] is evident in such late medieval instructional literature as Christine de Pizan's 1405 manual for a twelve-year-old princess, *The Book of the Three Virtues*, which recommends that governesses gain not only their young charges' attention but also their moral compliance by leavening instruction with amusing anecdotes and laughter. These examples reflect the long-held conviction that laughter is doubly serviceable to the persuasive professions (rhetors and teachers) because it enhances attention and retention and forges an affective bond between pedagogue and pupil. Contemporary instructional books for teachers on using humour in the classroom continue unanimously to reaffirm virtually unchanged the equation of humour with cognitive retention and interpersonal bonding. By using comic techniques to 'bring the Middle Ages to life', a phrase which is repeated throughout the media reviews of both programmes, it would appear that these series not only draw on a long tradition but participate in a proliferating contemporary phenomenon of history commodified as entertainment. My examination of the ways these series represent the medieval past as edutainment will take into account their intersecting usage of a range of comic techniques, and their overt and oblique allusions to the history of comedy as well as to social histories. Through examining these questions, it will explore the ways in which, as forms of medievalism, these series invite a different treatment from other more avowedly fictive forms of comic medievalism, and the ways in which they address their 'responsibility' to the past as comic-pedagogic texts.

Medieval Lives, as its title avers, is dedicated specifically to examining the lives of peasants, monks, damsels, minstrels, knights, outlaws, kings and philosophers in this period, which Jones defines as falling between the Norman Conquest and the Tudor period. *Worst Jobs*, however, ranges from

---

　5　Mary Carruthers, *The Book of Memory: A Study of Memory in Medieval Culture* (Cambridge: Cambridge University Press, 2008).

Figure 3. Tony Robinson as a medieval purple maker, *The Worst Jobs in History*.

the Roman period through to the Victorian. Nevertheless, the medieval period, which spans the 'Dark' and 'Viking' ages as well as the later Middle Ages, holds a central position in Robinson's series. Apart from the fact that pre- and post-conquest England features in three instalments in the series, Robinson explains in numerous interviews and on the first page of the book's introduction that the series originated out of a conversation about the Middle Ages with the historian Dr Mike Jones,

> who described in lurid detail the Formula-One type backup team that kept a knight-in-armour operational. My favourite team-member was the Arming Squire, the lowest rung on the ladder, who had to sluice out the sweat, urine and excrement that had accumulated in his master's armour after a day in the saddle. It seemed like the worst job in the world to me, but Mike insisted – as in the famous Monty Python sketch – that 'he was lucky. There were many worse ways to earn a living in the Middle Ages.'[6]

The Middle Ages, then, becomes both the starting point and the benchmark for 'fairly disgusting' occupations. This notion returns later into the series and in the book (which essentially transcribes the commentary from the series) when, discussing the Saxon churl, Robinson says 'life itself was a worst job';[7] furthermore, when discussing our modern perception of Norman and feudal England, he says 'it's tempting to think of the entire 400 years as one long, grim Worst Job, with imagery supplied by Monty Python's Holy Grail'.[8] While he goes on to claim that this is something of

6   Tony Robinson and David Willcock, *The Worst Jobs in History: Two Thousand Years of Miserable Employment* (London: Pan, 2005), pp. 7–8.
7   Ibid., p. 19.
8   Ibid., p. 44.

an exaggeration, when asked in numerous interviews to nominate the worst job he encountered in the making of the series, he nominates the medieval fuller, claiming that the appalling tedium of treading woven wool for eight hours was only outstripped by the nauseating horror of doing so in a vat of 'meat-smelling' aged human urine. The medieval period, then, becomes both paradigmatic and synechdochic of the vile history Robinson wishes to expose to his audience.

Taking things even further, *Horrible Histories* ranges from the 'Savage Stone Age' across classical, medieval and modern periods up to WWII; nevertheless, a disproportionate bulk of Deary's volumes and the ensuing programme deal wholly or in part with the Middle Ages and, more specifically, with what Deary calls 'medieval British' history, as evinced by the sketches that fall into the categories *Smashing Saxons, Stormin' Normans, Vicious Vikings, Cruel Kings and Mean Queens, Dark Knights and Dingy Castles* and, more broadly, *The Measly Middle Ages*. That the Middle Ages is a synecdoche of the past is expressed in the series' theme music, the rapid-fire punk/ska patter of which ends abruptly in a deep monastic chant intoning the words 'HOR-RIBLE HIS-TOR-IES'. Within the series' dominant medievalism, the Anglo-Saxon period has a particular significance, as it becomes both the template for the representation of grotesque 'pastness', and, as will be discussed later, its rupture by the Norman invasion makes it the historical switch-point at which Deary's concept of 'the modern' is ushered in.

Over the past few years there has been a flourishing of scholarship focused on the televisual representation of history, particularly in the context of Britain. Essay collections edited by Erin Bell and Ann Gray (2010 and 2012), Helen Wheatley (2007), David Cannadine (2004), Gary R. Edgerton and Peter C. Rollins (2001) and Graham Roberts and Philip M Taylor (2001), as well as a dedicated issue of the *European Journal of Cultural Studies* (2007),[9] have all examined what Gray calls the 'production ecology' in British televisual culture that led to what all agree has been an 'exponential' rise of historical programming on British television since the mid-1990s.[10] This scholarship engages closely with a range of questions pertinent to this chapter, such as

---

[9]   See Erin Bell and Ann Gray's edited collections *Televising History: Mediating the Past in Postwar Europe* (Houndmills, Basingstoke: Palgrave Macmillan, 2010) and *History on Television* (London: Routledge, 2012), Helen Wheatley, ed., *Re-Viewing Television History: Critical Issues in Television Historiography* (London: I. B. Tauris, 2007), David Cannadine, *History and the Media* (Houndmills, Basingstoke: Palgrave Macmillan, 2004), Gary R. Edgerton and Peter C. Rollins, eds, *Television Histories: Shaping Collective Memory in the Media Age* (Lexington, KY: University Press of Kentucky, 2001) and Graham Roberts and Philip M Taylor, eds, *The Historian, Television, and Television History* (Luton: University of Luton Press, 2001), as well as the special issue of the *European Journal of Cultural Studies* 10.1 (2007).

[10]   Ann Gray, 'Contexts of Production: Commissioning History', in Bell and Gray, *Televising History*, pp. 59–76 (p. 62).

the competing demands of professional and public forms of history, and the ways in which the pressures of the televisual medium shapes the genre of history TV, including the selection of hosts, settings, scripts and so on; but almost no attention has been paid to the comic iterations of this genre, or why, a decade after the 'history boom' on British TV began, it had begun to parody itself. Jerome de Groot's wide-ranging 2009 study *Consuming History* comes closest, examining the commodification of history within the context of Britain's popularised heritage culture, including such edutainment forms as docudrama, re-enactment series, historical cinema and children's historical television, but still he does not dwell on jocumentary. Meanwhile, research into medievalism on television has so far tended to deal primarily with fictional genres, with the exception of Angela Weisl's account of reality television. Interestingly, Weisl explores the opposite end of the affective spectrum from laughter, identifying a formulaic 'medievalizing rhetoric' in the public weeping of the reality show contestant. Furthermore, rather than identifying a deliberate evocation of the medieval that would be comparable to the jocumentary form, she points instead to reality TV's performative engagement with a residual medieval 'economy of sentiment'.[11]

If little has been said about comedy in medievalist historical television, an equal silence prevails over the intersection of the comic with the practices of historiography. The notion of 'history in the comic mode' as an academic practice most famously formulated by Caroline Walker Bynum in her influential 1991 study of medieval corporeality and incarnation theology, *Fragmentation and Redemption*, and has, in medieval studies, more recently been reanimated in the 2007 essay collection dedicated to Bynum *History in the Comic Mode* edited by Rachel Fulton and Bruce Holsinger. Bynum's notion of the comic does not engage centrally with register, or the solicitation of laughter or amusement, drawing rather on notions of the comic as a literary genre: she says that her call for comic history 'is ... not so much a plea for treating history with a sense of humor (although it is that) as a suggestion that the human condition requires us, as historians and as human beings, to accept limitation, artifice, compromise and paradox in telling the story of the past'.[12] She goes on:

> A comic stance toward doing history is aware of contrivance, of risk. It always admits that we may be wrong. A comic stance knows that ... doing history is, for the historian, telling a story that could be told in another way. For this reason, a comic stance welcomes voices hith-

---

[11]   Angela Weisl, 'Confession, Contrition, and the Rhetoric of Tears: Medievalism and Reality Television', in *Medieval Afterlives in Popular Culture*, ed. Gail Ashton and Daniel T. Kline (New York: Palgrave Macmillan, 2012), pp.129–43 (p. 130).

[12]   Caroline Walker Bynum, *Fragmentation and Redemption: Essays on Gender and the Human Body in Medieval Religion* (New York: Zone Books, 1992), pp. 304–5, n. 24.

ertofore left outside, not to absorb them or mute them but to allow them to object and contradict. Its goal is the pluralistic, not the total. It embraces the partial as partial.[13]

This appeal to a 'comic' idea of historical narration as reflexive about limitation and tolerant of multi-perspectival approaches would appear to be further strengthened in the scholarship that is beginning to emerge which examines the representation of history in comic screen genres. While much has been written about historical cinema in general, and medievalist cinema in particular, little has been said to date about the specific role of comic representation in conveying visions of pre-modernity. What has been argued, however, in Hannu Salmi's 2011 volume *Historical Comedy on Screen*, rests somewhat uncritically on assumptions about the subversive potential of comic representations of history. In her chapter in Salmi's volume, 'Comedy and Counter-History', Marcia Landy, a well-known film historian and theorist of historical cinema, argues that 'popular film and television through the lens of parody, farce, and satire are instrumental in offering a view of the past that runs counter to official historicizing'.[14] While she does not say so explicitly, the assumption behind this – an assumption that appears regularly in one strain of scholarship on comedy, humour and laughter – is that comedy is an effective instrument for speaking truth to power, and that eliciting laughter lands a blow against authority.[15] The key examples Landy uses in this chapter are, as mentioned in the previous chapter, Mario Monicelli's comic depictions of the Crusades in his two *Brancaleone* films, which deploy farce to satiric ends, with the effect, she contends, that 'The world of the Middle Ages has been portrayed from a bottom up view of historical events, pitting the threadbare rogues against more powerful forces.'[16] This suggests that the use of comic performative and cinematic approaches can collude with the comic historiographic approach described by Bynum.

How compatible are these claims with what we find in the three series under examination here? Do they too subscribe to the belief that comic method can service multi-perspectival history? Of the two hosts, Tony Robinson is more comfortable with adopting the social historian's idea that what is being offered is a counter-perspective of history that brings to

[13]   Ibid., p. 25.

[14]   Marcia Landy, 'Comedy and Counter-History', in *Historical Comedy on Screen*, ed. Hannu Salmi (Bristol: Intellect Press Ltd, 2011), pp. 177–98 (p. 177).

[15]   Among the large number of humour theorists who take this view, see Christie Davies, *Jokes and their Relation to Society* (Berlin: Mouton de Gruyter, 1998), Egon Larsen, *Wit as a Weapon: The Political Joke in History* (London: F. Muller, 1980). Hans Speier, 'Wit and Politics: An Essay on Power and Laughter', *American Journal of Sociology* 103, 5 (1998), and Marjolein C. 't Hart and Dennis Bos, *Humour and Social Protest* (Cambridge and New York: Press Syndicate of the University of Cambridge, 2007).

[16]   Landy, 'Comedy and Counter-History', p. 183.

light the everyday existence of 'the vast majority' and 'the unseen army' of labourers, whose lives have been eclipsed by the prominence of 'kings and queens, generals, prime ministers' in the historical narratives he learned as a school child. Although Robinson implies, in a trope common to him, Jones and Deary, that this 'upper-class' institutionally disseminated history operates to censor much of the past, he does not deny that the narrative of the victorious, wealthy and powerful should exist; rather, he argues, in a gesture very familiar to those who have dealt with history in the wake of Marxism, feminism, queer studies and postcolonialism, that this dominant narrative is only partial, and needs to be supplemented by other partial histories, other fragments that can be patched together to produce a necessarily disunified but more complete picture of the past.

Jones, however, does not fit as neatly as Robinson into the mould of 'comic history' as outlined by Bynum. From his direct address and the voice-over text in his programmes, it becomes apparent that despite his use of comic techniques, he is not interested in acknowledging either hermeneutic limitation or ideological pluralism in the narrating of 'true' history. Rather, he is overt in offering *Medieval Lives* not as a supplement but rather as a corrective to dishonest or censored history. As he states repeatedly in interviews, his programme is motivated by his objection to what he perceives as contemporary culture's misplaced preference for the Renaissance as the age of rationality qua medieval superstition, and of capitalist liberty qua feudal subjection – in short, as the 'early modern'. Robinson does issue correctives on a smaller scale, as for instance when he describes the myth of horned Vikings as the 'invention of cartoonists and hen-night male strippers',[17] itself an amusing parody of medievalists' usual tendency to blame nineteenth-century romanticism and Wagnerian opera for this misconception; but Jones is more comprehensive and more serious in his argument that people today have been misled about the truth of the Middle Ages. When Jones attributes these distortions to 'an unholy alliance of nineteenth-century novelists and painters with twentieth-century movie-makers',[18] it is hard to know whether he is being tongue-in-cheek or contrite about his own former participation in this myth-making, especially since, as will be discussed later, he alludes to and even actively reprises some of his Pythonesque roles in the series. Despite this, however, he is emphatic throughout the series that his audience has been deceived about the realities of medieval people's lives, which were not only more complex but 'more entertaining' than they realise (DVD jacket). For instance, the series' first episode, 'The Peasant', is devoted to demonstrating that the conventional story of the enslavement of the villein under feudalism is greatly exaggerated, and that they were in some ways

---

17 Robinson and Willcock, *The Worst Jobs in History*, p. 35.
18 Terry Jones, *Terry Jones' Medieval Lives* (London: BBC Books, 2005), p. 13.

better off than the worker under late capitalism. Indeed, it is difficult not to note the similarity of his argument to Thomas Carlyle's famously paternalistic argument in Book III of *Past and Present* (1843) that the medieval peasant 'lacks not his due parings of the pigs he tends', and hence was better off than the atomised labourers of contemporary England.[19] It is intriguing that when he cites the mythology of the abused villein, Jones as presenter says, somewhat pointedly, 'It must have been the worst job in history'. Robinson's series was not to appear on British television until eight months after Jones's, but Jones may have been aware it was forthcoming, and appears to be making a pre-emptive strike against Robinson's case about the onerous lot of medieval rural labourers.

Horrible Histories' famous catchphrase 'History with the nasty bits left in' clearly announces its intention to expose the conspiracy of 'niceness' that has led to the dissemination of ideologically cleaned-up and puritanically unfunny 'official' history, while its determination to offer a corrected version is advertised in its closing theme lyrics: 'gory, ghastly, mean and cruel, / Stuff they don't teach you at school'. That the Middle Ages are, of all periods, the greatest casualty of official misprision is suggested in the musical sketch 'It's Not True' (Season One), in which a teacher telling an Arthurian tale to her students is arrested for 'disseminating falsehoods to young children'. While popular myths about other periods are mentioned, the song is dominated by medieval examples: 'Galahad? No such lad / Lancelot? Lance-not / Guinevere? Dear, oh dear! ... Viking hat? No horn on that / King Alfred's cake? Big mistake / It never fried? The old books lied', and so on. Similarly, the syrupy mock-power-ballad 'Richard III' (Season Four) features an ingratiating Richard refuting the 'Tudor propaganda' about his reign, working through a long list of misconceptions while holding up and discarding handwritten placards in a parody of Bob Dylan's famous film clip to *Subterranean Homesick Blues*. This approach continues in televisual form what Deary originally formulated as his rogue pedagogy. He repeatedly opens his books with an anti-teacher topos that directly addresses his 6–12-year-old audience, and which is vital to interpellating them into his historical project. A self-described 'alternative education advocate', he frequently recounts how the rote-learning approach of his own childhood history lessons put him off the subject, and how his series is an attempt to restore to children both a primal fascination with history and (somewhat more disingenuously) the power to shape for themselves how they learn about the past. Although education scholar Margaret Scanlon, reading *Horrible Histories* as carnivalesque and anti-authoritarian, argues 'Deary makes it clear that *Horrible Histories* is *his* version of history', she is compelled to add the telling caveat 'albeit one which

---

[19] Thomas Carlyle, *Past and Present*, intro. Ralph Waldo Emerson (Boston: Little, Brown, 1843), p. 211.

he occasionally refers to as the truth'.[20] In the television version, numerous sketches are followed by commentary in which Deary's proxy Rattus Rattus, a puppet rat, assures viewers what they have just seen was '100% accu-rat'. The persistent assertion of corrective factuality in *Horrible Histories* is important to register because it reflects the extent to which this text, like Jones's *Medieval Lives*, is in fact using discursive strategies that make clear truth claims about its content which, as I will later discuss, both work with and strain against its use of comic technique.

Despite this difference between the programmes, what they do share is the conviction that the use of comedy is instrumental to producing historical narratives that will appeal to general audiences. The motif that is used most often is that of 'bringing history to life' for viewers; a motif which is literalised in all three programmes via a range of live action performance techniques. In Robinson's case, this involves re-enacting the lives of medieval workers, mostly in costume, all the while offering arresting and revolting facts (such as the use of dung as a bonding agent in Saxon wattle and daub walls) to amuse and to capture viewers' imaginations, while Jones brings history 'to life' via narration to camera while in costume, some re-enactment and the use of animated medieval illuminations, sometimes with Jones inserted into them as a character. *Horrible Histories'* approach to relating the past is through live action vignettes of a violent and/or scatological nature, with a focus on the 'everyday humanity' of medieval people. In spite of Jones's and Robinson's somewhat ironic (for viewers) scepticism about the medievalist distortions perpetuated by popular media, they both agree with Deary that history as it is received in institutional settings such as schools is duller than it should be; for both presenters, the ideological conspiracy to censor history is buttressed by a dry and conservative pedagogic approach that deters the historians of the future. Jones recalls 'I thought history lessons were going to be really interesting, and all about horror and heroism and ambition and cunningness and despair, but all I learned was this bunch of dates',[21] while Robinson's accounts of his truncated school career repeatedly emphasise his disengagement with the teaching he experienced while there.[22] Print media reporters have on the one hand colluded with this view of school history, suggesting that comic television history is superior both because of its engaging technique – 'Robinson is like the history teacher you never had at high school'[23] – and because of its apparently anti-elitist audience reach: 'with *Medieval Lives* [Jones] is destined to reach millions of people rather than addressing a few

---

[20] Margaret Scanlon, 'History Beyond the Academy: Humor and Horror in Children's History Books', *New Review of Children's Literature and Librarianship* 16 (2011), 69–91 (p. 76).

[21] *The Scotsman*, 17 November 2000.

[22] *The Guardian*, 13 September 2005.

[23] *Illawarra Mercury*, 21 May 2011.

dozen in a lecture theatre'.[24] Elsewhere, however, critical media responses to Jones's style have likened him to a school master who assumes 'we all suffer from Attention Deficit Disorder and may start carving our initials on the desks if we aren't given regular doses of jocularity – television's equivalent of Ritalin,'[25] and who 'worr[ies] about keeping the attention of the rowdier elements at the back of the class'.[26] So the discursive communities at whom the series are aimed are not entirely unanimous as to the success of historical edutainment as a genre.

Bynum says, further, of history in the comic mode: 'in such historical writing as in the best comedy, the author is also a character. Authorial asides and authorial musings are therefore welcome ... [as] part of, not a substitute for, doing history'.[27] In this respect, both Robinson's and Jones's programmes do engage in comic history, not just because of their hosts' physical insertion of themselves into the past via costumes and re-enactment, but also because the personae they have developed throughout their respective oeuvres are crucial to the particular kinds of authority they seek for their programmes. Both, first of all, are known and loved for their former roles as medieval characters, with Robinson in particular being identified with his long-running turn as the dogsbody Baldrick in *Blackadder*, which has made him metonymic of a comic view of the pre-modern. The vast majority of reviews of, and interviews on, this programme remind us of Robinson's time on *Blackadder*, even to the extent of just referring to him as 'Baldrick'. Many of the reviewers of *Medieval Lives* also disclose the long shadow cast by Jones's former Python roles, sometimes even weaving some of his best-known lines into their commentaries. Additionally, both presenters are known for their former hosting of historical television: Jones for a number of documentaries, including his *Complete and Utter History of Britain* (1969),[28] and the ambivalently received *Crusades* series of 1995; and Robinson for his hosting since 1994 of the Channel 4 pop-archaeology programme *Time Team*. With these hybrid personae, both openly present themselves in interviews and in their writings as autodidacts who have been brought to a love of history after and in spite of any formal education received. In Robinson's case, this has consolidated him, as de Groot rightly points out,[29] as the public face of autodidactic enthusiasm: on *Time Team*, as on *Worst Jobs*, he performs the role of unschooled audience proxy, asking the academic experts the naïve 'so what?'

[24] *Liverpool Daily Post*, 29 January 2004.
[25] *The Independent*, 10 February 2004.
[26] *The Times*, 20 May 2006.
[27] Bynum, *Fragmentation and Redemption*, p. 25.
[28] *The Complete and Utter History of Britain*, created by Terry Jones and Michael Palin (London Weekend Television, 12 January–16 February 1969).
[29] Jerome De Groot, *Consuming History: Historians and Heritage in Contemporary Popular Culture* (London: Routledge, 2009), p. 22.

questions that force them to democratise their knowledge for him and for the viewers. In the introduction to the *Worst Jobs* book, he distinguishes his approach from that of academic social history and admits he chooses 'colour and imagination' over displays of laborious research. Jones's relationship to his autodidacticism is more complex and ambivalent. On some occasions he insists that his research into the Middle Ages, such as his book on Chaucer's Knight and his recent speculative study *Who Murdered Chaucer?*, has been self-directed and 'iconoclastic', challenging academic orthodoxies and occlusions; he also disavows the title of historian, arguing that his interest is in similarities between the past and the present, rather than differences, which is the province of the historian. Yet on other occasions, such as his critique in Episode 1 of Froissart's account of the peasant uprising, he overtly aligns himself with 'professional historians'.[30] This ambivalence is echoed in his presentational style on *Medieval Lives*, which is wacky and donnish by turns. Furthermore, by jokingly describing his own comic medievalism as 'history with the boring bits put back' he craftily elevates himself above the juvenile populism of *Horrible Histories*, with its 'nasty bits left in'. Jones's implication here is that his combination of comic flair and erudition allow him to reinsert the 'boring bits' without losing audiences. Despite these differences, Jones and Robinson can both be inserted into a longer narrative of medieval studies' disciplinary development, in which the enthusiast has performed a vital public service adjacent to that of the universities. Jones's narrative of at first being reviled by the academy, then grudgingly tolerated, then embraced to the extent that he co-wrote *Who Murdered Chaucer?* with a number of eminent medievalists, puts us in mind of such famous amateur medievalists as F. J. Furnivall, whose editing of medieval texts, the *OED*, foundation of the early English Text Society, and leadership of the Philological Society are now regarded as invaluable, if imperfect, contributions to modern Anglophone study of the Middle Ages.

Despite their proudly amateur rejection of institutionally disseminated history, both have also, along with Deary, engaged vocally in the educational debates that have been raging in the UK over the past decade around the national curriculum and the reported drop in student interest in history, with Jones proclaiming to the *Liverpool Daily Post* 'I think history is really important and it's outrageous that it's not part of the national syllabus after

---

[30] Jones, *Terry Jones' Medieval Lives*, p. 17. Jones's alignment with the academy has recently been consolidated by the *Festschrift* dedicated to him, *The Medieval Python: The Purposive and Provocative Works of Terry Jones*, ed. R. F. Yeager and Toshiyuki Takamiya (Houndmills, Basingstoke: Palgrave Macmillan, 2012). It is noteworthy, however, that some of the 'professional historians' in this volume take polite issue with his views. See, for instance, Nigel Saul's rebuttal of Jones's 'provocative revisionism' in the chapter 'Terry Jones's Richard II', pp. 39–54 (p. 52).

the age of 14 any more',[31] while Robinson claims to *The Daily Telegraph* that 'Politicians … have been downplaying the importance of history as a subject in our schools but, if they had bothered to have a better grasp of history themselves, they might have avoided costly wars.'[32] Deary is clinched in a more complex dance with the British school system. On the one hand he rejects what he sees as the regimented, one-way institutional dispensing of facts stripped of their relevance, refusing categorically to do any school visits. He openly disavows any academic credentials, attributing the success of the franchise to the fact that he is not a historian but an entertainer by training.[33] On the other hand, he is not only aware that his texts are repeatedly cited within debates in the UK about the 'demise of history' as a secondary school subject, but to some degree inserts himself into these debates. His contributions are, it must be said, somewhat confused: for all his rejection of school history teaching (which he sometimes attributes to teachers and sometimes to a politicised national curriculum that favours testing over learning), Deary is not as jubilant as expected about the subject failing to attract upper secondary candidates. He both yearns for a world without schools and yearns for schools with good history lessons. He and his franchise also feature ambiguously within this and other debates. In 2009 there was a major public conversation on how to repackage history to lure back the presentist, distractable, mediatised tweens and teens of today, especially the 'lost boys' of history classes, with their love of interactive learning and gross-out humour. In this discussion Deary was cast as both victorious rival and salutary path-breaker from whom teachers can learn: 'It's not hard to see why schoolchildren prefer *Horrible Histories* to the National Curriculum. Terry Deary's mischievous mix of humour, sadistic statistics and corny jokes, padded out by Martin Brown's wry comic cartoons, has proved irresistible bedtime reading for millions' (*The Evening Standard*). Like Deary, Robinson and Jones view their comic historical approaches as attempts to reverse what they see as a national disregard for 'bringing history to life'. What is less clear is their understanding of whether their series are supplementing school-taught history, wooing people back to serious study via their entertaining introductions to the past, or supplanting academic pursuits by participating in the new mediatised sphere of popular history and antiquarianism.

Taking into account the discursive strategies discussed above, television is in fact the ideal medium for these programmes. Their 'conspiratorial' nature, in which the audience is interpellated, even recruited, into the mission of exposing the hidden truths of history, is well served by the intimacy of the

---

[31]   *Liverpool Daily Post*, 29 January 2004.
[32]   *The Daily Telegraph*, 28 April 2012.
[33]   Terry Deary, 'Horrible History Teaching', *BBC History Magazine*, October 2009 http://www.historyextra.com/feature/horrible-history-teaching (accessed 9 April 2013).

medium, which comes right into viewers' homes to let them in on the secret. From an industrial perspective, these programmes' free-to-air access (as opposed to paying to see them at the cinema) also bolsters their claim to be releasing hitherto hidden information. The role of the television in daily life also makes it a particularly appropriate medium for programmes that claim to be myth-busting by exposing the material realities of everyday life for people in the past. *Worst Jobs*' and *Medieval Lives*' regular use of medium-close up shots of the host addressing the camera or an expert of some kind, as well as reaction shots in which we see the host react with amusement and surprise to what he is learning, borrow from the distinctive shooting toolbox of the sitcom as described by television scholar Brett Mills. This 'reaction cross-shot' structure is described by Mills[34] as an editing technique that increases the humorous potential of a scene, as we see the weirdness of the content reinforced by the amused/bemused/amazed reaction of the character receiving the information. This use of sitcom technique is then fused with these series' parodic replaying of the historical documentary method, including the pithy scripts, handsome scenery, walk-into-shot segues and direct address used by other British celebrity historians such as Simon Schama and David Starkey, which reflects the ambivalence of Jones's and Robinson's relationship to even the televisual version of so-called 'official' history.[35] These programmes' use of parody is closer to that formulated by Linda Hutcheon in *A Theory of Parody*, that is, 'a form of repetition with ironic critical distance, marking difference rather than similarity'.[36] According to Hutcheon, parody allows the parodist

> to speak the language of the dominant (which allows you to be heard) but then to subvert it through ironic strategies of exaggeration, understatement or literalization. Parody is the mode that allows you to mimic that speech, but to do so through recontextualizing it and therefore without subscribing to its implied ideals and value.[37]

By mixing parodic documentary method with features from entertainment genres such as sketch comedy in *Horrible Histories*, pantomime and cartoon in the case of *Medieval Lives* and in *Worst Jobs*, techniques taken from what de Groot calls the 'postdocumentary' Reality History participatory re-enactment genre,[38] these programmes are able to partake of the authority of documentary at the same time as engaging the 'lower' pleasures of laughter

---

[34] Brett Mills, *Television Sitcom* (London: BFI, 2005), p. 39.

[35] *A History of Britain*, written and presented by Simon Schama (BBC One, 2000–2); and, *Monarchy*, presented by David Starkey (Channel 4, 2004–6).

[36] Linda Hutcheon, *A Theory of Parody: The Teachings of Twentieth-Century Art Forms* (Urbana: University of Illinois Press, 2000), pp. xii, 37.

[37] Kathleen O'Grady, 'Theorizing – Feminism and Postmodernism: A Conversation with Linda Hutcheon', *Rampike* 9.2 (1998), 20–2 (p. 22).

[38] De Groot, *Consuming History*, p. 177.

and amusement. As such their disposition toward the documentary genre might be described as ironic, in the sense described by Geoffrey Hartman, who argues that ironic utterance is 'language giving the lie to itself while relishing its power'.[39] When offered 'straight', the programmes lean heavily on zany, grotesque or titillating factoids taken from the medieval period to generate comic historical interest.

These programmes use this sophisticated generic hybrid to offer histories with clear ideological investments. Of these, the most conspicuous is the production of an English national history. All three series focus most concertedly on the 'British' Middle Ages (i.e. mostly English but occasionally using Welsh and Scottish examples) as an origin and analogue to the modern, although in some episodes Jones also makes brief references to continental examples. In interviews, the most-cited premise behind Jones's and Robinson's series' focus on British history is that it will 'tell us who we are' (the identity of the 'we' here is unclear, but presumably the British viewing public). This shared premise, however, takes the two in very different directions, deploying diverse models of power and class relations to describe this national past. As a result of his interest in labour history, Robinson's ideological vision of the medieval past cleaves to a Marxist historical materialist model, leading him to produce a history in which economic and material necessity was the key shaping force of people's lives. It is this materialist approach that allows Robinson to indulge his, and our, fascination with the risky, arduous, painful, visceral and excremental details of earlier British lives. Jones's series is more invested in a mixed culturalist-individualist version of the medieval past in which power is played out locally and in a more fluid, sophisticated and even opportunistic way, influenced by, as well as at times resistant to, complex cultural as well as economic factors, even under the apparently rigid structural hierarchies of feudalism. For instance, while Robinson's portrait of monastic life focuses sympathetically on the hardscrabble life of the early Celtic monks of Lindisfarne, Jones's account takes a more secularist, even anticlerical stance, pointing to monastic power and to medieval monks' economic, cultural and indeed sexual engagement with the temporal world. (*Horrible Histories*' 'Funky Monks' sketch in Season Two takes a middle path between these, presenting the discipline and privation of monastic life, yet also suggesting through its soul-singing brothers that many monks continued to enjoy clandestine pleasures.) The respective national audiences hailed in the two presenter-based series stand to 'know themselves' very differently from the historical exempla placed before them. Robinson's series portrays British workers historically as a hardworking, resilient and modest people who nevertheless, be they medieval peasants or Victorian match girls, stood

---

[39] Geoffrey Hartman, *Saving the Text: Literature/Derrida/Philosophy* (Baltimore, MD: Johns Hopkins University Press, 1981), p. 146.

up against exploitation when necessary. Jones's series, conversely, for all its greater display of erudition, offers a liberal humanist portrait of medieval people who, despite their different circumstances and worldview, were much like modern people: self-interested, secular, aspirational, amoral but resourceful. According to Stephen Wagg, a similar liberal humanism was already visible in the early Pythons' emphasis on silliness, which took the form of a scattergun anti-authoritarian social satire that stopped short of targeted political critique.[40] Except for the episode on women, 'The Damsel', which is incidentally also the most concerned with corporeal life, the implicit sympathy suffusing Robinson's account is not as conspicuous here.

Horrible Histories' comic depictions of medieval life mobilise a Marxian rejection of privilege which, while occasionally opening out to the continental Middle Ages, is most pointedly deployed in its sympathetic representation of the geo-political fortunes of the Saxons in the wake of the Norman invasion. The number of times the date 1066 appears in interviews with Deary reveals his preoccupation with it as a national, and indeed a global, watershed, and explains why the 'British' Middle Ages, especially a broadly defined Anglo-Saxon period, features so prominently in both the literary and televisual arms of his franchise. In its treatment of the conquest and its aftermath, the franchise reanimates for his young audiences the romantic nationalistic notion of the 'Norman Yoke', which argued that the brutal totalitarian nature of Norman rule, in particular its imposition of continental feudalism over the 'native' free institutions of Saxon England, led to the demise of Anglo-Saxon society. The sketches purvey many of the most recognisable tropes of the Norman Yoke thesis, including the imposition of feudalism ('Normanopoly', Season Four), the proto-panopticism of the Domesday book ('Domesday door-knock' sketch, Season One), as well as Scottian tropes of cruel yet effete Normans ('Historical desktops: King John', Season Four). In interview, Deary not only confirms his Norman Yoke perspective, but, moreover, nominates the post-conquest period as the crucible of modernity: 'The Normans is a huge period that is ignored, but it is one of the most significant parts for today's life. They destroyed a Saxon culture. That's important to learn about; 950 years after the conquest we are still burdened by their feudalism.'[41] From interviews it becomes evident that Deary's representation of Anglo-Saxon history is motivated additionally by a Northern regionalist agenda. Deary's scepticism of the dominance of contemporary southern English metropolitan culture, which he sees as resulting from the Norman invasion, stems from his persona as a proud Northerner looking to stimulate his local economy by

[40] Stephen Wagg, 'You've Never Had It So Silly: The Politics of British Satirical Comedy From *Beyond the Fringe* to *Spitting Image*', in *Come on Down? Popular Media Culture in Post-War Britain*, ed. Dominic Strinati and Stephan Wagg (London: Routledge, 1992), pp. 254–84 (pp. 268–75).

[41] Damian Whitworth, 'Is History So Horrible?' Education, *The Times*, 15 May 2009.

locating the proposed *Horrible Histories* Theme Park in County Durham. His regionalist politics are clearly evident in the attention given to The Harrying of the North (in the book *Stormin' Normans*, and revisited in the sketch 'Normanopoly'). His account of the depredations of the invaders and the doomed resistance of the locals discloses his sense of the North as a distinct culture in need of release from a prolonged decline that is a direct legacy of Norman oppression.

From the comic methods used in these series, it becomes apparent that the preoccupation with national histories is strongly reinforced by the use of methods that pay homage to comic lineages which are identified by comedy scholar Andy Medhurst as specifically English, but which could more accurately be described as British given that they were directed at UK audiences beyond England.[42] When narrating *Worst Jobs*, Robinson does make several references to *Monty Python and the Holy Grail*, speaking of its influence on today's popular impression of a grotesque Middle Ages, but its allusion to British comic history is overwhelmingly via its physical evocation, in Robinson's distinctive physiognomy, of his iconic career as Baldrick, a character aligned simultaneously with the Middle Ages but also with the simian stage of human evolution. The visual motifs most commonly associated with Baldrick in all four *Blackadder* series are turnips and rats, which also become metonymic of his continued connection to pre-modernity. Each time Robinson subjects himself to some degrading or repellent medieval ordeal, such as being sucked by leeches, dagging a sheep or drinking worm stew, it recalls the eternally medieval Baldrick's many trials and humiliations. The *Blackadder* allusion also buttresses *Worst Jobs'* rejection of social inequity.

Blackadder's satire of the medieval institution of monarchy was in part a response to the renewed interest in royal succession in the early 1980s because of the marriage of Prince Charles to Lady Diana Spencer in 1981, and the birth of their heir Prince William in 1982.[43] Anti-monarchists in Britain were horrified by the 'royal fever' that accompanied these events. The programme that channelled anti-monarchism most conspicuously in Britain was the satirical puppet show *Spitting Image*, which ran from 1984 to 1996, and on which Richard Curtis and Ben Elton, an outspoken critic of the Royal Family, were both writers at the same time as they were developing the scripts for *Blackadder* 1 and 2; *Blackadder* can, I argue, be seen as another, historicised, instance of this anti-monarchist satire. The stupidity, arrogance and undeserved privilege of royalty are running themes in the first three series of *Blackadder*, but in the first series this is particularly pointed by

---

[42] Andy Medhurst, *A National Joke: Popular Comedy and English Cultural Identities* (New York: Routledge, 2007).

[43] *Blackadder*, written by Rowan Atkinson, Richard Curtis and Ben Elton, produced by John Lloyd (BBC1, 1983–9).

having Edmund, the Black Adder, as an actual member of the royal family. Series One's lampooning of hereditary rule also engages with the outcry on the British left at the steady rejuvenation of the role of the House of Lords in British politics since the election of Margaret Thatcher's Tory government in 1979. This conferral of unelected parliamentary power was vigorously rejected as 'undemocratic' by the Labour opposition, who vowed that they would abolish the Upper House on their return to power.[44] Through the double allusion to *Monty Python and the Holy Grail* and *Blackadder*, *Worst Jobs* alludes to a larger twentieth-century British tradition of historical black comedy ranging from Sellar and Yeatman's *1066 and All That* (1930) to the present. First coined by André Breton, who described it in his *Anthology of Black Humor* as 'the mortal enemy of sentimentality',[45] black comedy's solicitation of laughter through an irreverent focus on the existential absurdity of death, violence, disease and cruelty, is a particularly apt vehicle for Robinson's comic treatment of the hardships of medieval workers. The fact that Breton nominates Swift's mordant 1739 satire *A Modest Proposal* as one of the *ur*-texts of black comedy reflects the extent to which it is conceived as a comic form in which this black absurdity is mobilised in the service of social critique – a conception on which Robinson relies to convey his critique of social inequity in the Middle Ages.

Medieval Lives' comic genealogy is also rich and spans a longer period. Most unavoidably, Jones's Python lineage is alluded to and even reanimated through the use of Pythonic visual elements, in particular the use of animated cartoons reminiscent of those by Terry Gilliam used in the *Flying Circus* series and *Monty Python and the Holy Grail*, as well as through historical and gender cross-dressing. When addressing the camera, Jones's facial expressions, which have attracted comment from some critics, channelled the simultaneously ribald and scandalised facial expressions common in the British camp tradition, epitomised on television by Frankie Howerd's *Up Pompeii* (1969–70) and in cinema by the bawdy *Carry On* comedy franchise. Jones's cross-dressing as a damsel also recalls his turns as Dennis's mother in *Monty Python and the Holy Grail* and as Mandy, mother of Brian in *Monty Python's Life of Brian* (1979) and, more distantly, the drag tradition that emerged in the burlesque and pantomime of the Victorian era. British music hall is even evoked in a surprisingly contradictory way in the episode devoted to the medieval minstrel. In this episode Jones likens the

44   For another account of *Blackadder* which is oriented more toward its representation of the Middle Ages, see Katherine J. Lewis, '"Accident My Codlings": Sitcom, Cinema and the Re-Writing of History in *The Blackadder*', in *Mass Market Medieval: Essays on the Middle Ages in Popular Culture*, ed. David Marshall (Jefferson, NC: MacFarland and Co., 2007), pp. 113–25.

45   Andre Breton, 'Lightning Rod', in *Anthology of Black Humor*, trans. Mark Polizotti (San Francisco: City Lights Publishing, 1997), p. xix.

displacement of minstrels at the Ricardian court by vernacular poets such as Chaucer to the more recent displacement of music hall performers by 'university educated satirists of the television age',[46] an allusion that cannot but evoke the Oxbridge credentials of the Python ensemble, and through which he tacitly places himself within a long Chaucerian lineage. Yet despite this, he physically aligns himself with the 'superseded' minstrels by dressing as one on-and-off throughout the programme. This example is indicative of a disjunction that goes throughout the series, in which Jones physically identifies himself with figures such as alchemists and monks at the same time as his verbal text suggests he identifies elsewhere, and in fact regards these figures with scepticism or even derision. His identification with Chaucer, which boosts his satiric credibility, is something Jones takes very seriously. He has openly located the series' origin in the tradition of Chaucerian estates satire, claiming in a 2004 *History Today* article that the series developed out of an original desire to base a series on Chaucer's characters as 'generic [medieval] types'.[47] In a historical irony that Jones would surely appreciate, the *Sunday Times'* description of him as a 'plump and jovial' satirist echoes closely Thomas Hearne's 1711 pen-portrait of Chaucer, then newly rehabilitated as a forefather of English satire, as a plump rosy blond of benign yet grave physiognomy.

Horrible Histories' sketch format has a clear grounding in Britain's rich televisual tradition of sketch-based ensemble comedy from the 1960s on, from *Do Not Adjust Your Set*, *Monty Python's Flying Circus* and *Not the Nine O'Clock News* through to more recent offerings such as *Little Britain*, *The Catherine Tate Show*, *That Mitchell and Webb Look* and so on. The production team have acknowledged the particular influence of the Pythons as well as *Blackadder* on the programme's conception, and this is strongly evident in its dominant use of black humour, epitomised in the recurrent sketch 'Stupid Deaths' in which historical characters who purportedly suffered absurd deaths, such as Edmund II or Henry I, are forced to confess the humiliating circumstances of their ends to a jeering Death in order to gain entry to the afterlife. While Robinson's and Deary's programmes are, as discussed earlier, more directly parodic of the historical documentary genre, *Horrible Histories* is merrily promiscuous in its parodic allusions, drawing on everything from newscasting ('The News at 1066'), to the Teutonic metal rock video format used for the Viking invasion song 'Literally' ('We're gonna set this sleepy town alight – literally! ... play that axe, Ragnor!') and reality television formats ('Historical Fashion Fix: Medieval Peasant' / 'My Big Fat Scottish

[46] Jones, *Terry Jones' Medieval Lives*, p. 57.

[47] Terry Jones, 'History with the Boring Bits Put Back', *History Today* 54 (2004), 62–63 (p. 63).

Medieval Wedding') to the infomercial ('Cash My Sin', a satire of the medieval trade in indulgences).

The episodic rather than chronological structure of Deary's books, which
make liberal use of gags, lists, *1066 And All That*-style quizzes and parodic
snippets of letters and newspaper articles, lends itself readily to sketch-form
adaptation, but there is also a case to be made for the greater success of
the televisual version. This is mostly to do with the nature of the gag as it
functions in Deary's books, a point worth considering because Deary has
stated that his interest in jokes preceded his interest in history.[48] He had been
commissioned in the 1980s by Scholastic press to write a book of Tudor gags
for children; out of this the series grew, largely retaining the gag form. Deary
has recently argued for the strength of offering history in 'bite-sized' vignettes
that can be consumed 'like a buffet'. But the ethics and dynamics of the gag
as a short form are complex in the case of the *Horrible Histories* franchise.
As Simon Critchley has argued in his meditation on humour, the relative
brevity of the gag means that it must quickly establish an exclusive shared
sociability and 'illuminate a social world that is held in common' between
teller and listener,[49] which is structurally achieved at the expense of the joke's
object or butt. While the comic target of Deary's books is ostensibly teachers,
in fact its joke form aims itself at medieval people. This sits at odds with his
professed aim to expose children to the injustices of authority by rescuing
the history of the 'little people' of the Middle Ages from oblivion, because
within the joke format these very people become depersonalised and instru-
mentalised, like the foreigner of xenophobic humour. While it has become
a truism among his fans that his humour provokes thought among children
about social issues, the subversive effect is, I argue, limited by his 'othering' of
medieval people by using the jokes narrated by an implicitly modern omniscient voice, which short-circuits sympathy for the Middle Ages where Deary
would wish to evoke it and reanimates caricatures of pre-modern barbarism,
bizarre superstitions, tolerance of filth, absurd customs and laws, thereby
confirming the greater civility, rationality and hygiene of modernity. Scanlon
notes that Deary's treatment of social inequity and hardship is more comic
and remote when he deals with earlier periods, whereas his approach to the
same experiences in the modern era is much more sombre and personalised,
as though it is worse to encounter such things in an 'enlightened' age, while
it is simply to be expected in pre-modern times.[50] While the television show
in many cases repeats the content of Deary's books, its superiority as comic
pedagogy is, I suggest, attributable in large part to its move from narrated
gag to sketch form, because the sketch as a performative mode of humour

48 'Delving into an Evil Past', *Birmingham Mail*, 5 June 2009.
49 Critchley, *On Humour*, p. 86.
50 Scanlon, 'History Beyond the Academy', pp. 85–6.

enables the viewer's sympathies to be directed more democratically toward the medieval 'butt' of the joke in addition to, or instead of, an omniscient modern voice framing the sketch. Furthermore, as with Jones's and Robinson's series, the live-action performance form of the televisual adaptation of Deary's books also reinforces the humanity of medieval people by having them embodied in the form of well-liked modern people. As numerous fan sites reveal, the cult status of a number of the programme's actors means that the characters they play are strongly identified by fans with the actors themselves (just as they had been in nineteenth-century burlesque), and gain approval, sympathy and humanity by association.

A question that is especially vital in the case of jocumentaries is whether the past whose facts they purport to represent is dignified, diminished or otherwise distorted by their comic methodologies. Is it an ethical failing for such texts to generate laughter out of comic portraits of the Middle Ages as either fundamentally grotesque or rife with hypocrisy, or are the stakes of laughing at medieval people ethically and ideologically lower than laughing at, say, foreigners, because there is no trajectory of cohabitation, with its accompanying ethical urgencies? Jones's response to these questions exposes the competing demands under which his series labours. He states that he has been 'exercised about what we think of the people of the Middle Ages because so many of their voices are ringing vibrantly in my ears – Chaucer's, Boccaccio's, Henry Knighton's, Thomas Walsingham's, Froissart's, Jean Creton's … writers … who seem to me just as individual, just as alive as we are today'.[51] By claiming that these people are deeply present to him, he expresses a sense of responsibility to do them justice in the way he would someone actually living alongside him. And yet the jocumentary genre, with its comic methods of 'bringing history to life', paradoxically licenses him to caricature and travesty these people in ways that risks the very injustice he fears. Deary licenses his methods by invoking a different notion of the medieval-past-in-the-present. This is most arrestingly expressed in his use of *translatio* at the end of *Stormin' Normans* in a way that 'modernises' the Normans by likening their imposts on the Anglo-Saxons to the Serbs' ethnic cleansing of the Kosovars in the 1990s Balkans conflict. By analogy, pre-conquest England is aligned with Kosovo as a powerful symbol of unbroken but endangered pre-modernity. So when Deary concludes that the Normans were 'the sort of people who would survive in today's world', he implies to his young readers that atavistic Norman bullies walk among them daily, thriving everywhere from the playground to the boardrooms, cartels and killing fields of the modern world.[52] This use of analogy to make

---

[51]   Terry Jones, 'The Middle Ages of Reason', *The Observer*, 8 February 2004.
[52]   Terry Deary, *Stormin' Normans*, in *Smashing Saxons and Stormin' Normans* (London: Scholastic, 2009), p. 266.

the Middle Ages more 'present' is further compounded by the interpretive licence granted by the series' commitment to entertainment, which despite soliciting greater sympathy for medieval people, potentially compromises its instructional agenda, and queries the truism that humour and pedagogy are natural bedfellows.

These three jocumentaries attempt, then, to address their divided pedagogical and comic ambitions by embracing an unstable logic in which historical alterity is acknowledged, but under the star of pre-modern weirdness. The historical Schadenfreude underpinning this representation of pre-modern alterity is, however, ultimately subsumed into a dehistoricised 'plus ça change, plus c'est la même chose' style of universal humanism that informs the series' black humour. Because of the existential nature of this black humour, with its universalising ambit, medieval people are absurd not because they are medieval, but because they are people, and in this black comic genre, all humanity becomes defamiliarised and mocked, so that the medieval lives could be our lives, historical jobs remind us of the shit, suffering and death that our modern lives let us pretend to forget, and 'horrible history' is in fact simply an ongoing revelation of horrible humanity.

7

Smelling the Past: Medieval Heritage Tourism and the Phenomenology of Ironic Nostalgia

QUESTION THAT HAS EXERCISED NUMEROUS THEORISTS of comedy, humour and laughter is what Simon Critchley has called 'the ethos and ethnos' of humour; that is, its reinforcement of cultural and ethnic distinctions through the ridicule of foreigners, minorities and other outsiders.[1] But, as discussed in the previous chapter, by contrast almost nothing has been said about how received ideas about the present, and about modern Western personhood, are perpetuated by humorous representations of the pre-modern past and its people. It is perhaps unsurprising that this question has not detained these theorists, whose concern has generally been with the social implications of exclusionary and objectifying comedy taking place within a single temporal dimension cohabited by teller, audience and object. Unlike racist, sexist or homophobic jokes, historicist humour has not warranted their attention because its cross-temporality would seem to render it a victimless offence, with the long-dead of the Middle Ages both oblivious and invulnerable to the mirth they generate for us moderns. While this might be true, it leaves unaddressed what comic value the past, and the medieval past in particular, has for later societies. The previous chapter examined the particular difficulties of introducing comic content, interpretation and tone into televisual texts that otherwise purport to be 'responsible', even pedagogic, representations of the historical past. The situation is even more complex in the case of the 'living' and 'interactive' medieval past offered through the experience of comic heritage tourism, which is the subject of this final chapter. Touristic sites' capacity to combine representational forms with the creation of a phenomenological experience means they can avail themselves of the full gamut of sensory 'contact points' with the past; as

[1] Simon Critchley, *On Humour* (London and New York: Routledge, 2002), p. 68.

well as the auditory, visual and temporal experiences offered by such forms as theatre, film and television, visitors can also experience the past through touch and spatial sensation, taste and, lastly but most intriguingly, smell. Focusing on tourist attractions that engage visitors' interest in the medieval past using the tools of edutainment, I will be exploring how the use of smell is a locus for the convergence of nostalgia, disgust and laughter.

Heritage tourism is a flexibly defined phenomenon with a range of separate and overlapping iterations. It can include specific historic buildings or sites (castles, gaols, battle fields and so on), purpose-built museums, galleries or heritage centres built on or near these sites, as well as, more loosely, themed tourist attractions featuring 'heritage'-based objects and/or narratives over which the sites have a more tenuous claim, such as 'medieval' castle attractions in places such as the US whose European settlement was modern. Although there has been some debate over whether heritage attractions are meaningful due to their own heritage value or due to visitors' understanding of how the attraction intersects with their own sense of heritage,[2] there is broad agreement that within the contemporary tourism market, heritage attractions seek to engage a range of stakeholders whose various claims they aim to accommodate. To take just one example, Stephanie Trigg has written searchingly on the particular pressures bearing on contemporary medieval cathedral tourism, which must moderate between the competing demands of scholarly visitors, nostalgic tourists and the practising faithful.[3] Simultaneously shaped by, and instrumental in, the increased commodification of 'heritage brands' in the form of merchandise and experiences, the entire industry has also been compelled, as de Groot argues, to commodify its pedagogic functions, adopting 'a market-sensitive approach to education and attendance',[4] seeking opportunities to put the past to work in the service of an edutainment that is the 'experiential' counterpart of the televisual form offered by Jones, Robinson and their kind.

As an industry that emerged in the wake of the nineteenth-century development of local or national 'heritage', which Svetlana Boym describes as an institutionalised response to nostalgic modernity,[5] heritage tourism cannot be analysed without some consideration of its imbrication within modern nostalgia. This is particularly the case with medievalist tourism, given the abiding prominence of the Middle Ages as a site of nostalgic projection. And yet in its contemporary incarnation, its relationship with nostalgic paradigms

---

    [2] Yaniv Poria, Richard Butler and David Airey, 'Clarifying Heritage Tourism', *Annals of Tourism Research* 28 (2001), 1047–9.

    [3] Stephanie Trigg, 'Walking Through Cathedrals: Scholars, Pilgrims, and Medieval Tourists', *New Medieval Literatures* VII (2005), 9–33.

    [4] Jerome De Groot, *Consuming History: Historians and Heritage in Contemporary Popular Culture* (London: Routledge, 2009), p. 240.

    [5] Svetlana Boym, *The Future of Nostalgia* (New York: Basic Books, 2001), p. 15.

is notably unstable. This agonised industry negotiates, often uncomfortably but also often ingeniously, a particular dilemma: it must signal its winking ironic scepticism about the possibility of nostalgic possession and the experience of medieval 'presence', while on the other hand honouring its contract to deliver precisely these things. Describing heritage tourism as 'ironic' does not imply that its fundamental project is merely flippant, or operating with a disposition of relativistic unbelief in the idea of a factual medieval past. Rather, it is more akin to the register of 'romantic irony' described by Friedrich Schlegel, in which 'everything should be playful and serious ... contain[ing] and arous[ing] a feeling of indissoluble antagonism between the absolute and the relative, between the impossibility and the necessity of complete communication'.[6] Within this schema, absolute truth cannot be represented fully but can be gestured to through the acknowledgment of the limitations of our knowledge. In the case of heritage tourism, it operates in the ironic and self-reflexive recognition of the inevitable partiality of its own representation of authentic history.[7]

This ironic disposition is expressed even more openly in the more comic iterations of heritage tourism, which have emerged as a response to the increasing pressure for heritage tourism to embrace the methods of edutainment. A number of sites to be discussed operate in a curious, though also enjoyable and thought-provoking, register of comic nostalgia in which the past is both longed for and laughed at. Offering a medieval past that must constantly evolve to meet the twenty-first-century touristic market's changing demands for edutainment, medievalist tourism strives, despite its postmodern reflexivity, to make the Middle Ages present to us in the form of 'living history'. The market pressures that insist on constant 'refreshing' make tourism an especially evanescent form of comic medievalism, so the forms of publicity and some of the displays to be discussed in this chapter have already changed at the time of writing, and will have changed further by the time of reading; but the comic-nostalgic strategies underlying them persist in other, more recent iterations as they grapple with the same quandaries of delivering a comic historical experience of the past.

The most conspicuous experience of presence heritage tourism offers is one that is explicitly figured via faciality, that is, the use of faces of serio-comic figures from the medieval past. This is perhaps best exemplified by the invitation issued on the recent front page of the Jorvik Viking Centre's website, 'Get Face to Face with Vikings', where the viewer looks directly into

---

6   Friedrich Schlegel, *Philosophical Fragments*, trans. Peter Firchow, foreword Rodolphe Gasché (Minneapolis and Oxford: Minnesota University Press, 1991), p. 13.

7   For a discussion of romantic irony, see Robert Sinnerbrink, 'The Volcano and the Dream: Consequences of Romanticism', in *Religion After Kant: Gold and Culture in the Idealist Era*, ed. Paulo Diego Bubbio and Paul Redding (Newcastle upon Tyne: Cambridge Scholars Press, 2012), pp. 38–59 (pp. 45–6).

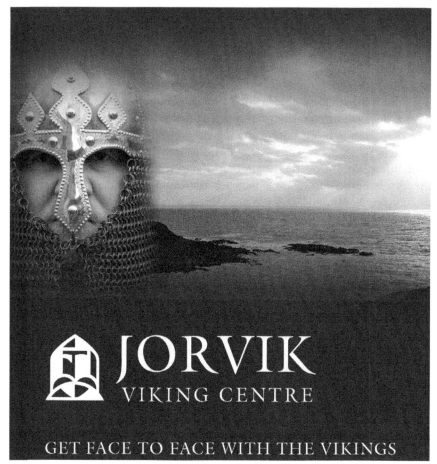

Figure 4. 'Get Face to Face with Vikings', from Jorvik Viking Centre webpage.

the stern helmeted visage of what we agree to see as a Viking, who also steadily meets our gaze.[8]

This concept of faciality, adapted here from Gilles Deleuze and Felix Guattari's *A Thousand Plateaus*, illuminates helpfully medievalist tourism's favoured tactics of historical representation, capturing perfectly this industry's engagement with a capitalist semiotics in which the medieval past is commodified and subjectified in the overcoded image of a pre-modern face. The conventional power of the face, within Deleuze and Guattari's conception, has been twofold. Its first capacity is that it guarantees, but also determines the parameters of, verbal signification: the unsmiling visage of the Jorvik Viking, for instance, leaves us in no doubt as to what the grim promise

---

[8]   Jorvik Viking Centre, www.jorvik-viking-centre.co.uk (accessed 5 November 2009).

that 'get[ting] face to face' with him entails. The subjectifying power of faces, furthermore, lies not in their reflection of individuality but rather, Deleuze and Guattari argue, in their capacity to form 'loci of resonance' that organise, assimilate and direct our perceptions so that they 'conform in advance to a dominant reality' indexed within that face.[9] While Deleuze and Guattari speak of the power of the face to overcode the meaning of the entire body, endowing it with a human subjectivity,[10] the Jorvik face goes even further, as it becomes the metonymic 'subjectivity' of an entire historical world. As visitors behold this face they consent to construe from the cultural codes it conveys that the 'world' of Viking England was a forbidding, austere, masculinist and violent place. Interestingly, although a more recent iteration of the website has replaced this face with a live-action animation in which a group of marauding Vikings jostle menacingly toward the visitor, at the end of the animation the visitor is still left with an image of grim helmeted faces conveying much the same message as their predecessors.

The Jorvik Vikings are, moreover, far from isolated figures. Even within the concentrated UK-based sample examined in this chapter, visitors to these tourist sites are bombarded with the face of the past. Whether it be the odd static mannequin faces of Chaucer's pilgrims at the Canterbury Tales attraction (Canterbury, UK), which are rendered in close-up in the centre's postcards and guidebooks, the disfigured and filthy faces featured at all of the sites in the Merlin' Entertainment Group's Dungeon franchise (situated in London, York, Edinburgh, Hamburg and Amsterdam), or the homely faces of the folk of tenth-century Jorvik projected in close-up on video screens in the Jorvik Centre's museum, there is a concerted attempt to facialise the past.

Moreover, they speak to visitors, either as ghostly video faces, as with the Jorvik folk, or as holograms, as with the William Wallace feature at the Edinburgh Dungeon, the eerie monk who greets at the York Dungeon and Eric Bloodaxe, the York Viking King who waits further within the same attraction. But when they open their mouths to address their visitors, the visitors are free to burst into laughter – whether at heavily coded 'pre-modern' modes of address or at 'pre-modern' bad hairstyles and rotten teeth, precisely because they know they cannot be seen or heard. They can experience the transgressive thrill of laughing in the faces of these medieval folk, with the ironic safety of knowing they are also doing it behind their backs.

For these hologrammatic faces are, as the tourist sites themselves acknowledge, spectres: the villagers from York's 'living history' are actually called the 'Jorvik ghosts'. They are traces, simulating presence in a way that openly

9 Gilles Deleuze and Félix Guattari, *A Thousand Plateaus: Capitalism and Schizophrenia*, trans. Brian Massumi (Minneapolis: University of Minnesota Press, 1987), p. 168.

10 Ibid., p. 170.

Figure 5. The Viking 'Ghost', Drifa, Jorvik Viking Centre display.

signals absence. This is brought home especially clearly if visitors linger long enough to witness the 'ghost' shows repeat their monologic loops, repeating the same pre-recorded scripts as the tourist traffic moves through the display space. Jacques Derrida argues that books, regarded in Western tradition as 'dead' repositories of deferred presence, can only repeat themselves in lieu of explaining themselves;[11] recalling this, it could be said that the 'talking heads' of medievalist tourism are really only facialised books. This is most literal in the case of the Canterbury pilgrims, who actually embody scenes and figures from a literary text, but it is also the truth of the hyperreal and so-called 'interactive' holograms, despite the effect of self-presence evoked by their voices.

By reminding visitors again of their virtual and machinic existence, these faces also evoke another kind of laughter that is unrelated to their grimy pre-modernity, a laughter famously described by Henri Bergson in his watershed 1900 study *Laughter: An Essay on the Meaning of the Comic*. This laughter, Bergson claims, results from the convergence of the human and the mechanical, such that 'we laugh every time a person gives us the impression of being

---

[11] Jacques Derrida, 'Plato's Pharmacy', in *Dissemination*, trans. Barbara Johnson (Chicago: University of Chicago Press, 1981), pp. 63–94 (p. 75).

a thing', with 'thing' (*machin*) referring specifically to a 'mechanical arrangement' whose distinguishing characteristic is a rigidity expressed through
unwitting and compulsive repetition. For Bergson this hijacking of human
by mechanical 'thinghood' is so insistently funny that he creates from it a
'new law' of laughter.[12] While, as Critchley has pointed out, what fascinates
Bergson is the comic convergence of the human and the mechanical in 'the
automaton, the world of the jack-in-the-box, the marionette, the doll, the
robot',[13] the hologrammatic effects of these medieval ghosts can certainly be
included as recent additions that Bergson was not able to imagine at the time
he wrote his essay. What this suggests is that there is an inevitable flirtation
with the comic in any medieval tourist attraction that resorts to short-play
animation as a technique for making the past present to its visitors.

The impossibility of embodying medieval presence also extends to the
live performing bodies of the Jorvik Centre, including the guides and the
re-enactors engaging in the activities of weaving and coin striking, who both
strive for, and comically break with, the mimetic representation of medieval
people. So noticeable is this mode of Romantic irony that Chris Halewood
and Kevin Hannam's study of Viking heritage tourism across Scandinavia and
Britain singles out Jorvik for the ironic nature of its approach.[14] In particular,
during a visit to the Centre in October 2009 (I have since returned three
times) I was intrigued by how the headgear worn by the desk- and guide staff
opted for the register of irony discussed earlier to negotiate the difficulties of
embodying Vikingness in a way that was historicist and postmodern in equal
parts. This was especially striking in the case of one young man who had
been employed as a guide not only because he was clearly conversant with
Viking England but also because of his stalwart build and impressive red-
blond beard which evoked the popular modern signifiers of the Scandinavian
warrior. While his costume approximated convincingly the reconstructed
medieval clothes worn by the mannequins in the Jorvik village display, on his
head he wore, along with a number of his colleagues, a headband crowned
with alien bobbles. This comic but jarring 'break from character' was a very
telling reflection of the necessity of evoking yet also avoiding the discredited
horned helmet image of the Viking. The Jorvik guidebook, which insists
repeatedly on the scholarly credentials of the Centre's displays ('every aspect
of the reconstruction at Jorvik Viking Centre is based on archaeological
evidence – nothing is made up'),[15] devotes a prominent early paragraph to
debunking the iconic myth of the horned Viking, sheeting home the blame,

---

[12]   Henri Bergson, *Laughter: An Essay on the Meaning of the Comic*, trans. Cloudesley
Brereton and Fred Rothwell (New York: The Macmillan Company, 1914), pp. 9–10.

[13]   Critchley, *On Humour*, p. 56.

[14]   C. Halewood and K. Hannam, 'Viking Heritage Tourism: Authenticity and
Commodification', *Annals of Tourism Research* 28:3 (2001), 565–80 (p. 575).

[15]   *Jorvik Viking Centre Guide* (York, UK: York Archaeological Trust, 2009), p. 13.

predictably enough, to nineteenth-century Romanticism;[16] so clearly the Centre's costumed Viking guides and re-enactors could not avail themselves of the convenient but anachronistic signifier of the horns.

Judging from Halewood and Hannam's study, as well as Wayne Fife's account of the Viking tourist sites at L'Anse aux Meadows in northern Newfoundland, this is a widespread problem for operators within this niche of the heritage tourism market,[17] although the blithe representation of horned Vikings in the York Dungeon guidebook shows that attractions at the kitsch extreme of heritage tourism entertain no such historicist scruples. The problem, then, is how a Viking tour guide at a tourist site of the non-kitsch variety can have a recognisable Viking head without horns. At L'Anse aux Meadows, Fife reports, the on-site re-enactors have taken it upon themselves to build salutary correctives into their performances, so that visitors are disabused of any 'fakeloric' horned fantasies and educated in the ways of authentic Vikings.[18] The Jorvik bobbles, on the other hand, operate within a more complex and riven logic of disavowal, attesting simultaneously to the impossibility of wearing the horns and the impossibility of entirely shedding them within an environment driven by medievalist commodification. They also express, somewhat unexpectedly, the logic of one variety of nostalgia – what Fife calls 'postmodern' touristic nostalgia[19] – for they acknowledge both the quest for the past and the past's unattainability. The bobbles also had the felicitous, though possibly unintended, effect of creating a comic but telling collocation between medieval people and extraterrestrials, suggesting that Vikings and ETs are alike in being the creations of fantasy, speculation and imaginative projection. They seem to suggest that when 'getting face to face with Vikings', we are really coming face to face with aliens, from a distant planet known as the past.

Yet, as mentioned earlier, these sites cannot completely abandon their pact with medieval presence, since it is central to their pedagogic mission and to the market sharehold they must maintain. In the case of the Dungeons franchise, the repeated appeal to, and production of, pre-modern presence through the medium of live performance has the purpose of maintaining the franchise's signature effect of sensational kitsch pantomime. But in the case of more avowedly historically researched places like the Canterbury Tales, Jorvik and some others that will be discussed later, the appeal to the 'presence of the past' is necessitated in large part by their pedagogic agenda. This agenda is expressed not only in the significant amount of written and verbal

---

[16]   Ibid., p. 6.

[17]   Wayne Fife, 'Semantic Slippage as a New Aspect of Authenticity: Viking Tourism on the Northern Peninsula of Newfoundland', *Journal of Folklore Research* 41(2004), 61–84 (p. 64).

[18]   Ibid., pp. 64–5.

[19]   Ibid., p. 65.

text accompanying the material displays in the Centre's museum section, but also an impressive calendar of activities that teach visiting groups of school-aged children about the medieval past. It is fairly safe to say that children are more likely to be engaged by an accessible Middle Ages that they can touch, see and wear than by tortured musings on the limits of historical positivism. But the Jorvik alien bobbles do not entirely dispatch the problem of how to side-step the trapdoors of historical representation in order to deliver on the promise of a comic but authentic experience of 'the medieval past'. I wish to suggest that arguably the most effective means of signifying unmediated pastness in the sites I visited was through their use of odour. I will examine odour in relation to a number of the British attractions I visited, and argue that its particular potency as a vehicle of both nostalgia and humour make it a crucial element in the production of these attractions' distinctive form of comic nostalgia. Although websites and printed guide materials are vital to contemporary heritage tourism's packaging of the Middle Ages, their strongly visual emphasis, taken in isolation from the tourist venues themselves, can tempt us to over-privilege the use of such techniques as 'heritage' faciality. When one passes through the actual venues, on the other hand, the importance of smell becomes strikingly, indeed unavoidably, apparent.

The active inclusion of smell as a feature, or even an attraction, is a distinctive aspect of heritage tourism. The few histories of tourism that have included an analysis of smell have tended to emphasise the capacity for odour to compromise the commercial aims of this industry. One example is Connie Chiang's analysis of Californian hoteliers' quests in the late nineteenth and early twentieth century to expel Chinese fishermen from the tourist precincts of Monterey because the offensive (and, by implication, 'Chinese') smells generated by their pursuit of a livelihood threatened to alienate the largely Anglo- and Euro-American visitors.[20] But in the case of comic medieval tourism a markedly different situation has emerged: for here is a form of tourism in which odour is in fact vital to its aims, playing a central role in this niche-industry's production of what historian Linda Austin has described as a powerful non-cerebral or embodied nostalgia[21] that is grounded in evoking the raw materiality of life in the Middle Ages. These attractions' attempts to make this nostalgic experience comic are less incongruous than they can initially seem. For just as nostalgia simultaneously engages bodily memory and cultural fantasy, so too laughter, according to theorists such as Peter L. Berger, is a phenomenon that is intensely corporeal yet also profoundly cultural: '*Homo ridens* ... stands at the intersection of what is most and what

---

[20] Connie Y. Chiang, 'Monterey-by-the-Smell: Odors and Social Conflict on the California Coastline', *Pacific Historical Review* 73 (2004), 183–214.

[21] Linda Austin, *Nostalgia in Transition, 1780–1917* (Charlottesville: University of Virginia Press, 2007), pp. 14–23.

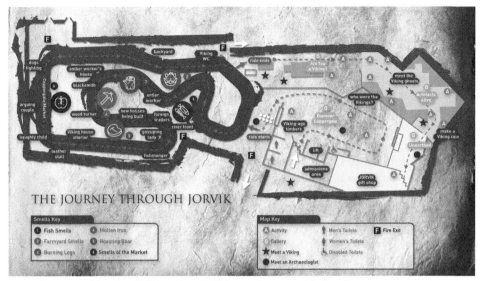

Figure 6. The Smell Map, Jorvik Viking Centre guide book.

is least animal about human beings.'[22] The same can be said of odour, which, as will be discussed, is experienced physically and culturally at the same time; so nostalgia, comedy and odour make for an apt, if counter-intuitive, triangulation in these touristic spaces. While of course odour is only one part of the sensorium of medieval heritage tourism, which also notably includes music and evocative sound-effects, it offers a suggestive entry point into developing what I want to call a phenomenology of comic nostalgia.

The evidence informing this discussion needs to be outlined briefly. Smell is a central element of the Jorvik Centre's recreative efforts: as visitors glide in their suspended pods through the Centre's life-scale reconstruction of the streets of Jorvik at 5.30 p.m. on 25 October AD 975, they are treated to a succession of the town's distinctive smells, released discreetly through narrow vents throughout the town display at a level apparently calculated to evoke the experience of medieval street-life without overwhelming visitors with its pungency. So vital are these smells to visitors' experience of this Viking street scene, the Centre's guidebook has produced a 'smell key' to help them interpret what they are smelling.

Similarly, when visitors walk into the first room of the Canterbury Tales attraction, which is a dimly lit recreation of Chaucer's Tabard Inn, with its slumbering bodies and dying fire, they are greeted by a smell that they are assured by the site's audio-tour guide is typical of inns in Chaucer's time.

---

[22] Peter L. Berger, *Redeeming Laughter: The Comic Dimension of Human Experience* (New York: Walter de Gruyter, 1997), p. 46.

While this smell is not taxonomised in the manner of the Jorvik smells, it is a pungent aroma redolent of smoke, leather and roasting meat. A remarkably similar smell can also be experienced in a rather more serious kind of touristic venue, the 'Works of God and Man' centre located at Rievaulx Abbey in North Yorkshire. Focusing on the working lives of the Abbey's monks, which it likens to the duties of contemporary workers within large corporations, the museum includes among its displays a cluster of metal cylinders whose lids can be lifted to allow visitors to inhale the olfactory by-products of Cistercian industry. We encounter the 'Tabard smell' in a cylinder that claims to offer a recaptured version of the aroma that would once have exuded from the monastery's tannery. Despite the centre's pedagogic earnestness, a placard accompanying the cylinder, evidently aimed at a junior audience, delights in communicating, with a glee not dissimilar to Tony Robinson's in *Worst Jobs*, that urine was a main ingredient used in leather tanning, and hence in the production of this smell. Finally the same smell (indeed, the extreme similarity leads one to ponder whether there is a niche 'medieval aroma' product available to these tourist operators, made to an industry standard) is found in the designated 'medieval' spaces of the York Dungeon, especially in the reconstructed Viking-ravaged tavern and in the Black Death room, where a re-enactor dons the distinctive beaked plague doctor mask while subjecting visitors to a stream of raillery in which they are insulted, diagnosed with plague and 'cured' via a range of comically brutal treatments. Within the Dungeon spaces, this smell performs a contradictory double function that is common to comic nostalgic tourism: on the one hand it provides an olfactory backdrop for the scatological joking that is central to the actors' comic-archaic performances, while on the other it grounds them in an authentic pre-modern materiality that licenses their departures from historical verisimilitude.

Where odour is not actually used, furthermore, it is repeatedly evoked metonymically. The many verbal and visual images visitors encounter of rotten teeth, unwashed faces, soiled clothes, lank hair and even plague buboes evoke the bodily stench that these exhibits insist was characteristic of 'ordinary' medieval people. Putrid medieval environments are evoked in the many lurid guidebook descriptions of medieval 'waste management', in which cesspits, fish markets, slaughterhouses and rotting food are staples. Both the Canterbury Tales attraction and especially the former annual exhibition 'Plague, Poverty, and Prayer' at the Barley Hall in York, a reconstructed fifteenth-century townhouse, treat visitors to nauseating spectacles of tabletop filth that strongly evoke the reek of putrefaction. The Jorvik Viking Centre takes us past a man defecating in a street-side latrine – one of the stars of the Centre's postcard series, with his straining face and wickerwork privy. Interestingly, however, despite the fact that this display is accompanied by a vivid soundscape of explosive flatulence, there is no change to the smellscape, and the odour he would presumably be creating is, in a missed comic opportunity, notably missing from the guidebook's Smell Key.

Perhaps the pièce de resistance of metonymic – or perhaps spectral – stench is the Jorvik Centre's eight-inch specimen of petrified Viking excrement, widely known, according to the *Rough Guide to Britain*, as the Lloyds Bank Turd (so-called because Lloyds was the building from under which it was excavated), which is proudly displayed at the entry to the museum section of the attraction. The stench of medieval battle is even evoked comically by its opposite, as in the souvenir Orsen the Norseman's Viking Hand Soap, available at most of these attractions' gift shops, which promises on its packaging to clean off the filth of 'plunder, pillage, and victorious celebration'.

Smell is, in short, not only everywhere in comic medieval tourism, but is given a privileged position. When the Canterbury Tales guidebook invites us, in a deliberately deflationary rhetorical triad, to 'experience the sights, sounds, and smells of a bygone era',[23] it on the one hand places smell at the bottom of a descending scale of sensual recognition (thereby seemingly reinforcing its status as one of what Mark M. Smith has called the 'so-called "lower", proximate senses')[24] but on the other hand situates it at the top of an ascending scale toward authentic and intimate presence. It is one thing to experience the sights and sounds, which can after all be recorded and disseminated, and thus experienced elsewhere, but touristic odour is, by definition, *in situ*: one has to be there to encounter it. It can only be experienced in its own spatio-temporal specificity, and thus seems to sit outside the disseminative flows of souvenir commodification. Although the Jorvik Centre appears to have managed to commodify medieval smell in its famous Scratch & Sniff souvenir postcard (featuring the man in the Viking latrine on one half, and the Viking Age Coppergate market on the other), the 'take-home' smells on the postcards offer what Smith has archly called 'modest heuristic returns',[25] being much less pungent than those experienced within the actual Jorvik township display, which elude full commodified reproduction.

But what is it about smell that makes it such an effective vehicle for the comic-nostalgic return to the medieval past? To begin to answer this question, it is instructive to look at scholarly work coming out of the burgeoning areas of sensory history and anthropology. In her comparative anthropological account of smell, 'The Odor of the Other', Constance Classen argues that 'through the act of smelling, one fills oneself with the presence of the other'.[26] Moreover, what Classen refers to as the 'transitive character of smells', their capacity to emanate and envelop, allows them to 'break down barriers'[27] and

[23] *Jorvik Viking Centre Guide*, p. 1.
[24] Mark M. Smith, 'Producing Sense, Consuming Sense, Making Sense: Perils and Prospects for Sensory History', *Journal of Social History* 40 (2007), 841–58 (p. 843).
[25] Ibid., p. 848.
[26] Constance Classen, 'The Odor of the Other: Olfactory Symbolism and Cultural Categories', *Ethos* 20 (1992), 133–66 (p. 156).
[27] Ibid.

to draw the visitor into a sphere of intimacy with their source, whether this be a facsimile Viking fishmarket or a recreated tavern in fourteenth-century Southwark. Even more pertinently for medieval tourism, this 'integrative' force of odour also allows it, Classen argues, to transgress the barriers of historical alterity.[28] In saying this she is careful not to characterise odours, or indeed the sense of smell, as merely pre- or sub-cognitive, acultural phenomena. Rather, it is 'because of its exclusion from the realm of the intellect [in the West] that smell is particularly associated with memory and the emotions'.[29] She does not deny the recollective power of humans' sense of smell, or the capacity for odours to prompt 'Proustian moments' of vivid personal reminiscence. But her point is more that we associate culturally the sense of smell with the act of remembering: hence the journey through touristic seeing, hearing and smelling is a journey that takes visitors deeper into the past. Classen is, moreover, in agreement with those historians of olfaction who argue that smell need not be tethered to personal history; rather, the odours we encounter are 'comprehensively encoded' with social and historical norms.[30] The odours of the Cistercian tannery, the Tabard Inn and the Plague Room are not the malodorous equivalents of Proust's madeleine, opening up at one sniff a nostalgic vista of lost childhood, although visitors certainly interpret them in part via what Smith calls their own modern 'olfactory cognates'[31] – the smells of their own lived experience, through which they evaluate aesthetically and culturally those encountered in medieval heritage attractions. What these touristic smells surround visitors with is an olfactory environment that they culturally and viscerally consent to recognise as 'the smell of the Middle Ages'. Boym says, elegantly, that nostalgia is never fully synthesisable, and hence 'seduces rather than convinces'.[32] This is certainly true of the experience of this medieval smell; made up equally of viscerality and enculturation, it generates an ineffable but unmistakable bodily nostalgia.

Some sensory historians, such as Peter Charles Hoffer in his 2003 study *Sensory Worlds in Early America*, argue that the accurate reproduction of past smells in 'living history' touristic venues can unlock for visitors the specifics of historical experience and thereby 'make the past live again'.[33] But the nostalgic olfactory experience offered by the British medievalist sites is more complex – and at the same time less grandiose – in its aims than Hoffer's account suggests tourism might be. While the Jorvik Centre may well have

[28] Ibid., p. 161.
[29] Ibid.
[30] Ibid.
[31] Smith, 'Producing Sense', p. 847.
[32] Boym, *The Future of Nostalgia*, p. 13.
[33] Peter Charles Hoffer, *Sensory Worlds in Early America* (Baltimore, MD: Johns Hopkins University Press, 2003), pp. 14, 253.

used a wealth of local archaeological evidence to reproduce a meticulously differentiated sequence of medieval smells, there appears to be no real expectation that these smells will be received by visitors as anything other than an olfactory medley of pre-modernity. Although the Smells Key appears to encourage an 'authentic experience' of a range of historically remote smells, insofar as it attempts to render them separately intelligible and even familiar to modern tourists, its very existence is itself an indication of the difficulty of distinguishing the smells from one another. Indeed, crowding all of these purportedly authentic smells into a compressed and tightly sealed sensory environment has the effect of creating a 'surround-smell' medieval milieu without any easily identifiable modern olfactory cognates. This seductive and impressionistic approach to recreating pastness is not the enemy of modern or even postmodern nostalgia, which is in any case more concerned with the historical longing than the attainment of its object. Rather, as Linda Austin has persuasively demonstrated in her study *Nostalgia in Transition 1780–1917*, nostalgia has long nurtured a tolerance of inauthenticity, and a capacity to take pleasure in copies and replicas of its 'original' object. Discussing the case of the pathologically homesick eighteenth-century student Joseph Frédéric Grammont, Austin traces how Grammont's therapeutic programme was bound up in his developing the ability to enjoy a countryside setting that he was happy to treat, to use his doctor Friedrich von Schiller's phrase, as an 'aesthetic semblance' or substitute for the home that was the origin of his longing.[34] The touristic smelling encouraged at these sites takes its place in what Austin sees as a modern nostalgic phenomenon of 'ownership [of the past] through semblance' which has increasingly come to manifest itself in corporeal acts of 'noncerebral remembering'.[35] By engaging in the act of touristic smelling, visitors come to possess what can be called a phenomenological semblance of medieval presence that is a species of what Halewood and Hannam call 'negotiated' authenticity that is tacitly but mutually agreed upon by creators and consumers of heritage tourism.[36]

Yet smells can disrupt nostalgic engagement, for if an odour is sufficiently unpleasant it can also generate disgust, which in turn can necessitate distance between its source and its recipient. Theorists of disgust routinely nominate taste and smell as the two senses most responsive to disgust, with Aurel Kolnai in his watershed study *On Disgust* placing odour first among those stimuli capable of eliciting this affective state, calling it 'the true place of origin of disgust'.[37] The power to elicit disgust means that the transitive, travelling nature of smell, more than other transitive phenomena such as

---

34   Austin, *Nostalgia in Transition*, p. 12.
35   Ibid., p. 14.
36   Halewood and Hannam, 'Viking Heritage Tourism', p. 574.
37   Aurel Kolnai, *On Disgust*, ed. and intro. Carolyn Korsmeyer and Barry Smith (Peru, IL: Open Court Publishing, 2004), p. 50.

sound, make a space disgusting in a way that is impossible to avoid except by moving away or even departing. In the case of these tourist attractions, this can lead to a compounding of physical and historical distance. Smell's transitive quality can mean that visitors need not approach too close, but can stand back in a state of anti-nostalgic revulsion, congratulating ourselves on our fortuitous birth into what Classen calls 'inodorate' modernity,[38] the age of hygiene, public sanitation and institutional medicine, a world away from the malodorous, insalubrious conditions of pre-modernity.

What this reveals is that while the disgust elicited by odour is experienced phenomenally, it is interpreted morally and socially. Anthropologists and sociologists of smell, examining the social symbolism attached to various scents and odours, have pointed to the function of odour in social classification, and especially in the production of cultural otherness. It is never we who smell, but them, whoever they are. This is strikingly similar, in anthropological and sociological terms, to the function of humour as a reinforcer of difference between groups, a fact which might explain the particular amenability of smell as a category of xenophobic ridicule, generating the 'contempt' that Ian William Miller describes as 'the first cousin' of disgust.[39] In many societies, as shown both by Classen and by Gale Largey and Rod Watson (2006), odour is associated most strongly with women, social inferiors, nature and ethnic others. To this list we can add the pre-modern other, whose ambient smelliness reassures us modern tourists of our own perfumed or apparently inodorate cleanliness.[40] Smith has called this the myth of the 'putatively pre-modern' nature of odour, as part of his perceptive critique of a persistent and problematic modern/pre-modern divide in the field of sensory history that he argues should not be left unchallenged.[41] His observation is certainly borne out by Classen's speculative alignment of 'societies that emphasise smell' with a range of cultural traits that correspond with nostalgically figured pre-modernity, such as 'a preference for content over form, spirituality over materialism, [and] synthesis over analysis'.[42] She does not name the Middle Ages specifically, but the characteristics listed here are echoed closely in the account of the Middle Ages as an odour-tolerant society in her co-authored study with David Howe and Anthony Synnott, *Aroma: The Cultural History of Smell*, where medieval Europe is presented *in toto* as a society in which 'foul odours were disliked ... but on the whole tolerated ... while unpleasant they tended to be accepted as a natural part of the

[38] Classen, 'The Odor of the Other', p. 149.

[39] Ian William Miller, *The Anatomy of Disgust* (Cambridge, MA: Harvard University Press, 1997), p. 9.

[40] Gale Largey and Rod Watson, 'The Sociology of Odors', in *The Smell Culture Reader*, ed. Jim Drobnick (Oxford and New York: Berg, 2006), pp. 29–40.

[41] Smith, 'Producing Sense', pp. 850–82 (p. 851).

[42] Classen, 'The Odor of the Other', p. 162.

cycle of life'.[43] Classen, Howe and Synnott's vivid characterisation of putrid medieval street-life in *Aroma* is corroborated in a much more recent essay by J. Douglas Porteous, where the medieval period is singled out with great relish as an era whose smells promise an abundant, though abject, yield for an olfactory historian. Porteous highlights particularly 'the medieval ripeness of houses, persons and foods; the characteristic smells of "occupational" streets in pre-modern towns, from Bristol's Milk Street to York's Shambles, where one would have encountered the raw reek of butchery and blood'.[44] So pervasive in scholarship of olfaction is the collocation of the pre-modern with odour that we find Largey and Watson suggesting modern associations of strident perfume with female promiscuity bear 'echoes of the Middle Ages', a period in which, they claim, 'perfumers were suspected of "moral laxity"'.[45] Here the Middle Ages are not inadvertently but in fact unapologetically, even piously, malodorous.

Laughter is intimately linked as a reflex-response to the disgust generated by smell. Nevertheless, scholars in osphresiology (the study of smell) maintain that this laughter does not simply appear as an expression of revulsion and, by extension, of ridicule, but also has a strongly recuperative function. In his analysis of the relationship between laughter and disgust, Winfried Menninghaus argues:

> disgust might well be considered a property no less characteristic of humanity than the capacity to laugh – a property, in fact, that represents the negative complement of laughter. The sudden discharge of tension achieves in laughter, as in vomiting, an overcoming of disgust, a contact with the 'abject' that does not lead to lasting contamination or defilement.

From this disgust and laughter are mutually imbricated. Laughter also paradoxically wards off disgust:

> Disgust ... and laughter are complementary ways of admitting an alterity that otherwise would fall prey to repression; they enable us to deal with a scandal that otherwise would overpower our system of perception and consciousness.[46]

Similarly, Paul Rozin et al. note the 'civilised pleasure', and the triumph over

[43] Constance Classen, David Howes and Anthony Synnott, *Aroma: The Cultural History of Smell* (London: Routledge, 1994), p. 57.

[44] J. Douglas Porteous, 'Smellscape', in Drobnick, *The Smell Culture Reader*, pp. 89–106 (pp. 98–9).

[45] Largey and Watson, 'The Sociology of Odors', pp. 30–1.

[46] Winfried Menninghaus, *Disgust: The Theory and History of a Strong Emotion* (Albany, NY: SUNY Press, 2003), pp. 10–11.

materiality which is at the heart of laughing at what otherwise produces disgust. By this argument, the laughter generated by contact with malodorous reconstructions of the medieval past can lead to incorporation rather than rejection of that past, ultimately restoring the sense of intimacy with the past that is risked by the introduction of disgusting 'pre-modern' smells.[47] This recuperative reflex, which has a strongly ironic tonality in the case of this touristic experience, is closely aligned to Anna Klosowska's description of camp as an 'integration of the disgusting element [which] allows the emergence of a position where two incompatible relations, disgust and longing, can be occupied simultaneously'.[48] This laughter thereby facilitates nostalgia in which the personal and the historical are intertwined. Although these tourist attractions do not explicitly invoke the troubling notion of the Middle Ages as the lost cultural infancy of the West, it threatens to return via the heavy emphasis on smell and, in some cases, their complementary recourse to scatological humour. Their collocation of the medieval with stench licenses a (pleasurably) puerile laughter response which, for adult visitors, acknowledges and then disavows disgust, creating its own form of comic nostalgia: through their comic-nostalgic response to the Middle Ages such visitors are able return to a past world of childhood humour in which smells feature prominently.

A contradiction thus operates in the use of smell in medieval heritage tourism which aims to present a medieval smellscape that is both confrontingly rank yet romantically natural. Judging from recent studies in Civil War re-enactment tourism in the US, there seems to be a Janus-faced nostalgia common among consumers of heritage tourism, in which sentimental longing for a more innocent though riskier (and smellier) past coexists with gratitude for the wonders of twenty-first-century sanitation and medicine.[49] The touristic use of medieval smell seems to service this ambiguous nostalgia by presenting us with a phenomenological metonym of a grotesque Middle Ages, in which, as discussed earlier, disease, decay and dental horrors are a part of everyday life in a way that is comic and hence comfortingly remote for us. This is the grotesque famously formulated by

---

[47] Paul Rozin, Jonathan Haidt and Clark McCauley, 'Disgust: The Body and Soul Emotion in the Twenty-first Century', in *Disgust and Its Disorders: Theory, Assessment, and Treatment Implications*, ed. Bunmi O. Olatunji and Dean McKay (Washington, DC: American Psychological Association, 2009), pp. 9–29 (p. 24).

[48] Anna Klosowska, 'The Eastern Western: Camp as a Response to Cultural Failure in The Conqueror', in *Queer Movie Medievalisms*, ed. Kathleen Coyne Kelly and Tison Pugh (Farnham, Surrey: Ashgate, 2009), pp. 97–114 (p. 99).

[49] See Elizabeth Carnegie and Scott Mccabe, 'Re-Enactment Events and Tourism: Meaning, Authenticity and Identity', *Current Issues in Tourism* 11 (2008), 349–68; and Nina M. Ray, Gary McCain, Derick Davis and Tracy L. Melin, 'Lewis and Clark and the Corps of Discovery: Re-Enactment Event Tourism as Authentic Heritage Travel', *Leisure Studies* 25 (2006), 437–54.

Mikhail Bakhtin, that is the realm of the lower bodily stratum, and 'those parts of the body that are open to the outside world' – what he calls its 'apertures or convexities',[50] which are the sites of abject production. In the case of the touristic medieval grotesque, we can also include those parts of the body that are sites of violence and entry points for the invasion of disease.

It is striking how heavily this grotesque representation relies on the satiric idiom associated with Monty Python. Predictably enough, this borrowing is most conspicuous in the case of the Dungeon franchise, whose guidebook underlines their comically gruesome portraits of plague victims with the phrase 'Bring out your Dead' – a phrase no-one can read or hear without recalling the hilariously filthy world of the medieval English proletariat in *Monty Python and the Holy Grail* (1976). But even the less overtly comic tourist attractions also participate in this Pythonesque satiric production of the Middle Ages, exposing its stench as the authentic obverse of the perfumed delusions of courtly culture and the incense-fumed world of religious superstition. The use of scatalogical humour is especially evident in their attempts to appeal to younger visitors. For instance, Dig, an interactive archaeological tourist attraction in York designed for a pre-teen market, advises its aspiring archaeologists, 'look out for the 2000 year old skull and the Viking-Age poo!' (presumably a replica of the Jorvik one), while the Barley Hall's 'Plague, Poverty, and Prayer' exhibition also cannot resist revelling, under its guise of sober medical history, in descriptions of abject medieval bodies. Along with the blood, mucus, vomit, semen, urine and excrement featured in the other attractions, the Barley Hall exhibit's exploration of the minutiae of pus and internal parasites deserves to be singled out for honourable mention, along with the plastic faeces the surprised visitor finds cheekily hidden in a portable privy in its parlour. As discussed earlier, theorists of comedy have not extended their analyses of socially discriminatory humour to consider how it might also negotiate temporal boundaries; yet the comic-nostalgic use of smell in heritage tourism shows that there is clearly a case to argue that the past can become the target of a species of 'othering' humour. While Critchley speaks of humour as being bound to a locality – 'the *ethos* of a place is expressed through laughing at those who are not like us'[51] – it is also clearly bound within temporality. Just as George Orwell once argued that British imperial pride was founded on the belief that 'foreigners are funny', so too presentist chauvinism rests just as surely on the conviction that premoderns smelt funny.

Yet these satiric spectacles of abject medieval corporeality walk a fine line common to much medievalist satire. In *The Battle of the Books* (1704), Jona-

---

[50] Mikhail Bakhtin, *Rabelais and his World*, trans. Hélène Iswolsky (Bloomington: Indiana University Press, 1984), p. 26.
[51] Critchley, *On Humour*, p. 68.

than Swift famously described satire as 'a sort of glass wherein beholders do generally discover everybody's face but their own';[52] and so it is with the satire of comic medievalist tourism, which is laughing not in the face of the past, but in ours. With comic heritage tourism, for all its olfactorily oriented satire of pre-modern grotesquery, there is arguably a crypto-nostalgic agenda also being played out. This is hardly surprising, given the proven amenability of nostalgia to function as a tool of anti-modernist satire. Satire's critique of the present, which is its temporal anchor, can of course be as easily conducted through futuristic or fantastic projection as through historical nostalgia; but it shares with nostalgia a fundamentally and powerfully utopian impulse. But what is the nature of this satire that uses smell as its central metonym? When we sniff the rank fumes of the Viking latrine, or the pungent brew of the Tabard and the Rievaulx tannery, what we are consuming is an olfactory symbol of life lived at a greater intensity and in greater proximity with nature than we in our deodorised and denaturalised world can achieve. Again, postmodern knowingness notwithstanding, these tourist attractions, like the historians of olfaction discussed earlier, happily mobilise the familiar nineteenth-century nostalgic tropes of pre-modern organic community and unalienated labour. The Jorvik village tour is a particularly pronounced instance of this, featuring scenes of artisans contentedly at work and of Viking neighbours bantering good-naturedly with one another. These tropes in turn dovetail with, and medievalise, the Horatian satiric yearning for a return to humanity's essential benevolence. But the use of smell brings these organicist fantasies into more intimate focus by conjuring up a medieval lifeworld of natural corporeality that offers satiric commentary on the bodily regimes of postmodern Western society.

One intriguing touristic leitmotif that is used to epitomise the grotesque but 'organically superior' nature of medieval corporeality and medicinal culture is the leech. The guidebook produced by the Dungeon franchise features typically lurid images of leeches writhing amid blood spatter across a four-page historical timeline. These leeches are a perfect image of the ambiguous nostalgic satire of medievalist tourism, for they symbolise on the one hand the quackery of medieval humoral medicine and on the other the deep pre-modern understanding of the healing properties of the natural world, a point reinforced by the guidebook's '21st Century Update' which informs us of the recent reintroduction of leeches in the practices of reconstructive surgery (The Dungeons Guide).[53] While the Barley Hall's exhibit on medieval medicine is altogether more respectful of the pre-modern use of natural cures, even offering visitors a complimentary booklet of medieval home remedies,

---

[52] Jonathan Swift, *A Tale of a Tub and Other Works*, ed. Angus Ross and David Woolley (Oxford: Oxford University Press, 1984), p. 104.

[53] *The Dungeons Guide* (Merlin Entertainments, 2009), unpaginated.

its treatment of leechcraft is not radically different in tenor from that of the Dungeons. Indeed in the Barley Hall's souvenir shop, which functions as a kind of kitsch appendix to the largely serious displays within the house, visitors are able to buy 'Make-Your-Own Leech' kits, a gross-out product clearly capitalising on the horror leeches provoke in contemporary Western society. But the displays that arguably best disclose these attractions' crypto-nostalgic tribute to the intensity of medieval corporeal existence are the skeletons. Both the Barley Hall and the Jorvik Centre house skeletons in rooms whose walls are densely covered in text and images detailing the horrors visited on medieval bodies by warfare, accident and disease. In Jorvik we encounter Bob, the skeleton of a youngish man, while the Barley Hall skeleton is that of an anonymous middle-aged woman. Both sites offer meticulous, even loving, forensic accounts of the hardships experienced by these two in life: Bob's pocked and fractured bones, whose injuries are minutely anatomised, bear witness to the misadventures of physical labour and the violence of combat, while the woman's warped and eroded frame testifies to the ravages of leprosy and a host of related maladies which are described in sometimes horrifying detail. Yet these are bodies whose proximity to death not only elicits dread and pathos but provokes a nostalgic fantasy of life lived more vividly because conducted in death's shadow, and with greater equanimity because the cycle of life was accepted.

Of course these exhibits' declared aim is to offer edutainment about medieval life and death, not to offer critiques of contemporary society, a point reinforced at Jorvik by the anatomical fact sheets stationed next to Bob. But there is, romanticism notwithstanding, an undeniable satiric force (and here I distinguish the critical intent of satire from the techniques of comedy) in the *memento mori* gesture of proffering such corpses for our nostalgic contemplation as members of a youth-obsessed society whose bodily disciplines, aesthetic regimens and consumerist habits reflect our collective disavowal of death's approach. These glass-encased skeletons are well beyond putrefaction, but they are the natural corollary of all of the odours in the exhibits, whose meaty, leathery and excremental fumes are all to some degree redolent of death. These skeletons are, finally, arresting because in them the ultimate absence is made literally and unavoidably present. A consideration of comic tourism, then, allows us to understand the often surprising nuances of our consumption of the pre-modern past, and to see that medievalist nostalgia thrives in the unexpectedly compatible company of humour, if only we care to sniff it out.

Afterword
Laughing into the Future

I N THE ESSAY 'A DRAMA OF DOLLS', which appeared in the 1911 volume *Alarms and Discursions*, G. K. Chesterton tells of a trip to the Yorkshire dales where he saw 'an old puppet-play exactly as our fathers saw it five hundred years ago'. This puppet show, based on the legend of Faust, leads Chesterton into a meditation on inversive medieval humour that could almost be described as Bakhtinian *avant la lettre*. Most striking in this short meditation, however, is the conclusion Chesterton draws about the strange, contradictory comedy of the medieval puppets and the effect it had on him: '[t]he dolls were at once comic and convincing; but if you cannot at once laugh at a thing and believe in it, you have no business in the Middle Ages. Or in the world, for that matter.'[1]

The idea that representing 'the medieval' generates a comedy that is at once sceptical and credulous, ironically distant yet emotionally invested, has been at the core of this book's investigation of comic medievalism. In the introduction, and throughout the subsequent chapters, the word that I have used most often to describe this paradoxical state is 'ambivalent'. Although this word is sometimes used synonymously with words such as hesitant, dubious or doubtful, and as such can carry a faintly negative charge, it should by now be clear that the ambivalence at the heart of comic medievalism, taken as a whole, should be understood not as implicitly apprehensive toward the medieval past, and thus given to ridicule, but as genuinely composed

---

[1] G. K. Chesterton, 'A Drama of Dolls', *Alarms and Discursions* (New York: Dodd, Mead and Company, 1911), pp. 38–44 (p. 38).

of opposite and contending impulses. For every instance in which medieval cultures are unreflectively ridiculed as superstitious and ignorant, or barbaric and violent or, alternatively, as pompous and effete, there are at least as many in which a genial comedy emerges from a corresponding notion of the period's conviction, vitality and romance, which in turn are contrasted with, or even presented as antidotes for, the nihilism, enervation and rationalism of modernity. Even in such mordant examples as Twain's *Connecticut Yankee*, where it is harder to argue that derision is counterbalanced by faith, it still becomes apparent that the sustained ridicule it directs at the benighted folk of Camelot harbours, as its obverse, the ridicule of modernity's arrogant rationalism and belligerent technophilia. And while it is true that some of the texts examined in this book rely for their comedy on under-nuanced depictions of the Middle Ages, others formulate comic visions of medieval cultures that accommodate complexity and internal contradiction. When, for instance, Chaucer and St Francis are held up as pre- and proto-modern exemplars of wit and radical farce, they are regarded as both representative of and exceptional to the medieval cultures in which they carried out their work.

Throughout the book this comic ambivalence has taken many forms, and been called many names, but its uniting impetus is more persistently goodwill than scorn. This is apparent in the chivalric parodies found throughout *Don Quixote*, in which mockery and discursive homage vie with one another. It is the impulse that underlies what Sontag has called the 'tender' camp of the Victorian burlesques, where flippant parodic content comes couched in lovingly reconstructed historicist scenery. It informs both Bynum's 'history in the comic mode', which cheerfully acknowledges the limitations of historical representation, and heritage tourism's ironic recognition that even when the medieval past is being made materially present, it eludes full recovery. This geniality is even ingeniously evident in cases where the Middle Ages are being exposed to unflattering satire, as in Mel Brook's use of Jewish comedy simultaneously to emphasise and leaven his treatment of medieval anti-Semitism.

To reiterate and reinforce the contention offered in the introduction and tested across the length of the study, it is very difficult to isolate comic representations that are simply laughing *at* the Middle Ages, with all the progressivist certainty that this entails. The multi-temporality of comic medievalism, its almost inevitable imaginative crossing of the medieval/modern divide, creates a sense of proximity between the subject and object of laughter that thwarts simple ridicule. What this suggests, then, is that the theories of humour discussed in the introduction, which dominate within current scholarship, should be applied with some caution to comic medievalism. Given its largely anachronistic nature, the formulation most compatible with comic medievalism is that of 'incongruity humour' which, as its name suggests, argues that the comic arises out of the initial dissonant surprise involved in encountering unexpected elements together. But in the end, this is a descriptive term, and does not offer a deep diagnosis of the cultural work being performed by comic medievalism. The idea of 'superiority humour', furthermore, the pleasure of which arises from a feeling of superiority to the object of ridicule, has, as has been demonstrated, only limited pertinence for describing the benevolent comedy of much medievalism. 'Relief theory', in which humour is used as a way of expressing anxiety or managing fear, is closer to the mark when it comes to considering the satiric function of comic medievalism; but, having diagnosed this, it does not account for the nuances of comic play within the texts themselves. This is not to say that these comic frameworks are wrong or irrelevant, but rather to urge attentiveness to what frameworks are demanded by the texts themselves, including the possibility that with any given medievalist text all three theories might pertain at once.

There is much still to be said about comic medievalism in general, and historical comedy more generally. This study has mapped out a territory but has not fully populated it. The case studies featured in this book were selected as much for the taxonomic purposes they could serve as for their quality as comic texts. There are many other texts that I have refrained from discussing, but which I very much hope to discuss in future, or to see others discuss. In particular, the proliferating culture of online medievalist humour is a domain not broached in this study but which would provide rich pickings, adding a comic angle to the developing study of the significance of the Middle Ages' afterlife in the digital age. Furthermore, although some European examples have been discussed in this book, the dominantly Anglophone focus could be expanded so that it gradually attains a more global compass.

In this study I have chosen to answer the question 'why have people laughed at the Middle Ages?' by examining key examples of *how* they have laughed. The question of 'why' seemed problematic to me because it invites an essentialising of both the Middle Ages and modernity in order to pinpoint 'the thing' that makes the earlier time comically appealing to the later. It may be that the 'why' can eventually be identified through a cumulative study of the many instances where the medieval period has proven amusing to post-medieval societies; but the extreme variability of medievalism militates against a single answer. Alternatively, perhaps the approach taken in this book can be supplemented by psychological approaches that can illuminate the impulses behind laughter, humour and comedy, and by phenomenological or existential approaches that can offer interpretations of how our sense of temporal being intersects with what we find amusing. It also seems to me, finally, that with the history of emotions assuming increasing prominence in recent medieval studies research, it can be both worthwhile and fascinating to supplement this with medievalist study of 'historical emotions', that is, affective states produced by material or imaginary contact with the historical past. It is my hope this study has at least made a start on such a project, showing how mirth and amusement offer vital insight into one of the most agreeable ways in which the medieval period has maintained, or even increased, its appeal throughout its long and prolific afterlife. It is serious business, then; but also a lot of fun.

Bibliography

Primary Texts

Books and Essays

Bergson, Henri, *Laughter: An Essay on the Meaning of the Comic*, trans. Cloudesley Brereton and Fred Rothwell (New York: The Macmillan Company, 1914)

Carlyle, Thomas, *Past and Present*, intro. Ralph Waldo Emerson (Boston: Little, Brown, 1843)

Cervantes, Miguel de, *Don Quixote*, trans. Edith Grossman, intro. Harold Bloom (London: Vintage Books, 2005)

Chaucer, Geoffrey, *The Riverside Chaucer*, ed. Larry D. Benson, 3rd edn (Oxford: Oxford University Press, 1988)

Chesterton, G. K., *Alarms and Discursions* (New York: Dodd, Mead and Company, 1911)

Deary, Terry, *Stormin' Normans*, in *Smashing Saxons and Stormin' Normans* (London: Scholastic, 2009)

—— *Vicious Vikings and the Measly Middle Ages*, illustrated by Martin Brown (London: Scholastic Children's Books, 2004)

Dryden, John, *The Poems of John Dryden*, ed. and intro. John Sargeaunt (London and New York: Oxford University Press, 1913)

Eco, Umberto, *The Name of the Rose*, trans. William Weaver (London: Vintage Books, 1998)

Fo, Dario, *The Tricks of the Trade*, trans. Joe Farrell, ed. Stuart Hood (New York: Routledge, 1991)

Hartley, L. P., *The Go-Between* (London: Hamish Hamilton, 1953)

Jones, Terry, *Terry Jones' Medieval Lives* (London: BBC Books, 2005)

Pasolini, Pier Paolo, 'Manifesto for a New Theatre', trans. Thomas Simpson, *PAJ: A Journal of Performance and Art* 29 (2007), 126–38

—— *The Savage Father*, trans. Pasquale Verdicchio (Toronto: Guernica Editions, reprint 1999)

Pope, Alexander, *Poems of Alexander Pope*, 7 vols, general editor John Butt (London: Methuen and Co., 1961-); comprising
—— *The Dunciad* in four books, in *Poems* vol. V, ed. James Sutherland
—— *An Essay on Criticism*, vol. I, ed. E. Audra and Aubrey Williams
—— 'Imitation of English Poets: Chaucer', in vol. VI, ed. Norman Ault and John Butt
—— 'Peri Bathous, or the Art of Sinking in Poetry', in *Alexander Pope: The Major Works*, ed. Pat Rogers (Oxford: Oxford University Press, 2006), pp. 195-238
—— 'The Wife of Bath Her Prologue' and 'January and May', in vol. II, ed. Geoffrey Tillotson
Robinson, Tony and David Willcock, *The Worst Jobs in History: Two Thousand Years of Miserable Employment* (London: Pan, 2005)
Sellar, W. C. and R. J. Yeatman, *1066 and All That: A Memorable History of England* (New York: Barnes & Noble, 1993)
Shaftesbury, Anthony Ashley Cooper, 'Sensus communis, an Essay on the Freedom of Wit and Humour', in *Characteristicks of Men, Manners, Opinions, Times*, 3 vols, vol. 1 (publisher unknown, 1744), pp. 49-135
Swift, Jonathan, *A Tale of a Tub and Other Work*, ed. and intro. Angus Ross and David Woolley (Oxford: Oxford University Press, 1986)
Thomson, James, 'Summer', in *The Works of James Thomson, in Four Volumes Complete*, vol. I (The Strand, London: A. Millar, 1757), pp. 49-116
Twain, Mark, *Life on the Mississippi* (Boston: James R. Osgood and Company, 1883)
—— *A Connecticut Yankee in King Arthur's Court*, intro. Roy Blount, Jr., illustrated by Daniel Carter Beard (New York: The Modern Library, 2001)
Waller, Edmund, *The Works of Edmund Waller in Verse and Prose* (London: Published by Mr Elijah Fenton, 1744)

Films and Television

The Adventures of Robin Hood, dir. Michael Curtiz and William Keighley (Warner Bros, 1938)
Andrei Rublev, dir. Andrei Tarkovsky (Mosfilm, 1966)
The Arabian Nights, dir. Pier Paolo Pasolini (MGM, 1974)
Bewilderness, dir. John Kaye Cooper (Talent Television, 2000)
Bill & Ted's Excellent Adventure, dir. Stephen Herek (De Laurentiis Entertainment Group (DEG), 1989)
Black Knight, dir. Gil Junger (Twentieth Century Fox, 2001)
Blackadder, written by Rowan Atkinson, Richard Curtis and Ben Elton, produced by John Lloyd (BBC1, 1983-9)
Brancaleone alla Crociate, dir. Mario Monicelli (Fair Film, O. N. C. I. C., 1970)
The Cable Guy, dir. Ben Stiller (Columbia Pictures, 1996)
The Canterbury Tales, dir. Pier Paolo Pasolini (Image Entertainment, 1972)
The Complete and Utter History of Britain, created by Terry Jones and Michael Palin (London Weekend Television, 12 January-16 February 1969)
A Connecticut Yankee in King Arthur's Court, dir. Tay Garnett (Paramount Pictures, 1949)

The Court Jester, dir. M. Frank and N. Panama (Dena Enterprises, 1955)

Crimes and Misdemeanors, dir. Woody Allen (Jack Rollins & Charles H. Joffe Productions, 1989)

The Decameron, dir. Pier Paolo Pasolini (MGM, 1971)

Erik the Viking, dir. Terry Jones (MGM, 1989)

Everything You Always Wanted to Know about Sex* But Were Afraid to Ask, dir. Woody Allen (United Artists, 1972)

Fawlty Towers, dir. John Howard Davies and Bob Spiers (BBC Worldwide, 1976–9)

The Flowers of St Francis, dir. Roberto Rossellini (Cineriz, Rizzoli Film, 1950)

History of the World Part 1, dir. Mel Brooks (Brooksfilms, 1981)

Horrible Histories, dir. Steve Connelly, Dominic Brigstocke and Chloe Thomas (CBBC/BBC 1, 2009–12)

How to Train Your Dragon, dir. Dean DeBlois and Chris Sanders (Dreamworks Animation, 2010)

Just Visiting, dir. Jean-Marie Poiré (Hollywood Pictures, 2001)

A Kid in King Arthur's Court, dir. Michael Gottlieb (Tapestry Films, Trimark Pictures, Walt Disney Pictures, 1995)

A Knight in Camelot, dir. Michael Young (Rosemont Productions and Walt Disney Television, 1998)

L'armata Brancaleone, dir. Mario Monicelli (Fair Film, Les Films Marceau, Vertice Film, 1966)

Les Visiteurs, dir. Jean-Marie Poiré (Alpilles Productions, 1993)

Medieval Lives, dir. Nigel Miller (Oxford Film and Television, 2004), hosted by Terry Jones

'Medieval Helpdesk', *Øystein og jeg* (Norsk Rikskringkasting 2000). Skit with English subtitles (NRK, 2001). URL: http://www.youtube.com/watch?v=pQHX-SjgQvQ

Monty Python and the Holy Grail, dir. Terry Gilliam and Terry Jones (National Film Trustee Company Ltd, Python (Monty) Pictures, Michael White, 1975)

The Navigator: A Mediaeval Odyssey, dir. Vincent Ward (Arena Film, Australian Film Commission, John Maynard Productions, 1988)

Robin Hood: Men in Tights, dir. Mel Brooks (Brooks Films, Gaumont, 1993)

Time Bandits, dir. Terry Gilliam (HandMade Films, 1981)

Uccellacci e Uccellini, dir. Pier Paolo Pasolini (Water Bearer Films, 1966)

Unidentified Flying Oddball, dir. Russ Mayberry (Walt Disney Productions, 1979)

Up Pompeii, dir. Bob Kellett (Anglo-EMI, Associated London Films, 1971)

Up Pompeii (TV), dir. David Croft and Sydney Lotterby (BBC TV, 1969–70)

Up The Chastity Belt, dir. Bob Kellett (Associated London Films, Anglo-EMI, Virgin Films, 1971)

Up The Front, dir. Bob Kellett (Anglo-EMI, 1972)

Worst Jobs in History (Channel 4, 2004–7), hosted by Tony Robinson

Your Highness, dir. David Gordon Green (Universal Pictures, 2011)

Plays

Beaumont, Francis, *The Knight of the Burning Pestle* (Manchester, UK: Manchester University Press, 1984, revised 2004)

Brooks, Shirley, *The Exposition: A Scandinavian Sketch, Containing As Much Irrelevant Matter As Possible – In One Act* (London: T. H. Lacy, 1851)

Brough, William, *Joan of Arc! A New and Original Burlesque* (London: T. H. Lacy, 1869)

Byron, Henry J., *Esmeralda; or, The 'Sensation' Goat!* (London: T. H. Lacy, 1861)

Byron, Henry J., *Ivanhoe! In Accordance with the Spirit of the Times – An Extravaganza* (London: T. H. Lacy, 1862)

Fitzball, Edward, *Robin Hood; or, the Merry Outlaws of Sherwood: A Dramatic Equestrian Spectacle – In Three Acts* (London: T. H. Lacy, 1860)

Fo, Dario, *Francis, The Holy Jester*, trans. Mario Pirovano (London: Beautiful Books, 2009)

—— 'Mistero Buffo', in *Plays: 1*, trans. Ed Emery, intro. Stuart Hood (London: Methuen, 1992)

Gay, John, *The Wife of Bath: A Comedy* (1713 version), Gently Modernized by Ross G. Arthur (Cambridge, Ontario: In Parenthesis Publications Restoration Drama Series, 2001)

Mayakovsky, Vladimir, 'Mystery Bouffe', in *Classic Soviet Plays*, ed. and intro. Alla Mikhailova, trans. Dorian Rottenberg (Moscow: Progress Publisher, 1979), pp. 95–172

Reece, R., *Whittington, Junior, and his Sensation Cat: An Original Civic Burlesque* (London: T. H. Lacy, 1870)

Newspapers

Birmingham Mail
The Daily Telegraph
The Guardian
Illawarra Mercury
Illustrated London News
Liverpool Daily Post
The Observer
The Scotsman
The Times

Secondary Texts

Aberth, John, *A Knight at the Movies: Medieval History on Film* (New York: Routledge, 2003)

Allen, John J., 'The Transformation of Satire in Don Quixote: "Dine With Us As An Equal" in Juvenal and Cervantes', in *Ingeniosa Invención: Essays on Golden Age Spanish Literature for Geoffrey L. Stagg in Honor of His Eighty-Fifth Birthday*, ed. Ellen Anderson and Amy Williamson (Newark, DE: Juan de la Cuesta Press, 1999), pp. 1–7

Aronson-Lehavi, Sharon, "'The End": Mythical Futures in Avant-Garde Mystery Plays', *Theatre Research International* 34 (2009), 116–23

Ashton, Gail and Daniel T. Kline, eds, *Medieval Afterlives in Popular Culture* (New York: Palgrave Macmillan, 2012)

Attardo, Salvatore, *Linguistic Theories of Humour* (Berlin and New York: Mouton de Gruyter, 1994)

Auerbach, Erich, *Mimesis: The Representation of Reality in Western Literature*, trans. William Trask (Princeton, NJ: Princeton University Press, 1953)

Austin, Guy, 'Body Comedy and French Cinema: Notes on *Les Visiteurs*', *Studies in French Cinema* 6 (2006), 43–52

Austin, Linda M., *Nostalgia in Transition, 1780–1917* (Charlottesville, VA: University of Virginia Press, 2007)

Bailey, Peter, *Popular Culture and Performance in the Victorian City* (Cambridge: Cambridge University Press, 1998)

Bakhtin, Mikhail, *Rabelais and His World*, trans. Hélène Iswolsky (Bloomington: Indiana University Press, 1984)

Ballerini, Luigi, Giuseppe Risso and others, 'Dario Fo Explains: An Interview', *The Drama Review* 22 (1978), 33–48

Bayless, Martha, 'Danny Kaye and the *Fairy Tale* of Queerness in *The Court Jester*', in *Queer Movie Medievalisms*, ed. Kathleen Coyne Kelly and Tison Pugh (Farnham, Surrey: Ashgate, 2009), pp. 185–200

—— *Parody in the Middle Ages: The Latin Tradition* (Ann Arbor: University of Michigan Press, 1996)

Behan, Tom, *Dario Fo: Revolutionary Theatre* (London: Pluto, 2000)

—— 'The Megaphone of the Movement: Dario Fo and the Working Class 1968–70', *Journal of European Studies* 30 (2000), 251–70

Bell, Erin and Ann Gray, eds, *History on Television* (London: Routledge, 2012)

—— eds, *Televising History: Mediating the Past in Postwar Europe* (Houndmills, Basingstoke: Palgrave Macmillan, 2010)

Berger, Peter L., *Redeeming Laughter: The Comic Dimension of Human Experience* (New York and Berlin: Walter de Gruyter, 1997)

Bildhauer, Bettina, *Filming the Middle Ages* (London: Reaktion Books, 2011)

Black, Georgina Dopico, 'Canons Afire: Libraries, Books, and Bodies in Don Quixote's Spain', in *Cervantes' Don Quixote: A Casebook*, ed. Roberto González Echevarría (Oxford and New York: Oxford University Press, 2005), pp. 95–123

Bloch, R. Howard and Stephen G. Nichols, eds, *Medievalism and the Modernist Temper* (Baltimore, MD: Johns Hopkins University Press, 1996)

Booth, Michael R., *Theatre in the Victorian Age* (Cambridge: Cambridge University Press, 1991)

—— *Victorian Spectacular Theatre 1850–1910* (Boston: Routledge & Kegan Paul, 1981)

Bowden, Betsy, ed., *Eighteenth-Century Modernizations from the Canterbury Tales* (Cambridge: D. S. Brewer, 1991)

Boym, Svetlana, *The Future of Nostalgia* (New York: Basic Books, 2001)

Braet, Herman, Guido Latré and Werner Verbeke, eds, *Risus Mediaevalis: Laughter in Medieval Literature and Art* (Leuven: Leuven University Press, 2003)

Bremmer, Jan and Herman Roodenburg, eds, *A Cultural History of Humour: From Antiquity to the Present Day* (Cambridge, MA: Polity Press, 1997)

Breton, André, *Anthology of Black Humour*, trans. Mark Polizotti (San Francisco: City Lights Publishing, 1997)

Brewer, Derek, *Geoffrey Chaucer, the Critical Heritage* (New York: Routledge, 1995)

—— ed., *Medieval Comic Tales* (Cambridge: D. S. Brewer, 1996)

Bryant, Brantley L., *Geoffrey Chaucer Hath A Blog: Medieval Studies and New Media* (New York: Palgrave Macmillan, 2010)

Buckingham, David and Margaret Scanlon, 'Selling Learning: Towards a Political Economy of Edutainment Media', *Media, Culture & Society* 27 (2005), 41–58

Buczkowski, Paul, 'J. R. Planché, Frederick Robson, and the Fairy Extravaganza', *Marvels & Tales* 15 (2001), 42–65

Burt, Richard, 'Getting Schmedieval: Of Manuscripts and Film Prologues, Paratexts, and Parodies', *Exemplaria* 19 (2007), 217–42

Bynum, Carolyn Walker, *Fragmentation and Redemption: Essays on Gender and the Human Body in Medieval Religion* (New York: Zone Books, 1992)

Callaway, Anita, *Visual Ephemera: Theatrical Art in Nineteenth-Century Australia* (Sydney: UNSW Press, 2000)

Cannadine, David, ed., *History and the Media* (Houndmills, Basingstoke: Palgrave Macmillan, 2004)

Cannon, Christopher, 'The Myth of Origin and the Making of Chaucer's Wit', *Speculum* 71 (1996), 646–75

Capozzi, Rocco, 'Palimpsests and Laughter: The Dialogical Pleasure of Unlimited Intertextuality in The Name of the Rose', *Italica* 66 (1989), 412–28

Carnegie, Elizabeth and Scott McCabe, 'Re-Enactment Events and Tourism: Meaning, Authenticity and Identity', *Current Issues in Tourism* 11 (2008), 349–68

Carruthers, Mary, *The Book of Memory: A Study of Memory in Medieval Culture* (Cambridge: Cambridge University Press, 2008)

Celebrating Jorvik, *A New Look at the Viking-Age Artefacts from the Coppergate Excavation 1976–1981* (York, UK: York Archaeological Trust, 2009)

Chapman, Graham, Terry Jones and others, *Monty Python and the Holy Grail (Book)* (London: Methuen, 1977; repr. 1989, 2002)

Chedgzoy, Kate, 'Horrible Shakespearian Histories: Performing the Renaissance for and with Children', in *Filming and Performing Renaissance History*, ed. Mark Thornton Burnett and Adrian Streete (Houndmills, Basingstoke: Palgrave Macmillan, 2011), pp. 112–26

Chiang, Connie Y., 'Monterey-by-the-Smell: Odors and Social Conflict on the California Coastline', *Pacific Historical Review* 73 (2004), 183–214

Ciment, Michael, Luda Schnitzer and Jean Schnitzer, 'The Artist in Ancient Russia and in the New USSR', in *Andrei Tarkovsky: Interviews*, ed. John Gianvito (Jackson: University Press of Mississippi, 2006), pp. 16–31

Classen, Albrecht, ed., *Laughter in the Middle Ages and Early Modern Times: Epis-*

temology of a Fundamental Human Behavior, its Meaning, and Consequences (Berlin: de Gruyter, 2010)

—— *The Medieval Chastity Belt: A Myth-Making Process* (New York: Palgrave, 2007)

Classen, Constance, 'The Odor of the Other: Olfactory Symbolism and Cultural Categories', *Ethos* 20 (1992), 133–66

Classen, Constance, David Howes and Anthony Synnott, *Aroma: The Cultural History of Smell* (London: Routledge, 1994)

Cleto, Fabio, ed., *Camp: Queer Aesthetics and the Performing Subject – A Reader* (Ann Arbor: University of Michigan, 1999)

Close, Anthony J., *Cervantes and the Comic Mind of His Age* (Oxford: Oxford University Press, 2000)

—— *Cervantes: Don Quixote* (Cambridge: Cambridge University Press, 1990)

—— 'The Legacy of Don Quijote and the Picaresque Novel', in *The Cambridge Companion to the Spanish Novel: From 1600 to the Present*, ed. Harriet Turner and Adelaida López de Martínez (Cambridge: Cambridge University Press, 2003), pp. 15–30

Codelli, Lorenzo, 'Mario Monicelli: 1915–2010', *Positif* 600 (2011), 56–7

Connell, Philip, 'British Identities and the Politics of Ancient Poetry in Later Eighteenth-Century England', *The Historical Journal* 49 (2006), 161–92

Cowan, Susan, 'Dario Fo's Throw-away Theatre', *The Drama Review* 19 (1975), 102–13

Critchley, Simon, *On Humour* (New York: Routledge, 2002)

D'Arcens, Louise, 'Dario Fo's *Mistero Buffo* and the Left-Modernist Reclamation of Medieval Popular Culture', in *Medieval Afterlives in Popular Culture*, ed. Gail Ashton and Daniel T. Kline (New York: Palgrave Macmillan, 2012), pp. 57–70

—— 'Deconstruction and the Medieval Indefinite Article: The Undecidable Medievalism of Brian Helgeland's *A Knight's Tale*', *Parergon* 25 (2008), 80–98

—— *Old Songs in the Timeless Land: Medievalism in Australian Literature 1840–1910* (Turnhout, Belgium: Brepols, 2011)

Davies, Christie, *Jokes and their Relation to Society* (Berlin: Mouton de Gruyter, 1998)

—— *The Mirth of Nations* (Piscataway, NJ: Transaction Publishers, 2002)

Davis, Kathleen, *Periodization and Sovereignty: How Ideas of Feudalism and Secularization Govern the Politics of Time* (Philadelphia: University of Pennsylvania Press, 2008)

Davis, Paul, 'After the Fire: Chaucer and Urban Poetics, 1666–1743', in *Chaucer and the City*, ed. Ardis Butterfield (Woodbridge: Boydell & Brewer, 2006), pp. 177–92

Day, David D., 'Monty Python and the Holy Grail: Madness with a Definite Method', in *Cinema Arthuriana: Twenty Essays*, ed. Kevin J. Harty (Jefferson, NC: McFarland, 2002), pp. 127–35

Deary, Terry, 'Horrible History Teaching', *BBC History Magazine*, October 2009 http://www.historyextra.com/feature/horrible-history-teaching (accessed 9 April 2013)

De Grazia, Margreta, 'The Modern Divide: From Either Side', *Journal of Medieval and Early Modern Studies* 37 (2007), 453–67

De Groot, Jerome, *Consuming History: Historians and Heritage in Contemporary Popular Culture* (London: Routledge, 2009)

Deleuze, Gilles and Félix Guattari, *A Thousand Plateaus: Capitalism and Schizophrenia*, trans. Brian Massumi (Minneapolis: University of Minnesota Press, 1987)

Dell, Helen, 'Nostalgia and Medievalism: Conversations, Contradictions, Impasses', *Postmedieval* 2 (2011), 115–26

Derrida, Jacques, 'Plato's Pharmacy', in *Dissemination*, trans. Barbara Johnson (Chicago: University of Chicago Press, 1981), pp. 63–94

Di Carpegna Falconieri, Tommaso, *Medioevo militante: La politica di oggi alla prese con barbari e crociati* (Turin: Einaudi, 2011)

Dinshaw, Carolyn, *Getting Medieval: Sexualities and Communities, Pre- and Postmodern* (Durham, NC: Duke University Press, 1999)

—— *How Soon is Now? Medieval Texts, Amateur Readers, and the Queerness of Time* (Durham, NC, and London: Duke University Press, 2012)

Doebler, Peter, 'Screening the Silly: The Christian Iconography of Roberto Rossellini's Francesco, Giullare di Dio', *Journal of Religion and Film* 15 (2011) http://www.unomaha.edu/jrf/Vol15.no1/Doebler_ScreeningSilly.html (accessed 17 November 2011)

Duckworth, George E., *The Nature of Roman Comedy: A Study in Popular Entertainment*, 2nd edn, with foreword and bibliographic appendix by Richard Hunter (Norman, OK: University of Oklahoma Press, 1994)

Edgerton, Gary R. and Peter C. Rollins, eds, *Television Histories: Shaping Collective Memory in the Media Age* (Lexington, KY: University Press of Kentucky, 2001)

Ellis, Steve, *Chaucer at Large: The Poet in the Modern Imagination* (Minneapolis: University of Minnesota Press, 2000)

Farrell, Joseph, *Dario Fo and Franca Rame: Harlequins of the Revolution* (London: Methuen, 2001)

Farrell, Joseph and Antonio Scuderi, eds, *Dario Fo: Stage, Text and Tradition* (Carbondale: Southern Illinois University Press, 2000)

Farrell, Thomas J., *Bakhtin and Medieval Voices* (Gainesville, FL: University Press of Florida, 1995)

Fasolini, Diego, 'The Intrusion of Laughter into the Abbey of Umberto Eco's *The Name of the Rose*: The Christian Paradox of Joy Mingling with Sorrow', *Romance Notes* 46 (2006), 119–29

Faulk, Barry J., *Music Hall and Modernity: The Late-Victorian Discovery of Popular Culture* (Athens, OH: Ohio University Press, 2004)

Fife, Wayne, 'Semantic Slippage as a New Aspect of Authenticity: Viking Tourism on the Northern Peninsula of Newfoundland', *Journal of Folklore Research* 41 (2004), 61–84

Finke, Laurie A. and Martin B. Schichtman, *Cinematic Illuminations: The Middle Ages on Film* (Baltimore, MD: Johns Hopkins University Press, 2010)

Forni, Kathleen, ed., *Chaucerian Apocrypha: A Selection* (Kalamazoo, MI: Medieval Institute Publications, 2005)

—— *Chaucer's Afterlife: Adaptations in Recent Popular Culture* (Jefferson, NC: McFarland & Company, Inc., 2013)

Fotheringham, Richard, ed., *Australian Plays for the Australian Stage 1834–1899* (St Lucia: University of Queensland Press, 2006)

—— *An Entirely New Sensation: the Early Australian Stage* (Civic Square, A.C.T: Interact Theatre of Canberra, 1987)

Foucault, Michel, *The History of Sexuality Vol. 1: An Introduction*, trans. Robert Hurley (New York: Pantheon Books, 1978), pp. 17–35

Fradenburg, Aranye, "'So That We May Speak Of Them": Enjoying the Middle Ages', *New Literary History* 28 (1997), 205–30

Freccero, Carla, *Queer/Early/Modern* (Durham, NC: Duke University Press, 2006)

Frye, Northrop, *Anatomy of Criticism: Four Essays* (Princeton, NJ: Princeton University Press, 1957)

Fulton, John, 'Religion and Politics in Gramsci: An Introduction', *Sociological Analysis* 48 (1987), 197–216

Fulton, Rachel and Bruce W. Holsinger, eds, *History in the Comic Mode: Medieval Communities and the Matter of Person* (New York: Columbia University Press, 2007)

Gramsci, Antonio, *Letters from Prison*, ed. Frank Rosengarten, trans. Raymond Rosenthal (New York: Columbia University Press, 1994)

Gray, Ann, 'Contexts of Production: Commissioning History', in *Televising History: Mediating the Past in Postwar Europe*, ed. Erin Bell and Ann Gray (Houndmills, Basingstoke: Palgrave Macmillan, 2010), pp. 59–76

Green, Dennis Howard, *Irony in the Medieval Romance* (Cambridge: Cambridge University Press, 1978)

Greene, Naomi, *Pier Paolo Pasolini: Cinema as Heresy* (Princeton, NJ: Princeton University Press, 1990)

Greene, Thomas M., 'History and *Anachronism*', in *Literature and History: Theoretical Problems and Russian Case Studies*, ed. Gary Saul Morson (Stanford: Stanford University Press, 1986), pp. 205–20

Gumbel, Andrew, 'Nobel Prize: Dario Fo, the Showman, Wins Nobel Literature Prize', *The Independent*, 10 October 1997, http://www.independent.co.uk/news/nobel-prize-dario-fo-the-showman-wins-nobel-literature-prize-1234928.html (accessed 17 November 2011)

Guthrie, Steve, 'Time Travel, Pulp Fictions, and Changing Attitudes toward the Middle Ages: Why You Can't Get Renaissance On Somebody's Ass', in Gail Ashton and Daniel T. Kline, eds, *Medieval Afterlives in Popular Culture* (New York: Palgrave Macmillan, 2012), pp. 99–111

Haines, John, *Music in Films on the Middle Ages: Authenticity vs. Fantasy* (New York and Oxon: Routledge, 2014)

Halewood, C. and K. Hannam, 'Viking Heritage Tourism: Authenticity and Commodification', *Annals of Tourism Research* 28 (2001), 565–80

Hall, James, 'Introduction', in *Understanding Popular Culture: Europe from the Middle Ages to the Nineteenth Century*, ed. Steven L. Kaplan (Berlin, New York: Mouton, 1984), pp. 5–18

Hansen, Elaine Tuttle, *Chaucer and the Fictions of Gender* (Berkeley: University of California Press, 1992)

Harrington, C. Lee and Denise D. Bielby, eds, *Popular Culture: Production and Consumption* (Malden, MA: Blackwell Publishers, 2000)

Hartman, Geoffrey, *Saving the Text: Literature/Derrida/Philosophy* (Baltimore, MD: Johns Hopkins University Press, 1981)

Harty, Kevin J., ed., *Cinema Arthuriana: Twenty Essays* (Jefferson, NC: McFarland, 2002)

—— *The Reel Middle Ages: American, Western and Eastern European, Middle Eastern and Asian Films about Medieval Europe* (Jefferson, NC: McFarland, 1999, repr. 2006)

Haydock, Nickolas, *Movie Medievalisms: The Imaginary Middle Ages* (Jefferson, NC: McFarland, 2008)

Haydock, Nickolas and E. L. Risden, eds, *Hollywood in the Holy Land: Essays on Film Depictions of the Crusades and Christian–Muslim Clashes* (Jefferson, NC: McFarland, 2009)

Heng, Geraldine, *Empire of Magic: Medieval Romance and the Politics of Cultural Fantasy* (New York: Columbia University Press, 2003)

Hewitt, Barnard, 'Mrs. John Wood and the Lost Art of Burlesque Acting', *Educational Theatre Journal* 13 (1961), 82–5

Hoffer, Peter Charles, *Sensory Worlds in Early America* (Baltimore, MD: Johns Hopkins University Press, 2003)

Hoffman, Donald L., 'Not Dead Yet: *Monty Python and the Holy Grail* in the Twenty-first Century', in *Cinema Arthuriana: Twenty Essays*, ed. Kevin J. Harty (Jefferson, NC: McFarland, 2002), pp. 136–48

Holsinger, Bruce, *The Premodern Condition: Medievalism and the Making of Theory* (Chicago, IL: The University of Chicago Press, 2005)

Holsinger, Bruce and Ethan Knapp, 'The Marxist Premodern', *Journal of Medieval and Early Modern Studies* 34 (2004), 463–71

Howells, W. D., *My Mark Twain: Reminiscences and Criticisms*, ed. and intro. Marilyn Austin Baldwin (Baton Rouge: Louisiana State University Press, copyright 1967)

Huizinga, Johan, *Homo Ludens: A Study of the Play Element in Culture* (Boston: Beacon Press, 1955)

Hunt, Tristram, 'Reality, Identity, and Empathy: The Changing face of Social History Television', *Journal of Social History* 39 (2006), 843–58

Hutcheon, Linda, *A Theory of Parody: The Teachings of Twentieth-Century Art Forms* (Urbana: University of Illinois Press, 2000)

Ife, B. W., 'The Historical and Social Context', in *The Cambridge Companion to*

Cervantes, ed. Anthony J. Cascardi (Cambridge: Cambridge University Press, 2002), pp. 11–31

—— *Reading and Fiction in Golden-Age Spain: A Platonist Critique and Some Picaresque Replies* (Cambridge: Cambridge University Press, 1985)

Iffland, James, 'Laughter Tamed', *Bulletin of the Cervantes Society of America* 23 (2003), 395–435

Jäckel, Anne, 'Les Visiteurs: A Popular Form of Cinema for Europe?' in *European Identity in Cinema*, ed. Wendy Everett (Bristol: Intellect, 2005), pp. 41–9

Jones, Terry, 'History with the Boring Bits Put Back', *History Today* 54 (February 2004), 62–3

Jones, Terry, Robert Yeager and others, *Who Murdered Chaucer? A Medieval Mystery* (London: Methuen, 2003)

Jorvik Viking Centre, www.jorvik-viking-centre.co.uk (accessed 5 November 2009)

Jost, Jean E., ed., *Chaucer's Humor: Critical Essays* (New York: Garland, 1994)

Kelly, Kathleen Coyne and Tison Pugh, 'Introduction', in *Queer Movie Medievalisms*, ed. Kathleen Boyne Kelly and Tison Pugh (Farnham, Surrey: Ashgate, 2009), pp. 1–17

Klopp, Charles, 'Fiction in Italy since the Years of Lead', *World Literature Today* 79 (2005), 35–8

Klosowska, Anna, 'The Eastern Western: Camp as a Response to Cultural Failure in *The Conqueror*', in *Queer Movie Medievalisms*, ed. Kathleen Coyne Kelly and Tison Pugh (Farnham, Surrey: Ashgate, 2009), pp. 97–114

Kolnai, Aurel, *On Disgust*, ed. and intro. Carolyn Korsmeyer and Barry Smith (Peru, IL: Open Court Publishing, 2004)

Kooper, Erik, ed., *Sentimental and Humorous Romances: Floris and Blancheflour, Sir Degrevant, The Squire of Low Degree, The Tournament of Tottenham and the Feast of Tottenham* (Kalamazoo, MI: Medieval Institute Publications 2005)

Kramnick, J. Brody, 'The Making of the English Canon', *PMLA* 112 (1997), 1087–101

Kundera, Milan, *The Curtain*, trans. Linda Asher (New York: Harper Collins, 2005)

Landy, Marcia, 'Comedy and Counter-History', in *Historical Comedy on Screen*, ed. Hannu Salmi (Bristol: Intellect Press Ltd, 2011), pp. 177–98

Largey, Gale and Rod Watson, 'The Sociology of Odors', in *The Smell Culture Reader*, ed. Jim Drobnick (Oxford: Berg, 2006), pp. 29–40

Larsen, Egon, *Wit as a Weapon: The Political Joke in History* (London: F. Muller, 1980)

Le Doeuff, Michèle, *The Philosophical Imaginary*, trans. Colin Gordon (London: Athlone, 1989)

Le Goff, Jacques, 'Laughter in the Middle Ages', in *A Cultural History of Humour: From Antiquity to the Present Day*, ed. Jan Bremmer and Herman Rodenburg (Cambridge: Polity Press, 1997), pp. 40–53

Lewis, Katherine J., '"Accident My Codlings": Sitcom, Cinema and the Re-writing of History in *The Blackadder*', in *Mass Market Medieval: Essays on the Middle*

Ages in Popular Culture, ed. David Marshall (Jefferson, NC: MacFarland and Co., 2007), pp. 113–25

Lewis, Paul, 'The Muhammad Cartoons and Humour Research: A Collection of Essays', *Humor* 21.1 (2008), 1–46

Liu, Benjamin, *Medieval Joke Poetry: The Cantigas d'Escarnho e de Mal Dizer* (Cambridge, MA: Harvard University Press, 2004)

Lockyer, Sharon and Michael Pickering, eds, *Beyond a Joke: The Limits of Humour* (Houndmills, Basingstoke: Palgrave Macmillan, 2005)

Lund, Roger D., 'Wit, Judgement, and the Misprisions of Similitude', *Journal of the History of Ideas* 65 (2004), 53–75

Lundquist, Lynne, 'Myth and Illiteracy: Bill and Ted's Explicated Adventures', *Extrapolation* 37 (1996), 212–23

Lynch, Andrew, 'King Arthur in Marvellous Melbourne: W. M. Akhurst's Burlesque Extravaganzas', *Australian Literary Studies* 26 (2011), 45–57

Maceri, Domenico, 'Dario Fo: Jester of the Working Class', *World Literature Today* 72 (1998), 9–14

Mackie, Craven, 'Frederick Robson and the Evolution of Realistic Acting', *Educational Theatre Journal* 23 (May 1971), 160–70

Mancoff, Debra N., ed., *King Arthur's Modern Return* (New York: Garland, 1998)

Manselli, Raoul, *St. Francis of Assisi* (Chicago: Franciscan Herald Press, 1988)

Martín, Adrienne L., 'Humor and Violence in Cervantes', in *The Cambridge Companion to Cervantes*, ed. Anthony J. Cascardi (Cambridge: Cambridge University Press, 2002), pp. 160–85

Marvin, Roberta Montemorra, 'Verdian Opera Burlesqued: A Glimpse into Mid-Victorian Theatrical Culture', *Cambridge Opera Journal* 15 (March 2003), 33–66

Maslen, R. W., 'The Afterlife of Andrew Borde', *Studies in Philology* 100 (2003), 463–92

McMorran, William, '*Les Visiteurs* and the Quixotic Text', *French Cultural Studies* 19 (2008), 159–72

Medhurst, Andy, 'Carry on Camp', *Sight and Sound* 2 (1992), 16–19

—— *A National Joke: Popular Comedy and English Cultural Identities* (New York: Routledge, 2007)

Meisel, Martin, *Realizations: Narrative, Pictorial, and Theatrical Arts in Nineteenth-Century England* (Princeton, NJ: Princeton University Press, 1983)

Meisel, Perry, *The Myth of Popular Culture from Dante to Dylan* (Chichester, UK: Wiley-Blackwell, 2010)

Mennighaus, Winfried, *Disgust: The Theory and History of a Strong Emotion* (Albany: State University of New York Press, 2003)

Meyer, Moe, *The Politics and Poetics of Camp* (New York: Routledge, 1993)

Milburn, D. Judson, *The Age of Wit: 1650–1750* (New York: The Macmillan Company, 1966)

Miller, Ian W., *The Anatomy of Disgust* (Cambridge, MA: Harvard University Press, 1997)

Mills, Brett, *Television Sitcom* (London: BFI, 2005)

Mitchell, Tony, *Dario Fo: People's Court Jester*, 2nd edn (London: Methuen, 1986)

Monicelli, Mario and Andrea Palazzino, 'Il Medioevo di Monicelli: Una Parodia Molto Vera', *Babel: Littératures plurielles* 15 (2007), 11–16

Morreall, John, *Comic Relief: A Comprehensive Philosophy of Humor* (Chichester, UK: Wiley-Blackwell, 2009)

—— ed., *The Philosophy of Laughter and Humor* (Albany, NY: State University of New York Press, 1987)

—— *Taking Laughter Seriously* (Albany, NY: State University of New York Press, 1983)

Morrison, Susan Signe, *Excrement in the Late Middle Ages: Sacred Filth and Feco-poetics* (New York: Palgrave Macmillan, 2008)

Nikolopoulou, Anastasia, 'Medievalism and Historicity in the English Gothic Melodrama: Maturin's Bertram: or, The Castle of St. Aldobrand', *Poetica* 39–40 (1994), 139–53

Nobel Prize Website, 'The Nobel Prize in Literature 1997: Awarded to Dario Fo', http://www.nobelprize.org/nobel_prizes/literature/laureates/1997/

Nollen, Scott A., *Robin Hood: A Cinematic History of the English Outlaw and his Scottish Counterparts* (Jefferson, NC: McFarland, 1999, reprinted 2008)

O'Grady, Kathleen, 'Theorizing – Feminism and Postmodernism: A Conversation with Linda Hutcheon', *Rampike* 9.2 (1998), 20–2

Patterson, Lee, *Chaucer and the Subject of History* (Madison, WI: The University of Wisconsin Press, 1991)

Pfister, Manfred, ed., *A History of English Laughter: Laughter from Beowulf to Beckett and Beyond* (Amsterdam: Rodopi, 2002)

Phiddian, Robert, 'Are Parody and Deconstruction Secretly the Same Thing?' *New Literary History* 28:4 (1997), 673–96

Piccolo, Pina, 'Dario Fo's giullarate: Dialogic Parables in the Service of the Oppressed', *Italica* 65 (1988), 131–43

Pionke, Albert D., 'A Ritual Failure: The Eglinton Tournament, the Victorian Medieval Revival, and Victorian Ritual Culture', *Studies in Medievalism* 16 (2008), 25–45

Porìa, Yaniv, Richard Butler and David Airey, 'Clarifying Heritage Tourism', *Annals of Tourism Research* 28 (2001), 1047–9

Porteous, J. Douglas, 'Smellscape', in *The Smell Culture Reader*, ed. Jim Drobnick (Oxford: Berg, 2006), pp. 89–106

Prendergast, Tom and Stephanie Trigg, 'What is Happening to the Middle Ages?' *New Medieval Literatures* 9 (2008), 215–29

Pugh, Tison and Angela Jane Weisl, *Medievalisms: Making the Past in the Present* (London: Routledge, 2012)

Ray, Nina M. and others, 'Lewis and Clark and the Corps of Discovery: Re-Enactment Event Tourism as Authentic Heritage Travel', *Leisure Studies* 25 (2006), 437–54

Riley, E. C., *Cervantes's Theory Of The Novel* (Oxford: Clarendon Press, 1962)

—— 'Literature and Life in Don Quixote', in *Cervantes' Don Quixote: A Casebook*, ed. Roberto González Echevarría (Oxford: Oxford University Press, 2005), pp. 125–40

Robb, Frank Maldon, ed., *Poems of Adam Lindsay Gordon* (London: Oxford University Press, 1912)

Roberts, Graham and Philip M. Taylor, eds, *The Historian, Television, and Television History* (Luton: University of Luton Press, 2001)

Roberts, J. F., *The True History of the Black Adder: The Unadulterated Tale of the Creation of a Comedy Legend* (London: Preface Publishing, 2012)

Robertson, Ritchie, *Mock-Epic Poetry from Pope to Heine* (Oxford, New York: Oxford University Press, 2009)

Rogers, Pat, *Essays on Pope* (Cambridge: Cambridge University Press, 1993)

Rossellini, Roberto, 'The Message of *The Flowers of St. Francis*', in *My Method: Writings and Interviews*, ed. Adriano Apra, trans. Annapaola Cancogni (New York: Marsilio Publishers, 1992)

Rozin, Paul, Jonathan Haidt and Clark McCauley, 'Disgust: The Body and Soul Emotion in the Twenty-first Century', in *Disgust and its Disorders: Theory, Assessment, and Treatment Implications*, ed. Bunmi O. Olatunji and Dean McKay (Washington, DC: American Psychological Association, 2009), pp. 9–29

Russell, Robert, 'The Arts and the Russian Civil War', *Journal of European Studies* 20 (1990), 219–40

Salmi, Hannu, ed., *Historical Comedy on Screen* (Bristol: Intellect Press Ltd, 2011)

Saul, Nigel, 'Terry Jones's Richard II', in *The Medieval Python: The Purposive and Provocative Work of Terry Jones*, ed. R. F.Yeager and Toshiyuki Takamiya (New York: Palgrave Macmillan, 2012), pp. 39–54

Sayad, Cecilia, 'The Auteur as Fool: Bakhtin, Barthes, and the Screen Performances of Woody Allen and Jean-Luc Godard', *Journal of Film and Video* 63 (2011), 21–34

Scanlon, Margaret, 'History Beyond the Academy: Humor and Horror in Children's History Books', *New Review of Children's Literature and Librarianship* 16 (2011), 69–91

Scham, Michael, 'Don Quijote and the Art of Laughing at Oneself', *Cervantes* 29 (2009), 31–55

Schiffman, Zachary Sayre, *The Birth of the Past* (Baltimore, MD: Johns Hopkins University Press, 2011)

Schlegel, Friedrich, *Philosophical Fragments*, trans. Peter Firchow, foreword Rodolphe Gasché (Minneapolis, Oxford: Minnesota University Press, 1991)

Schoch, Richard, *Not Shakespeare: Bardolatry and Burlesque In the Nineteenth Century* (Cambridge: Cambridge University Press, 2002)

—— *Shakespeare's Victorian Stage: Performing History in the Theatre of Charles Kean* (Cambridge: Cambridge University Press, 1998)

—— *Victorian Theatrical Burlesques* (Aldershot: Ashgate, 2003)

Scuderi, Antonio, *Dario Fo: Framing, Festival, and the Folkloric Imagination* (Lanham, MD: Lexington Books, 2011)

—— 'Dario Fo and Oral Tradition: Creating a Thematic Context', *Oral Tradition* 15 (2000), 26–38

—— 'Unmasking the Holy Jester Dario Fo', *Theatre Journal* 55 (2003), 275–90

Shuffelton, George, 'Chaucerian Obscenity in the Court of Public Opinion', *The Chaucer Review* 47:1 (2012), 1–24

Simmons, Clare A., 'Small-Scale Humor in the British Medieval Revival', in *The Year's Work in Medievalism, 2004*, ed. Gwendolyn Morgan (Eugene, OR: Wipf and Stock, 2006)

Sinnerbrink, Robert, 'The Volcano and the Dream: Consequences of Romanticism', in *Religion After Kant: Gold and Culture in the Idealist Era*, ed. Paulo Diego Bubbio and Paul Redding (Newcastle upon Tyne: Cambridge Scholars Press, 2012), pp. 38–59

Sitter, John, *Arguments of Augustan Wit* (Cambridge: Cambridge University Press, 1991)

Smith, Mark M., 'Producing Sense, Consuming Sense, Making Sense: Perils and Prospects for Sensory History', *Journal of Social History* 40 (2007), 841–58

Sontag, Susan, 'Notes on Camp', in *Against Interpretation and Other Essays* (New York: Farrar, Straus and Giroux, 1966)

Sogliuzzo, A. Richard, 'Dario Fo: Puppets for a Proletarian Revolution', *Drama Review* 16 (1972), 71–7

Speier, Hans, 'Wit and Politics: An Essay on Power and Laughter', *American Journal of Sociology* 103, 5 (1998), 1352–401

Spurgeon, Caroline, *Five Hundred Years of Chaucer Criticism and Allusion, 1357–1900, vol. 1* (New York: Russell & Russell, 1925, reprinted 1960)

—— *Shakespeare's Imagery and What it Tells Us* (Cambridge: Cambridge University Press, 1935, reprinted 1971)

Strinati, Dominic, *An Introduction to Theories of Popular Culture*, 2nd edn (London: Routledge, 2004)

't Hart, Marjolein C. and Dennis Bos, *Humour and Social Protest* (Cambridge and New York: Press Syndicate of the University of Cambridge, 2007)

Tarkovsky, Andrei, *Sculpting in Time: Reflections on the Cinema*, trans. Kitty Hunter-Blair (Austin: University of Texas Press, 1986, reprinted 2005)

Terry, Richard, 'Literature, Aesthetics, and Canonicity in the Eighteenth Century', *Eighteenth-Century Life* 21 (1997), 80–101

Trigg, Stephanie, *Congenial Souls: Reading Chaucer from Medieval to Postmodern* (Minneapolis: University of Minnesota Press, 2002)

—— 'Walking Through Cathedrals: Scholars, Pilgrims, and Medieval Tourists', *New Medieval Literatures* 7 (2005), 9–33

Vighi, Fabio, 'Pasolini and Exclusion: Žižek, Agamben, and the Modern Sub-Proletariat', *Theory, Culture and Society* 20 (2003), 99–121

Von Geldern, James, *Bolshevik Festivals 1917–30* (Berkeley: University of California Press, 1993)

Wagg, Stephen, 'You've Never had it so Silly: The Politics of British Satirical Comedy From *Beyond the Fringe* to *Spitting Image*', in *Come on Down? Popular Media Culture in Post-War Britain*, ed. Dominic Strinati and Stephan Wagg (London: Routledge, 1992), pp. 254–84

Weisl, Angela, 'Confession, Contrition, and the Rhetoric of Tears: Medievalism and Reality Television', in *Medieval Afterlives in Popular Culture,* ed. Gail Ashton and Daniel T. Kline (New York: Palgrave Macmillan, 2012), pp. 129–43

Wheatley, Helen, ed., *Re-Viewing Television History: Critical Issues in Television Historiography* (London: I. B. Tauris, 2007)

Whitworth, Damian, 'Is History So Horrible?' *The Times,* Education, 15 May 2009

Williams, Raymond, *Keywords* (London: Fontana, 1983)

Wilson, Diana de Armas, 'Cervantes and the New World', in *The Cambridge Companion to Cervantes,* ed. Anthony J. Cascardi (Cambridge: Cambridge University Press, 2002), pp. 206–25

Winton, Calhoun, *John Gay and the London Theatre* (Lexington, KY: University of Kentucky Press, 1993)

Wood, James, *The Irresponsible Self: On Laughter and the Novel* (New York: Picador, 2005)

Wroth, Warwick, *Cremorne and the Later London Gardens* (Paris: E. Stock, 1907, reprinted Whitefish, MO: Kessinger Publishing, 2010)

—— *The London Pleasure Gardens of the Eighteenth Century,* foreword A. H. Saxon (London: Macmillan, 1896, reprinted 1979)

Yeager, R. F. and Toshiyuki Takamiya, eds, *The Medieval Python: The Purposive and Provocative Work of Terry Jones* (New York: Palgrave Macmillan, 2012)

Young, Deborah, 'Poverty, Misery, War and Other Comic Material: An Interview with Mario Monicelli', *Cinéaste* 29 (2004), 36–40

Zitner, Sheldon P., ed., 'Introduction', to Francis Beaumont, *The Knight of the Burning Pestle* (Manchester, UK: Manchester University Press, 1984, new edn 2004)

Index

Medievalism

Printed and bound by CPI Group (UK) Ltd, Croydon, CR0 4YY

13/04/2025

14656520-0002